THE
BEIJING
FACTOR

THE
BEIJING
FACTOR

How Christianity Is
Transforming China and Changing
the Global Balance of Power

DAVID AIKMAN

MONARCH
BOOKS

Oxford, UK and Grand Rapids, Michigan

This edition first published in the UK 2005.
Reproduced from the American edition first published
in the USA by Regnery Publishing, Inc.

First published in the UK by Monarch Books
(a publishing imprint of Lion Hudson plc),
Mayfield House, 256 Banbury Road, Oxford OX2 7DH
Tel: +44 (0) 1865 302750 Fax: +44 (0) 1865 302757
Email: monarch@lionhudson.com
www.lionhudson.com

UK ISBN 1 85424 715 8

Distributed by:
UK: Marston Book Services Ltd, PO Box 269,
Abingdon, Oxon OX14 4YN

British Library Cataloguing Data
A catalogue record for this book is available
from the British Library.

THIS BOOK IS DEDICATED TO THE MEMORY OF ALL CHRISTIANS, CHINESE AND FOREIGN, WHO DIED IN CHINA AS MARTYRS FOR THEIR FAITH, FROM A.D. 635 TO MODERN TIMES.

CONTENTS

INTRODUCTION

I FIRST BECAME INTERESTED IN THIS STORY while working in Hong Kong in the 1970s as a correspondent for *Time* magazine. It was difficult for Westerners to enter China at all in that period, though I made three visits to China during 1972–1976. But every reporter in Hong Kong on the China-watching beat tried hard to piece together what was going on in the country from the fragmentary information available. There were, of course, the official New China (or Xinhua) News Agency stories, carefully crafted to ensure political precision. Like Kremlinologists of yore, many of us in Hong Kong pored over stories of such epochal events as, say, a visit to Beijing by the foreign minister of San Marino, to see which Chinese officials showed up at the official banquet. But enticing tidbits of information were also leaking out of south China through the thousands of Hong Kong Chinese and overseas Chinese who were permitted to visit relatives in China.

Many of these visitors, especially those from Hong Kong, were churchgoing Chinese Christians who snatched at any information they could about the status of fellow believers in China as the nation staggered to pull itself together after the chaos of the Cultural Revolution. It was from such visitors that remarkable stories of an incipient Christian revival inside China began to emerge.

Later, in the mid-1980s, I lived in China for nearly two years as the *Time* bureau chief in Beijing. Foreigners, especially foreign reporters, were watched carefully by the Chinese government at the time. It was possible to visit privately with ordinary Chinese, but at some risk to them. I used to show up unannounced in the dilapidated home of one Christian family in north Beijing after donning a thick Chinese cotton peasant coat, a surgical face mask, and a large fur hat and bicycling through the city streets after dark. An elderly Chinese Christian physician loved to tell me stories of peasant evangelists from the countryside who dropped by to pick up Bibles or Christian literature. Her son, a Communist Party member, was also a believer.

I returned briefly to Beijing in June 1989, in time to witness first-hand the PLA crackdown on protesting students and citizens in the city on June 4. I came back to China again several times during the 1990s, at first while still with *Time* and later as a freelance journalist. Each time I sought out longtime contacts among China's Christian community or developed new ones.

The genesis of this book goes back to 1998 when, with another reporter, Mark O'Keefe, then of *The Oregonian* newspaper, I was introduced by a Chinese contact to top leaders of China's largest networks of Christians in the "house churches," unregistered gatherings of Christians who wanted nothing to do with the Three Self Patriotic Movement or the Catholic Patriotic Association. The secret meeting in a safe house on the outskirts of Zhengzhou, capital city of Henan province, required elaborate arrangements for Mark and me to attend without putting at risk any of the Chinese participants. It turned out to be the first occasion on which China's "house church" leaders, sometimes referred to outside China as "underground," had agreed not just to meet with reporters from Western news organizations, but to be photographed and openly identified by their own names as well. The participants compiled their first official collective statement of opinion for the benefit of both the TSPM and China's government. We later published this in the United States. The document was interesting not just because it was the first deliberate effort of house church network leaders to reveal themselves, but also because it showed that

China's underground Christians, despite decades of persecution, did not consider themselves *political* dissidents, and in fact took pride in proclaiming their Chinese patriotism. (Specifically, they opposed political independence for either Tibet or Taiwan.)

I returned to China again in 1999, arriving in Shanghai during the climax of China's celebrations of the first fifty years of Communist rule. I myself saw the fireworks, but spent much of the time furtively wandering the city looking up old house church contacts.

Finally, to gather the bulk of reporting for this book, I returned to China for three months in the summer of 2002. I traveled extensively around China (though not to Tibet, nor on this occasion to the far western region of Xinjiang), talking to as many people as I could, inside and outside of China's Christian community, to try to peer into the situation. I was given remarkably free access, especially by senior leaders of China's various house church groups, most of whom I had met at the historical meeting in August 1998.

Chapter One

JESUS COMES TO BEIJING

THE EIGHTEEN AMERICAN TOURISTS visiting China weren't expecting much from the evening's scheduled lecture. They were already exhausted from a day of touring in Beijing. But what the speaker had to say astonished them.

"One of the things we were asked to look into was what accounted for the success, in fact, the pre-eminence of the West all over the world," he said. "We studied everything we could from the historical, political, economic, and cultural perspective. At first, we thought it was because you had more powerful guns than we had. Then we thought it was because you had the best political system. Next we focused on your economic system. But in the past twenty years, we have realized that the heart of your culture is your religion: Christianity. That is why the West has been so powerful. The Christian moral foundation of social and cultural life was what made possible the emergence of capitalism and then the successful transition to democratic politics. We don't have any doubt about this."

This was not coming from some ultra-conservative from a think tank in Orange County, California, or from Jerry Falwell's Liberty University in Lynchburg, Virginia. This was a scholar from one of China's premier academic research institutes, the Chinese Academy of Social Sciences (CASS) in Beijing, in 2002. Though CASS has had a reputation since its inception for gently pushing the envelope of acceptable areas of research in China, it is hardly a viper's nest of liberal dissent.

We'll call the speaker Dr. Wu—an urbane academic in his late thirties who spoke excellent English, specialized in the study of religion, and was deeply knowledgeable about not just China but the history of the West in general and the U.S. in particular. During his presentation to the American visitors, he let them take notes and even record his voice, but he didn't want to be filmed or identified by name.

The Americans were not typical of the 12 million foreign tourists who flock to China every year. Although they made the requisite stops at the Great Wall, the Summer Palace, and a large Peking duck restaurant during their eight-day excursion, their tour was called "A Christian Heritage Tour of China." The group was made up of twelve middle-class professionals—most of them Christian ministers—almost all from California or Texas, and six of their wives, and they were in China to see what was still left of the historic Christian legacy in China.

Though China's tourism authorities were happy enough to indulge a quaint American taste for ecclesiastical archaeology, the tourists were more likely expecting to hear the official old Communist dogma about religion being the opium of the people and missionaries being tools of Western imperialism, not this enthusiastic reference to Christianity by a member of China's academic elite.

Had Christianity reached far deeper into Chinese culture and society than most people inside or outside China hitherto thought? My own answer is, definitely yes, as this book, based upon decades of interest in the topic and extensive reporting in China in the summer and fall of 2002, will show.

HOW MANY CHRISTIANS IN CHINA?

Just how many Christians are there in China? The answer is not a simple one.

As part of their tour, the Americans had visited several large churches that are allowed by the Communist government to operate formally in both Beijing and China (beginning in the late 1970s). Some of these had been constructed decades earlier in the era of vigorous missionary activity in China. The visitors had been surprised to discover how packed these churches were, not just on Sundays, but even during mid-week worship or other teaching occasions.

The only Protestant Chinese organization that is permitted by the Communist Party to function openly is the China Christian Council (CCC), a sort of organizational umbrella for China's officially approved Protestant churches. The CCC was formed in the early 1980s to provide China's Protestant Christian church hierarchy just a little distance from the government organization established by the Communist Party in the 1950s to take control of Chinese Protestantism. This was the Three Self Patriotic Movement (TSPM), an administrative entity designed to ensure that all the activities of China's officially approved Protestant churches conformed to Beijing's political and social objectives. As we shall see, the relationship of the CCC and the Three Self from the beginning has been overlapping. The only Catholic organization permitted to function is the Catholic Patriotic Association (CPA).

The CCC routinely claims to have some 15 million baptized believers on its church rolls throughout China. The CPA says its churches have registered 6 million baptized Catholics.

But these figures are not considered credible even by China's own Public Security Bureau, the official police force, which in the past few years has indicated privately that there are at least 25 million Christians in China. Both Chinese within China and visiting outside observers generally believe that the numbers of Christians who attend churches not approved by the government—unofficial, so-called "house churches"—may exceed by a factor of three or four those under the various Chinese government-approved umbrellas.

In effect, the number of Christian believers in China, both Catholic and Protestant, may be closer to 80 million than the official combined Catholic-Protestant figure of 21 million. But, the reality is simply that no one knows for sure. All we do know is that Christianity has grown at a staggering speed since 1979, when China began to relax the fierce restrictions on religious activity that had been imposed during the Cultural Revolution in the 1960s.

CHRISTIANS EVERYWHERE

It was already clear in the 1980s that Christians were beginning to show up, though almost never identified as such, within the Chinese Communist Party. But during the 1990s it became clear that something else was happening too. I began to meet intellectuals, academics, social scientists, businessmen, artists and musicians, some of them party members, most of them not, who were unmistakably Christian believers, and who acknowledged this privately.

I began to meet increasing numbers of visitors to China, some of them ethnic Chinese, some of them Westerners, who had extraordinary tales of their own about visits with Christian contacts across China while visiting the country. I was unprepared for the dimensions of what I learned.

In 2000, I was in Guangzhou, to which several leaders of the Fangcheng fellowship, one of China's largest house church networks, traveled in order to update me on their views of the latest condition of Christianity in China. By then, it had long since become clear to me that the progress of Christianity in China was not something that belonged just in the annual newsletter of some church missionary group in America's Bible Belt.

From the grassroots of the peasantry to high within China's establishment, the country was being seeded with believing Christians. In numerical terms they were still a small minority, perhaps 7 to 8 percent of the country's 1.2 billion population. But they were being noticed, and they kept turning up in the most unexpected places.

Consulate officers. I learned, for example, that at least three of the six Chinese consulates in the United States have Christian believers among their officers. The embassy in Tokyo has at least one. It is very probable that Christians are among the officers of Chinese embassies all over Europe, Asia, Africa, and Latin America. I discovered that there are deputy provincial governors, judges, and lawyers in China who are Christians, and that legal experts were working hard behind the scenes to try to implement laws of religious freedom and the larger concept of the rule of law—not just for Christians to be able to worship without harassment, but for followers of all faiths.

Entrepreneurs. There are Christian entrepreneurs at every level of Chinese society, including some of the richest men in the country. Zhang Jian, thirty-eight, is the founder and CEO of Broad air conditioners, founder and president of the Hai'er Air-Conditioning Company, and the first Chinese to own his own helicopter. Jian has also been a Christian for more than a year now and is eager to link up with other Christian businessmen around the country.

Actors, singers, and more. There are Christian actors, singers, and conductors in China, and these have been able to acknowledge their faith with much greater openness than those in other professions. For the second year in a row, in December 2002, Beijing's Forbidden City Concert Hall resonated to the solos and choruses of Handel's *Messiah*, performed in Chinese by the choir of the National Symphony Orchestra and the China Film Symphony Orchestra, under the baton of Su Wenxing, an openly professing Chinese Christian. Perhaps even more remarkable than the performance itself was the report in the official English-language newspaper, *China Daily*, on the event, and on Su himself. "Many great composers such as Bach and Handel were loyal Christians," the paper quoted Su, who also goes by the Christian name of Timothy, as saying. "Since I became a Christian [in 1996], I have had a new understanding of them and interpret them much better." The paper, noting Su's youthful age of thirty, quoted a renowned Chinese conductor describing Su as "one of the best conductors in the country for oratorio and religious songs."[1]

There are Christians in journalism at both the national and the local levels, but it is harder for them to indicate their beliefs to colleagues and outsiders because, in an authoritarian regime, journalism is always considered primarily a government propaganda tool to control and influence thought.

There are Christian-run homes for old people, Christian-run orphanages and hospitals, and Christian private schools the length and breadth of China.

The Communist Party and the People's Liberation Army. I heard from many Chinese Christians that there are Christian officers and enlisted men in the People's Liberation Army. I have not been able personally to meet any, and for obvious reasons I would not reveal their identity if I had.

Chinese officials have acknowledged several times that there are Christians within the Communist Party, though we do not know how high up they go, any more than we know how high up Christians can be found in China's government apparatus. I have certainly met a few.

What we do know is that several of the sons and daughters of current or past Chinese leaders have become Christian and been baptized. Li Peng, a former premier whose last post before retirement in the spring of 2003 was chairman of the National People's Congress, has a daughter who studied in Japan and was baptized a Christian there. Wang Guangmei, widow of Mao's primary political target during the Cultural Revolution, Liu Shaoqi, has three daughters, all of whom have been baptized as Christians.

Students and scholars. In fact, perhaps half of all of China's students and scholars studying in the U.S., estimated to number as many as 150,000, according to statistics from the Ministry of Education, attended church at least once during their time in the United States. Many, of course, become Christians and get baptized while they are here.

Zhang Boli, a former student dissident who was on the police list of the twenty-one most-wanted student leaders of the 1989 Tiananmen Square protests, became a Christian while on the run in his own country before escaping in 1991. Now a pastor of two Chinese churches in the Washington, D.C., area, he estimates that as many as 20 percent of all Chinese at universities outside of China may by now have become Christian.

Political dissidents. Zhang Boli notes that he is one of at least two Christian clergy from the original twenty-one most-wanted student protest leaders, both now in the U.S. The other is Xiong Yan, who had been part of the Tiananmen hunger strike team and one of the student representatives who met, futilely, with leaders like Li Peng himself in an effort to defuse the tensions shortly before the June 4, 1989, crackdown. Xiong is now preparing to be a chaplain for the U.S. Army.

Two other Tiananmen protest leaders are also Christian. One of them, Wu Er Kaixi, currently lives in Taiwan with his Taiwanese wife. Originally of Uighur ethnic minority background in Xinjiang province, Wu was baptized in Taiwan by Zhang Boli in 2002. The other is Han Dongfang, the founder of the Beijing Autonomous Workers' Federation. Han actually walked into a police station in July 1989 to protest his inclusion on the most-wanted lists, convinced that he had done nothing wrong during the student protests. He was promptly arrested and was thrown into a cell in the infectious diseases ward of a prison, where he contracted tuberculosis and nearly died in prison. Released and permitted to go to the U.S. in 1992 on medical grounds, he was converted in an overseas Chinese church in New Jersey in 1993. He now resides in Hong Kong, broadcasting to China about Chinese labor problems for Radio Free Asia.

Some other Christian dissidents include Wang Xizhe, who was imprisoned for helping pen a "big-character" protest poster in Guangzhou in 1974 and subsequently spent seventeen years in prison in China. He was baptized as a Christian in California in 2001. Two other prominent dissidents who became Christian while in exile are Dr. Wang Bingzhang and Dr. Yang Jianli; both were arrested within the past two years and are currently serving prison terms.

THE IMPACT OF A CHRISTIANIZED CHINA

Clearly, Christianity is filtering into multiple aspects of Chinese society. But what does this mean? During three months of reporting the situation of Christianity in China in 2002, I was startled to discover other aspects of the Christian growth that are of profound importance to how the world responds to Islamic-origin terrorism in the wake of the events of September 11, 2001.

One journal of Chinese Protestant house church Christians, printed clandestinely, admitted that some Chinese had applauded the terrorist attacks on American civilians, but pointed out—quite accurately—that a number of Chinese (along with citizens from more than seventy other nations) had died in the New York World Trade Center attacks. Therefore, the magazine pointed out, President George W. Bush's decision to claim war against the terrorists was to maintain justice, and so was Biblical in nature.

The vast majority of China's Protestant house church Christians, it turns out, are deeply pro-American and determined to evangelize the Muslim world, something Americans generally have been too frightened to do with much boldness. Among Chinese Christians themselves is the belief—indeed some Chinese Christians refer to it as a divine calling—for Christian believers from China to bring the Gospel to the Muslim nations of the world.

"Muslims prefer Chinese to Americans. They don't like Americans very much," one Chinese Christian said boldly. He outlined several reasons why Chinese Christians can succeed where Westerners have failed. "The Chinese government supports [Middle Eastern] terrorism [he didn't mean literally, only in the sense of supporting the anti-American objectives of some political groups in the Middle East] so the Muslim nations support China. Besides, we have a lot of experience of persecution. As Chinese missionaries, wherever we go, when we arrive in a place we always see what the escape route will be."

This Chinese Christian articulated the view that Chinese believers would play a major role in the circumnavigation of the teachings of Jesus back to the Middle East. "We have the view that Chinese missionaries will be part of the mainstream on the highway back to Jerusalem. The Muslim religion is the biggest obstacle on the road back to Jerusalem," he said.

A Christianized China is poised to change the face not just of Christendom worldwide, but potentially of the world of Islam.

AN OPPORTUNE TIME FOR CHRISTIANITY

ECONOMIC GROWTH AND THE "OPEN DOOR"

China has never been as intellectually and philosophically open to the outside world as it is today. Deng Xiaoping, who came to power in 1978, opened China up both to its own latent internal creative energies and to the outside world with his famous "open door" policy. To unleash the considerable energy and creative talents of China's entrepreneurs and workers, the regime took a conscious decision to loosen many of the clamps that had been fastened in place on Chinese social and civil life for decades.

For example, until the 1980s, every Chinese was at the mercy of his or her work unit, the *danwei*, a control system that determined residence location, job description, often even whether marriage was permissible or not. As the demand for flexible labor deployment grew, the *danwei* system, though still in place in much of the country, began to break down.

As China came to require a much deeper knowledge than hitherto allowed of the outside world in order to compete economically in the global marketplace, it became possible for ordinary Chinese to have contact with foreigners, then to travel overseas, and more recently, to have access to foreign-source information—including much information about China—through the Internet. Though the Chinese Communist Party still blocks key Internet sites, and occasionally resorts to blocking search engines like Google, overall, China's authorities have permitted their people unprecedented freedom of intellectual investigation and social activity at the *private* level for most of the past decade.

An inquisitive Chinese in China today would have no difficulty finding out the name of the prime minister of Montenegro, the total size of the U.S. defense budget, or for that matter, what the Christian theological issues at stake were in the fourth-century dispute between Arius and Athanasius. A Chinese interested in religion can attend, without fear of the consequences, any officially approved Protestant or Catholic church, can purchase books that explain, even sympathetically, the nature of Christian belief, can buy a Bible (but only at a TSPM or CPA church, not in any ordinary bookstore), and can openly question a pastor or priest about the differences between, say, Premillennialist Dispensational eschatology and that of the Protestant Reformed tradition.

Foreign capital, technological expertise, and management skills flowed into the country. From 1979 until the late 1990s, China's GDP grew at an annual rate of 9.5 percent, in some years reaching into the superheated zone of 14 percent. Things have slowed down somewhat since then, but not by much. Annual growth rate for the period 1996–2000 has been about 8.3 percent, and it appears to have slowed down by only about one percentage point in the two years since then.

Yet, the headlong growth of the economy has brought along plenty of downsides, including company collapses, stock market volatility, and dangerously widening income gaps between China's rich coastal cities and the impoverished inland provinces. The migration from countryside to city has led to a "floating population" of millions of illegal squatters in Beijing and other major cities and has depressed industrial wages in many parts of the country. Working conditions in many of China's urban factories may well be worse today than at any time in China's Communist history. Corruption in China is broadly acknowledged, and regularly deplored, at the very highest level of political leadership. Virtually every American business executive who has had anything to do with China can rattle off personal encounters with corruption. Beyond the occasional high-profile arrests and executions, little is done to fix the problems.

"In China you can do anything you like if you have money. The only thing you can't do is what you can't think up to do," said a Chinese who lives in the United States but visits his home country several times each year. One of his good friends, a senior judge in an inland province, told him that, for 30,000–50,000 yuan (approximately $3,750–6,250), even a man on death row could buy his freedom. Furthermore, if the sentence were commuted to fifteen years in prison, not even that would have to be served. Many Chinese, the judge told this Chinese, will actually do the prison time for you if you pay them, say, $30 a month.

China's Communist regime still ruthlessly represses people for any explicit display of political protest, as practitioners of the Falungong meditation practice discovered to their painful cost during 1998–2001. At the local level, sadistic provincial officials also can, and do, take the law into their own hands for arbitrary purposes. Christians who choose to meet together without formal authorization or registration of their organization can be, and have been, right up through 2003, arrested, beaten, and tortured without compunction by local officials of the Public Security Bureau.[2]

But compared with the blanket of desolate socialist totalitarianism that smothered the creative springs of China's culture and thought-life from the late 1950s until about 1978, today's civic freedom is a heady breath of intellectual liberty.

These factors—economic growth, increasing access to information, added civic freedoms, and the need for a consciousness to combat the social ills of prosperity—combine to create an opportune atmosphere for the growth of Christianity in China both as a movement and as an ideology.

FILLING AN IDEOLOGICAL VACUUM

It is significant that Christianity is emerging in China at a time when there is a massive ideological vacuum left in society by the nationwide collapse of belief in Marxism-Leninism.

Mao's catastrophic Cultural Revolution had "cured" almost all Chinese of any belief in the veracity of Communist theory. It is hard to find anyone in China today who truly believes in the theoretical truth of China's official political ideology, ponderously called "Marxism-Leninism, Mao Zedong thought." Marxism was tried in the extreme form during Mao's nearly two decades of utopian economic and social tinkering (1958–1976) and it was found to be irremediably destructive.

The Communist Party has managed to maintain power for more than a decade after the Tiananmen Square demonstrations in 1989, despite predictions that it would probably fade from power quite soon, for two reasons: sheer inertia and the fear among most ordinary

Chinese of *luan,* or chaos, that destructive anarchic condition that many foreigners thought was China's natural condition in the past two centuries. Fewer than four years after the 1989 crackdown, in 1993, I spoke to Chinese intellectuals at several of the nation's universities. The consensus was uniform: democracy, yes, but please not next week. They did not want to see any political change come *quickly* to China.

When Deng launched his "open door" movement of internal reforms and access to China of foreign capital and expertise, Chinese quickly grasped that, from an economic point of view, capitalism was now becoming the system of choice to make China strong. With straight-faced chicanery, the regime called the new system "socialism with Chinese characteristics."

This phrase obscured a more important point: what way of looking at life in general should Chinese now adopt? Marxism-Leninism itself was a dead letter. Confucianism, the ethical and moral system that China's ruling dynasties and ordinary people had sought to emulate for millennia, was certainly admired for its emphasis on family cohesion and mutual responsibility. But most Chinese considered it an unwieldy philosophy, incapable of the social change, capitalistic creativity, and entrepreneurial success needed in the newly globalized world of economic competition.

Many Chinese wondered: is capitalism just a way of doing business, or did it come with concrete ethical and philosophical foundations? Many Chinese sociologists note that, in the coastal city of Wenzhou, in Zhejiang province, south of Shanghai, Christianity in the 1980s seemed to surge proportionately to the success of Wenzhou retailers in making money. In fact, a decade ago, some Chinese, thinking about capitalism, Christianity, and Wenzhou, were making the intellectual connection between religion and the rise of capitalism, the central thesis of R. H. Tawney in his influential book with the same name, *Religion and the Rise of Capitalism.*[3]

Perhaps, some Chinese began to think, Christianity itself, which had been such a powerful, if not fully understood, ingredient in the global pre-eminence of Western civilization, may be a worldview, even a metaphysic, that could guide China's pathway into the twenty-first century. Perhaps it could even provide a lens for Chinese to understand their own history with greater insight than ever before.

A NEW WORLDVIEW FOR THE CHINESE?

By the early 1990s, a new kind of Chinese had come into existence at Chinese universities and research institutions: "cultural Christians." Many reject the name, as we shall see later, and prefer to use the ponderous phrase "Chinese scholars interested in Christianity." But the phenomenon was real enough: highly educated Chinese who were not satisfied that either the Marxist interpretation of religion or the standard Western Darwinian understanding of life adequately explained the human condition in general and the Chinese condition in particular.

Nor was it among just Western-trained academics or Shanghai yuppies that these ideas began to be discussed. Early in 2002, China's then president and Communist Party leader, Jiang Zeming, attended a dinner party in the private home of another senior Chinese political figure in the heart of Beijing. The conversation turned to the party's upcoming sixteenth congress, a momentous, once-every-five-years gathering then scheduled for the late autumn of 2002 (the Congress eventually met November 7–15, 2002).

The company was relaxed, the mood ebullient. "Comrade Jiang," a guest asked, "if, before leaving office, you could make one decree that you knew would be obeyed in China, what would it be?" Jiang put on a broad smile and looked around the room. "I would make Christianity the official religion of China," he replied.[4] Jiang, of course, formally relinquished the reins of power at the sixteenth party congress to his successor as party general secretary, Hu Jintao, and even if he wanted to implement that wish, is no longer in a position to do so. But even if he were being merely playful with his fellow guests, his whimsical comment was telling.

In 1949, the world's most populous nation adopted the materialist philosophy of a nineteenth-century German and a twentieth-century Russian in its search for wealth and power after a century of foreign encroachments on its government and culture. That philosophy turned out to be bankrupt and China is almost self-consciously casting around for something to replace it. Christianity has not yet been embraced as that replacement by the Chinese people, but today it is in a very good position to do so.

Foreigners, and especially foreign Christians, have for centuries yearned for China to change in a direction they considered desirable for both Chinese and themselves. Often, their hopes and aspirations have been illusory or just plain naïve. But China, whether it becomes Christian or goes in another direction, *is* changing right before our eyes. It is the Christian component of that change, and the remarkable potential that it contains, that this book is about.

Chapter Two

PATHFINDERS

ON A SUMMER'S AFTERNOON, the Forest of Steles Museum (formerly called the Shaanxi Provincial Museum) in the heart of Xian, Shaanxi Province, dozes through temperatures in the nineties. Squads of tired-looking American and French tourists come and go, while city hawkers make desultory efforts at peddling fans, bottled water, and postcards. Nestled close to the southern wall of the old city of Xian, the museum is actually located within an old Confucian temple. It is famous, among other things, for being probably the oldest continuously established museum in China. The first collection of ancient stone tablets with carved inscriptions, still on display in the various halls of the museum, was established more than 900 years ago, in 1090, when officials of the Song Dynasty sought to protect the texts of the Chinese Classics that had been carved in stone more than two centuries earlier during the Tang Dynasty.

The Forest of Steles Museum is not the most famous site in the Xian area. That honor belongs to the Museum of Qin Shi Huang, outside of the city. Tour groups alighting in Xian head straight for this remarkable destination. The museum's terra-cotta warriors, lined up in relentless ranks like a ghostly regiment, speak to the achievements of one of the most brilliant and ruthless national leaders of all antiquity. Qin Shi Huang, founder of China's short-lived Qin Dynasty (221–206 B.C.), conquered six rival kingdoms through guile, patience, and sheer brutality, to force together what became China, one of the great cultural centers of human history. He started the building of the Great Wall, killing hundreds of thousands of forced labor workers in the process, unified the system of writing and of weights and measures, and buried alive hundreds of scholars of preexisting Chinese culture and other presumed political opponents, so that he could, as it were, start the nation from scratch.

Years earlier I had already visited the terra-cotta warriors. Now I was back in Xian to see something in the Forest of Steles Museum that was central to the story of how Christianity first arrived in China: the Nestorian Tablet, a two-ton stone tablet standing more than nine feet tall and three feet wide, and inscribed with 1,900 beautifully carved Chinese characters. It was an official account of the first major Christian mission to China, an event that took place in A.D. 635, a short years after the start of the Tang Dynasty (A.D. 618–906), one of the most brilliant eras in China's history.

The stele had been inscribed in the year 781 at the orders of the Emperor Dezong. For eight and a half centuries, it lay mysteriously buried in the earth in the countryside outside Xian. It was not until 1623 that workers digging the foundation of a house came across the tablet.[1] By one of those strange historical coincidences, the magistrate of the area where it was found just happened to know of the small handful of Western scholars and priests, the foreign Jesuit community, then living in Peking.[2] Realizing that the tablet had something to say about the earliest known appearance of Christianity in China, he sent them a paper rubbing of the inscription. To their delight and surprise, this was an official account detailing the arrival of Nestorian Christians in China nearly one thousand years earlier.

The tablet stands upright, encased in glass, upon the back of a carved stone tortoise. A cross rising out of lotus lilies tops the arrow-shaped heading of the inscription. Below, the heading in large Chinese characters reads "The Record of the Transmission of the Religion of

Light of the West in China." The Chinese characters that follow set forth not only the theology of those early Christian travelers from Central Asia, but also the story of how they were received by the imperial authorities in Changan, site of the present-day city of Xian.

According to the stele, an impressive-looking delegation of foreigners arrived in the city of Changan, the capital of the Tang Dynasty, in the year 635. Their leader was a revered representative of a new religion (to the Chinese) who wore a long flowing white robe and was attended by followers carrying various carved images (probably a crucifix and small sculptured portrayals of the Virgin Mary). The leader's name was Aluoben[3] and he had come from Persia via the well-traveled trade route of the ancient Silk Road, the main thoroughfare of trade between China and the Mediterranean world for millennia. As far as the courteous Tang Dynasty court was concerned, Aluoben had come simply from "the West," a phrase that translates the habitually used characters *da qin* (pronounced *da chin*).[4] At the time of Aluoben's journey in 635, according to the tablet, *da qin* meant the political domains west of China's long reach into Central Asia, and often referred to Persia, where there was a large and vigorous Christian community.

NESTORIANS FROM "THE WEST"

The Christian community from which Aluoben had come, however, was neither Western, i.e. Catholic, nor Greek Orthodox. It was a branch of Christianity that called itself the Church of the East, also known as the "Nestorian Church." A former bishop of Constantinople, Nestorius (circa A.D. 390–451) was deposed from his see in 431 A.D. by the Council of Ephesus. He had objected to the official church use of the term Mother of God (*theotokos* in Greek) as applied to the Virgin Mary, and he held that the human and divine nature of Christ were not united in one person, as Christian orthodoxy maintained, but were separate entities. Nestorius was exiled to the Libyan desert, but his followers migrated to Persia, where they took over the existing Christian church, assuming the name of the Church of the East.

The official language was, and remains, Syriac, and the community, now numbering several hundred thousand, is usually called the Assyrian Church. It is based in modern Iraq.[5]

The Nestorians, as these adventurous Christians of the Church of the East came to be called, were zealous missionaries, introducing Christianity first to the oases and towns in Central Asia along the Silk Road, then to the Western, Turkic-speaking regions of China occupying present-day Xinjiang province. It is the Syriac alphabet, turned ninety degrees so it was read top to bottom instead of left to right and named the Uighur script, that became the official writing system first of the Turkic peoples of Western China, the Uighurs, then of the Mongols, and finally of the Manchus, the last foreign conquerors of China.

The Nestorian stele makes it clear that the purpose of Aluoben's visit and that of his delegation in 635 had nothing to do with tribute giving, the traditional reason for foreigners to request an audience with the emperor. His sole purpose was to introduce a new religion into China, referred to by the Chinese characters *jing jiao,* and variously translated as "religion of light" or "luminous religion." The stele describes the beliefs of these visitors from Persia.

The "teachings" contained in the Nestorian stele are certainly a recognizable expression of basic Christian doctrine. "In the beginning," says the inscription, "was the natural constant, the true stillness of the origin and the primordial void of the Most High. Then, the spirit of the void emerged as the Most High Lord, moving in mysterious ways to enlighten the old ones. He is Joshua [i.e., Jesus], my True Lord of the Void, who embodies the three subtle and wondrous bodies, and who was condemned to the Cross so that the people of the four directions can be saved." The "teachings" go on to speak of the influence of Satan (in the Garden of Eden) and "My Lord Ye Su [Jesus], the one emanating in three subtle bodies," who "became human, and came on behalf of the Lord of Heaven to preach the good teachings. A virgin gave birth to the Sacred in a dwelling in the Da Qin Empire."[6]

So far, it is obvious that the stele is talking about Christianity. But there is enough in the phrasing and vocabulary of the Nestorian stele to suggest that it is a strongly syncretistic version of Christianity. A leading scholar of the Nestorian stele, Englishman Martin Palmer, asserts that that the version of Christianity brought to the Tang court by Aluoben had already been deeply influenced by Daoist philosophy.[7] Palmer believes that the flowery, philosophical language of the Nestorian stele, as well as the lotus-leaf symbol at its top, indicates that the Nestorians had absorbed Daoist concepts even as they sought to bring the "religion of light" to the Chinese court.

The stele refers to the worship style of these eighth-century Christians. "At seven [in the morning]," it reads, "we gather for service to pray for the salvation of all. Every seven days we have an audience with heaven. We purify our hearts and return to the simple and natural way of the truth."[8]

According to the tablet, the Nestorian community gained great favor from the imperial Chinese authorities early on. "When the emperor heard their teachings," the stone relates, "he realized deeply that they spoke the truth." The emperor then issued a decree: "Proclaim the teachings everywhere for the salvation of the people. Aluoben, the man of great virtue from the Da Qin empire, came from a far land and arrived at the capital to present the teachings and images of his religion. His message is mysterious and wonderful beyond our understanding."[9] Thereafter the teachings were translated into Chinese, and Christian communities were established throughout Tang China.

According to the stele, the first 150 years of these Christian missionaries in China constituted a period of great favor and success, though there was a temporary setback in 698 when Buddhists hostile to the growing Christian success initiated a brief period of persecution. By the first part of the eighth century, the Nestorians seem to have recovered from this setback and even improved their situation, according to the stele. During the reign of the Tang emperor Xuanzong, a senior Tang general was ordered to attend the consecration of an important church in the vicinity of Changan (present-day Xian), referred to as the Five Saints Church. This occurred around A.D. 742. By the time of the inscription of the stele in 781, Nestorian Christianity in China may have been at its apogee.

But then disaster struck. In Central Asia the new expansionist faith of Islam was already moving rapidly to conquer new areas of the world. In 751 Muslims defeated the Chinese armies in Central Asia. The Turkic-speaking Uighur kingdoms, largely Christianized for several hundred years, were taken over by Islam. The Silk Road, along which Aluoben and his delegation had traveled, was now in hands unfriendly to Christianity. Meanwhile, in China itself a strong reaction again foreign religions set in at the Tang court. In 845, an imperial decree, lashing out at any religion considered "foreign," ordered the three thousand monks belonging to "the Religion of Light" and the Zoroastrian religion to return to lay life, "so that they will not adulterate the customs of China."[10]

Who carved the stele and why was it hidden in the ground for over eight centuries? The stele itself says that it was carved by the monk Jingjing of the Da Qin Monastery. Englishman Palmer speculates that the Nestorian stele was carved to commemorate the significant event of the founding of that monastery. A twentieth-century Japanese scholar of early Chinese Christianity, P. Y. Saeki, drew a map in the 1930s in which he indicated that there was indeed a Da Qin monastery, or at least the remaining pagoda of such an establishment, still standing, some fifty miles southwest of Xian. In 1998 Palmer, using Saeki's map, suddenly rediscovered Da Qin, which was visible to the naked eye west of a prominent Daoist monastery. A seven-story pagoda leaning, Pisa-like, dangerously to one side, it was not in any tourist guidebook and had for years been thought of as a Daoist relic. An old Buddhist nun occupying a little hut-like temple close by the pagoda casually told Palmer on his first visit that though the pagoda had been taken over by Daoists, it had originally been established by "monks who came from the West and believed in one God."[11] A year later, Palmer revisited the site, and in the company of local officials and archaeologists and historians, climbed up into the pagoda to scrutinize two statues, both of them damaged, that had survived from the pagoda's very beginnings back in the eighth century. One of them was of the Virgin and Child, and the other of Jonah in Nineveh. Palmer realized that he had stumbled upon the oldest surviving Christian church in China, more than twelve centuries old. The Nestorian stele dug up in 1623 may well have been at this site, whose establishment it honored.

In the summer of 2002, I hired a driver/guide and rode out to Da Qin, a good ninety minutes from central Xian. You can't drive up the hillside to the pagoda, so we parked the car at the foot of the hill, and for about $1.50 each rented two horses for the ascent. It's a nice ride up the lush hillside on an unpaved dirt road that winds through fields thick with corn and kiwi fruit. I learned on arrival that about one hundred foreigners each year made their way to this earliest location of Christian worship in China. A toothless old Buddhist monk, who takes care of a little cubbyhole shrine at the ground level of the pagoda, shuffled out of his hut to insist that I buy Buddhist joss sticks before being permitted into this shrine. In the extremely basic, one-room "museum" next to the pagoda are framed English and Hong Kong newspaper clippings from 1999. "Beyond Belief," reads a head-line from *The Independent* of October 1999: "an obsessed English-man made one of the most important archeological finds of the century." The official caretaker of the museum, an unkempt, unshaven man in dirty pants and shirt called Li Huixiong, said that I could have entered the pagoda itself if I had given them a day's notice and been willing to pay the $50 required to bring up the necessary ladders. I hadn't known about that.

I asked Mr. Li what had happened to the church building that stood next to the pagoda for many centuries. "Destroyed by Red Guards," he said curtly, referring to an incident that took place almost certainly in 1966 or 1967, when Mao's Red Guards were most aggressive in stamping out opposition and any visible trace of religion across China. Mao's teenage acolytes had succeeded in eliminating the main building of the Da Qin monastery. But not even they had been able, or courageous enough, to topple the Christian pagoda.

The Nestorians not only survived the antiforeign purges of the late Tang but even the upheavals during the Mongol conquest of China in the twelfth and thirteenth centuries. Marco Polo and other visitors from the West reported the presence of Nestorian Christians in various parts of China. One of the most famous Chinese Nestorians, Rabban Sauma, actually of Turkic ethnic background in a China then ruled by the Mongols, traveled to Western Europe in the thirteenth century in an effort to enlist European cooperation with the Mongols to liberate Jerusalem from the Muslims. Rabban Sauma was courteously, even enthusiastically, received by Edward I of England and by Pope Nicholas IV. Both King Edward and the pope received communion from Rabban Sauma, an indication that, at least by this time, the "Nestorian" Church of the East was not considered heretical.

Neither Rome nor Byzantium, the two centers of Western and Eastern Christendom for hundreds of years, had any notion of what the Nestorians had accomplished in China until a terrifying threat to the very existence of Europe swept in upon them from the East: the Mongols. A gifted leader of a small subtribe of the nomadic Mongols, Temujin (1167–1227), had united the Mongol tribes by the year 1206 and taken on the name he has been known by throughout history, Chingis Khan (traditionally, and incorrectly, spelled Ghengis Khan), or "universal ruler." He and his sons and grandsons then embarked on some of the most ferocious and broad-ranging campaigns of global conquest that the world had ever seen. By 1215 Chingis had overrun north China. In 1219 the Mongols decimated Persia. Though Chingis himself died in 1227, his sons Jochi, Chagatai, Ogedei, and Tolui and his grandsons Guyuk, Mongke, and Kublai continued the expansion of the Mongolian Empire eastward and westward. The Russians were initially defeated in battle in 1222, though Moscow was not actually conquered until the second Mongol invasion of 1238. Kiev was taken in 1240. In 1241 at the Battle of Liegnitz, a German-Polish army was decimated. The Hungarians were crushed at the Battle of Mohi in 1242. Everywhere the Mongols conquered, they slaughtered men, women, and children by the millions. After conquering Herat in Persia, they killed 1.6 million people, after Khoresm 1.2 million, after Merv 1.3 million, and after Nishapur 1.7 million. Not until the twentieth century did any conquering power slaughter as many subject peoples in such a short period of time.

In 1242, Europe braced itself for a renewed onslaught of these savage armies from the steppes of Central Asia. But Europe was spared. The death of Ogodei, the third son of Chingis, and the need to select a new great khan diverted the Mongol armies from further devastation of Europe and drew them back to the Mongol capital for the election of a new leader.

At this point, in 1243, the newly elected pope in Rome, Innocentius IV, decided to take the initiative in reaching out to the Mongols with a message from Christendom before they resumed their conquests of Europe. He selected an overweight but intelligent and zealously evangelical sixty-year-old Franciscan friar, Giovanni da Plano Carpini, to take a letter from the pope to Guyuk Khan, the emergent Mongol leader, warning him that he would be under divine judgment if he attacked the Christians of Europe.

Traveling barefoot because he belonged to a mendicant order, Plano Carpini and his chief companion, Brother Benedict from Poland, set off from Italy in 1245, arriving in Karakorum, capital of the main Mongol army, in 1246, just in time for the enthronement ceremonies of Guyuk Khan. The Franciscan monk delivered the message from the pope and made earnest efforts to persuade Guyuk of his need to become a Christian. While politely declining to take that course, Guyuk sent Carpini back to Rome with a menacing letter of his own to the pope. The Vicar of Christ on earth, Guyuk said, should show up at Guyuk's court at the head of a delegation of all of the kings of Europe. He added, "[I]f you do not observe God's command, I shall know you as my enemy. Likewise if you do otherwise, God knows what I know. Whoever recognizes and submits to the Son of God and Lord of the World, the Great Khan, will be saved, whoever refuses submission will be wiped out."[12]

Europe was once again spared from the Mongols by internal divisions within the Mongol Empire itself. Guyuk died in 1248, not long after Carpini had began his long and arduous journey back to Europe, and there were furious internal disputes among the Mongols over who would succeed him.

Seven years later, in 1253, French King Louis IX took the initiative, sending another Franciscan off to Mongolia—Willem de Rubruck, an intelligent observer and debater who had accompanied

Louis on an abortive crusade to retake the city of Acre in the Holy Land. Rubruck's diplomatic purpose in traveling to Mongolia was quite different from Carpini's: Louis believed that the Mongols could be recruited to join the Western European nations in their fight against the Saracens.

Rubruck was summoned to a sort of interreligious debate in the presence of the khan at the end of May in 1254. The khan rather courteously declined Rubruck's vigorous efforts to turn him into a Christian, and also sent him back to the pope, though without such a minatory message as had been carried by Plano Carpini. Once back to Europe, Rubruck reported that Nestorian Christians were prominent among the family members of Guyuk. By this time, however, the Nestorians seem to have lost whatever legitimacy they had shown on their original arrival in China centuries earlier. Rubruck described them as "absolutely depraved," given to drunken feasts and to marrying multiple wives.[13]

The next significant Westerner to meet with the new ruler of the Mongols, and of China, was Marco Polo. The young Venetian adventurer first met Kublai Khan, grandson of Chingis Khan, in 1266 north of Peking. Though certainly no missionary, Polo had originally set off to Asia with two Dominican missionaries assigned by the pope to accompany him. The Dominicans got cold feet en route and dropped out, but Marco Polo came back to Europe with a remarkable request from the khan. He would like Europe to send to China, he said, one hundred missionaries, "wise men of learning in the Christian religion and doctrine." These men should know "the seven arts," meaning Western science and learning, "and be fitted to teach [the Chinese and Mongol] people and . . . should know well how to argue and how to show plainly to [Kublai] and to the idolaters and to the other classes of people . . . that all their religion was erroneous . . . that the Christian faith and religion is better than theirs and more true than all the other religions." If the pope could send such missionaries, Kublai promised, "he and all his potentates would become men of the church."[14]

But despite being confronted suddenly with one of history's most amazing open doors, Rome dithered. Instead of the hundred missionaries requested by Kublai, a solitary Franciscan, Giovanni of Monte Corvino (1246–1329), arrived in Peking, at the time called Khanbalik (also spelled Cambaluc), in 1294, after Kublai's death. Monte Corvino was given support by Kublai's successor, grandson Timur Oljeitu (who ruled 1294–1307) and by Prince George of the Onguts, who had converted to Roman Catholicism from his original Nestorian faith. Despite furious opposition from China's jealous Nestorians, the Catholics slowly built up a base in China's capital. Monte Corvino built a church in 1299, and six years later claimed that at least six thousand Chinese and Mongols had been baptized. In 1307 the pope of the day, Clement V, appointed him archbishop of Peking. With further clerical reinforcements sent from Rome, the Catholics in China established a thriving community in the port of Quanzhou,[15] on the coast of Fujian Province.

But the tide was now turning once again against Christians in China. The *pax mongolica* that had made possible rapid and relatively safe (with Mongol approval) travel across Eurasia and which had been at the outset distinctly favorable to Christians, was being altered from within by the growing conversion of Mongols to Islam.

Though the Nestorians existed in large and powerful communities up through the Yuan (Mongol) Dynasty (1268–1372), they suffered severely during the antiforeign Chinese nationalist upsurge at the beginning of the Ming Dynasty, which replaced the Mongols. The Ming Dynasty itself rode into power in Peking on the back of a peasant rebellion led by Zhu Yuanzhang, who became the first Ming emperor. Zhu had previously been part of a revolt against Mongol rule organized by a religious rebellion called the "Red Turbans," and many of the rebels believed that the change of dynasty would make possible the coming of the Maitreya Buddha, a messianic figure, to rule China and the world.

In addition, it seemed to most Chinese that the country's Christians belonged to a foreign religion, since their initial support had come from an alien and conquering dynasty, and they continued to rely on material support from other foreigners, inside or outside of China. By the time the Ming rebel armies swept into Peking in 1368, Chinese culture was already in the throes of one of its periodic paroxysms of antiforeignism that was hostile to Christianity in either its Nestorian form or the better organized and more recently arrived Catholics. By the end of the fourteenth century, Christianity had all but disappeared from China. It was not to be the last virtual disappearance.

Despite its incipient antiforeignism, the Ming Dynasty in China was to astonish the world by its voyages of discovery across the Indian Ocean, and down the South China Sea, and if a recent book is accurate, across both the Pacific Ocean and the Atlantic Ocean to America between 1405 and 1433 under a brilliant eunuch admiral, Zheng He.[16] Gigantic, ocean-going sailing junks, the largest of them close to 400 feet in length,[17] bore precious Chinese wares to all of the trading ports they visited, and returned to China with exotic African animals, precious stones, and ambassadors of the nations the ships had visited. But in 1433, the expeditions were suddenly ordered to stop; the oceangoing junks were destroyed, along with almost all surviving manuscript accounts of the voyages. China once again turned in upon itself.

JESUITS

It took more than two centuries before Christianity in any organized form returned to China from the outside. The Portuguese voyages of discovery of the fourteenth and fifteenth centuries, and growing European demand for access to the spice trade of Southeast Asia, led to epic sea journeys to Asia even before Columbus sighted the New World in 1492. But it was the European Reformation of the sixteenth century, and the Roman Catholic response to it, the Counter-Reformation, that sparked a renewed European effort to bring Christianity to China. This time, the carriers of the religion were highly educated priests of the newly established arm of Roman Catholicism, the Society of Jesus.

Francis Xavier, a Spanish missionary, had been a protégé of Ignatius Loyola, the founder of the Jesuits, as the Society of Jesus came to be known, in 1534. He spent most of the rest of his life as a Jesuit evangelizing in Asia, traveling, preaching, baptizing, and organizing in India, the Malayan Peninsula, the Moluccas, and Japan. In 1552 he died on the island of Shangchuan off the coast of China not far from modern Guangzhou, waiting in vain for permission to enter China.

Xavier's ardent desire to bring the Gospel into China was taken up by many other Jesuits, of which the most important was an astonishingly gifted Italian named Matteo Ricci. Just thirty when he landed in 1582 on the Portuguese-held enclave of Macau, off the southern coast of China's Guangdong Province, Ricci, whose Chinese name was Li Matou, may well be one of the most intellectually talented missionaries in all of Christian history. Almost all of the Jesuit missionaries at the time were trained in many of the advanced sciences of Europe thrown up by the Renaissance. Ricci, for example, had been trained by European experts in memorization techniques. Once he was accepted into Chinese society, Ricci astonished Chinese dinner guests with his ability to hear or read a classical Chinese poem just once and then recite it perfectly from beginning to end.[18]

Ricci worked his way into China and toward Peking slowly, first establishing a foothold in Guangdong Province and then receiving permission from the initially suspicious Chinese authorities to live in China's capital in 1601. The nine years he spent there before his death were richly fruitful for Christianity in China. His approach to China was to enter, if possible, the mindset of China's ruling intelligentsia. When he first entered China, he dressed in the robes of a Chinese Buddhist priest, but when he discovered that religious clergy from either Buddhism or Islam were less respected than members of the scholar-gentry class, Ricci changed and adopted the clothing of a Confucian scholar. He studied both spoken and written Chinese intensely and was able to write many literary works in Chinese explaining Christian concepts to an educated Chinese audience. But it was his skill as a clockmaker that provided him an entry into the court of the emperor himself. Ricci in his initial meeting with the emperor presented him with a clock, which none of the Chinese court mechanics knew how to rewind and adjust.

Ricci and other intellectually gifted Jesuits who followed him sought to acquire influence in the imperial court through their various mechanical, mathematical, cartographical, and astronomical skills, as well as through some brilliant personal diplomacy. Their initial success was remarkable. By 1605 Ricci claimed that there were more than one thousand Chinese who had been baptized as Catholics. Five years after Ricci's death, that figure had risen to more than five thousand and was growing. Ricci and his successors converted a significant number of the court eunuchs and women to the Christian faith. A Chinese scholar called Li Chowu wrote the following to a friend after meeting Ricci in the early years of the seventeenth century: Ricci "is an extraordinarily impressive person. His mind is lucid and his appearance is simple."[19] Fellow Jesuits noted that Ricci simply "wanted to become Chinese" and sought to impart Christianity as being in accord with the ethical principles of Confucian thinking. In 1632, one of Ricci's early converts, Xu Guangqi (1562–1633), was appointed grand secretary to the emperor, one of the highest positions obtainable in the Confucian bureaucracy.

As evidence of their diplomatic skill, the Jesuits were not toppled from their powerful influence in Peking even when the Ming Dynasty fell in 1644 and was replaced by the Manchus, another foreign dynasty of conquerors that had come into China from the northeast. Two of Ricci's most gifted successors, the German Adam Schall von Bell and his successor Ferdinand Verbiest, were given imperial appointments in the important arena of astronomy. The Jesuits had demonstrated that they could predict astronomic events such as eclipses more accurately than China's domestically trained observers of the stars. Their linguistic skills also benefited China in its diplomatic contacts with outside powers. In 1689, at the Treaty of Nerchinsk, which established the terms of relations between China and the emerging power of Russia, the main negotiators on each side were Latin-speaking Jesuits.

Schall died in 1666. His successor Verbiest established close personal relations with Kangxi (1654–1722), the second of the Manchurian Qing Dynasty emperors and, in the view of many historians of China, one of the most gifted Chinese imperial rulers in two millennia. Kangxi trusted Verbiest implicitly and loved to ask him probing philosophical questions. In return, Verbiest tried hard to persuade

Kangxi to adopt the Catholic faith and proclaim himself a Christian in public by being baptized. Kangxi politely but firmly declined. He was conscious of his own role as a theological linchpin in Chinese culture. One of the last century's most thoughtful historians of China's relations with the West made this analogy: "The conversion of the Chinese emperor to a foreign religion would have seemed almost as monstrous [to the ruling Chinese gentry class] as if the Pope had become a Mohammedan and still remained head of the Catholic church."[20]

Yet it seems possible that Kangxi did, in fact, come close to Christian belief, with or without the formal sacrament of Catholic baptism. Many Chinese Christians like to point to two remarkable classical Chinese poems attributed to Kangxi. One is called "The Cross," and the other "Poem on Truth." They believe these poems strongly suggest the conviction of the Christian faith. For example, "The Cross":

———

The blessed door was closed a long time for an ancient people
A mission fulfilled when the blood from the Cross became a stream
And grace a hundred-fold flowed from the West.
His body surrounded by soldiers walking the midnight road,
A disciple turned his back three times before the rooster crowed.
As five thousand whips broke his arm,
Six feet tall, he hung there, together with two thieves.
Tragedy shoot the furthest places and the highest officials.
After seven words it was finished and millions of souls cry out.
The way to Heaven depends on God's Son.[21]

———

But the Jesuits did not have a monopoly on Catholic missionary enterprise in China. They were followed by the Franciscan, Dominican, and Augustinian orders, which eschewed the patient cultivation of the literary ruling class of China in favor of direct outreach to China's lower classes. As the fame of the Jesuit achievement in China became known in Europe, organizational jealousies and theological disputes also arose. Most controversial of all was the so-called "rites controversy." Ricci and his Jesuit successors in China had argued that Chinese ancestor veneration, acted out in formal ceremonies within Chinese households, was a purely cultural phenomenon unrelated to issues of Christian faith. But other Catholics differed. Was the veneration of ancestors not a form of pagan polytheism, they argued? The debate gathered intensity during the late seventeenth and early eighteenth centuries, with the Jesuits themselves finally appealing to the Emperor Kangxi for his own ruling. Well informed about Christian doctrine— and perhaps even a Christian believer—he supported the traditional Jesuit position: the rites were cultural only, not spiritual.

In Europe there were also attacks upon the Jesuits, especially by the French followers of the French-speaking theologian Otto Jansen, founder of what became known as "the Jansenist movement" in the seventeenth century. Jansen's followers argued that Jesuits had put too much emphasis on free will and works, in contrast to grace and faith, and had compromised core Christian theology in their eagerness to please the scholar-gentry class of China. In a 1715 papal bull, the pope explicitly criticized the Jesuits for compromising Gospel truth in their acquiescence to Chinese cultural traditions.

Kangxi was infuriated not just by this papal judgment but by the way it was transmitted to him—through papal diplomats who were insultingly unfamiliar with Chinese language and culture. Kangxi began to speak of banning foreign Christian activity altogether within China. He did not live to do so, dying in 1723. But the following year his successor, Emperor Yong Zheng , issued a decree called "Edict of Expulsion and Confiscation." Throughout China, though not with uniform severity, church buildings were wrecked or turned into granaries, schools, or assembly halls. There may, at this point, have been about 300,000 Christians in China. Through local persecution and the suppression of foreign pastoral activity, that number began to dwindle in the next few decades.

The tiresome theological squabbles and intrigues among competing Catholic groups in China certainly contributed to the imperial crackdown. But another factor was probably the sheer decline in the quality of the Jesuits who served in the imperial bureaucracy. The Kangxi emperor himself complained that none of the foreign Christians performing official roles at the court toward the end of his life had a competent knowledge of Chinese.[22] Once this long-serving patron of Jesuit activity in China had died, there was no longer a strong personal connection between China's throne and Western Christians serving in the country.

Catholic missionary priests from the West, however, continued to operate at great risk inside China in the late eighteenth and early nineteenth centuries. The communities they served as pastors came under immense pressure from various forms of persecution. Several Western priests were martyred in the first half of the nineteenth century. Yet, in the year 1807, there were more than 1,800 adult Roman Catholic baptisms in China, evidence of a powerful, continuing presence of the Catholic faith in a country where it had once been welcome at the imperial court. But all in all, it seemed possible that Christianity in China, brought there with such promising auguries during the late Ming dynasty, was once again in danger of withering away to the point of vanishing.

ANGLO-SAXON PROTESTANTS

That it didn't was the product of the next major outside missionary effort to evangelize China, this time by Anglo-Saxon Protestants. From its unimpressive beginnings, this effort was considered by many to be weak and ineffective, and the early statistics show that it did not achieve to great success. The first Protestant missionary on Chinese soil won only ten converts in twenty-seven years of work. Yet Protestantism within a half century would very nearly overthrow the dynasty with quasi-Christian rebel forces. And in just over a century, it would provide China with a revolutionary leader who was a Christian believer. As we shall see, the long-term effects of these Protestant missions to China are to become seedbed for the growing Christianization of the country today.

OPIUM BOATS AND CHRISTIAN TRACTS

On September 4, 1807, a thin-looking, twenty-five-year-old Englishman, Robert Morrison, stepped off an American steamer in the southern Chinese port of Canton (today called Guangzhou) and headed for the American "Factory," the business and living quarters of the small group of Americans permitted by the Chinese government, between September and March, to trade in this city. The American "Factory" ("factory" meant not a place of manufacture but a place where merchants, "factors," conducted their trade) was one of several "factories" in the trading area, with the British being the nationality with by far the largest community.

Morrison had formed a passion to evangelize China and was recruited in London by the London Missionary Society in 1805 as an "agent" who would eventually move to Asia—the LMS originally thought he should go to Penang, an ethnically Chinese-dominated island off the coast of Malaysia—to translate the Bible into Chinese. However, during the Napoleonic wars, the only British ships traveling to Canton belonged to the British East India Company, which was at the time emphatically hostile to missionaries anywhere. So Morrison sailed first to the U.S. and then boarded an American sailing ship to China. The ship owner was skeptical. "And so, Mr. Morrison, you really expect that you will make an impression on the idolatry of the great Chinese Empire?" he asked.

"No, sir," said Morrison. "I expect God will."[23]

Morrison quickly set to work to study Mandarin Chinese, hiring Chinese teachers who took immense risks by instructing him. A Chinese who taught a foreigner to speak or read Chinese was, if caught, punishable by death. Morrison's Chinese soon became so good that he was hired by the British East India Company, even though the company acknowledged with some distaste the private motivation for Morrison's studies.

Beavering away, in the off-trade months, in a small house in Portuguese-administered Macau, Morrison translated the New Testament by 1813 and the Old Testament by 1819. Seven years after his initial landfall, in September 1814, he baptized in great secrecy the first Chinese convert to Protestantism. Only nine more Chinese were to be baptized through Morrison's own ministry before he died in 1834.

One of Morrison's major difficulties, and in fact what turned out to be a monstrous albatross for Protestant Christianity in China for more than a century, was the association of Western missionaries with Western traders who came to Canton to make money trading opium. Opium, to be sure, was not invented by the Westerners, and it had been used as a narcotic in China for decades before Morrison arrived in 1807. But the British East India Company (BEIC), in control of most of India from 1759 onward, specifically encouraged the growing of opium in India in order to raise money from trade with China. Even after the BEIC lost its monopoly of Asian trade in 1833, other British companies carried on with the opium trade to China. The British government turned a blind eye to the entire business and did not officially admit that it had anything to do with bringing opium into China. But, of course, it had.

Some Western Protestant missionaries were eager to have access to China by any means. One of the most linguistically gifted Protestant missionaries, the German-born Charles (Karl) Gutzlaff, knowingly took on employment with Jardine Matheson—a major British company of the era that engaged in opium smuggling—in order to be able to bring Chinese Christian tracts into China. The BEIC had discovered in the eighteenth century that the sale of opium grown in British-controlled India to the Chinese was a valuable source of revenue for the control of India. Jardine Matheson and other British companies also discovered that the sale of opium could more than pay for the quantities of tea, silk, rhubarb, and porcelain being demanded by a growing middle class in England. From the 1830s through the 1840s, Gutzlaff acted as an interpreter both for Jardine Matheson and for the British authorities. He made several pioneering trips into China, sometimes distributing Christian tracts from the same sailing ships that were importing opium into China.

Chinese demands that the British authorities curtail the opium trade clashed with British merchant demands that China open its ports for international trade unencumbered by bureaucratic restrictions, and this led to the Opium War of 1831–1839. British troops defeated the

Chinese imperial forces sent to expel them, and in 1842 a momentous new treaty was forced upon China, the Treaty of Nanking. This not only conferred the island of Hong Kong upon Britain, but also made five treaty ports on the Chinese coast available to foreign trade for both the British and other foreign powers: Fuzhou, Xiamen, Ningpo, Canton (Guangzhou), and Shanghai. The "treaty ports" were, however, more than simple market places for international trade. Within the ports' boundaries foreigners enjoyed "extraterritoriality" and were thus not subject to Chinese law. The Chinese saw this as a series of "unequal treaties" forced upon them by the Western powers.

Defeat in war by foreign powers further undermined the prestige of the Qing Dynasty government just as China was entering a period of dynastic decline: growing corruption in the official bureaucracy, bad harvests, landlessness and discontent among the peasantry. At this point, Christianity, or at least an adulterated version of it, entered the mainstream of Chinese life at the grassroots.

TAIPING REBELLION

Back in 1816, a Protestant missionary, William Milne, baptized a Macau-based Chinese printer called Liang Fa (1789–1855). This brave Chinese convert to Christianity was to have an impact upon Chinese history quite different from what he or his first Christian teacher, Morrison, could possibly have had in mind. In 1834, Liang Fa handed a Chinese Christian tract to Hong Xiuquan, a candidate for the official examinations for entry into the scholar-gentry class, in Guangdong Province. Hong didn't read it carefully or make sense of the contents until nine years later, when yet another failure in the examination process enraged him against the Manchu rulers of China. Strange dreams and visions led him to believe that he was called by God, very much the Old Testament Jehovah, to cleanse China of its corruption and ills and to overthrow the dynasty.

Getting started in 1854, Hong's "Society of God-Worshippers" practiced at first an austere lifestyle stressing segregation of men and women and a pious approach to *shangdi*, or God, as translated by a traditional Chinese term. He announced his rule as the Taiping

Kingdom, *taiping* in Chinese meaning "heavenly peace." Initial Protestant Christian enthusiasm for the new movement was considerable. Although that enthusiasm evaporated after Hong announced that God had told him that he was the younger brother of Jesus, some foreign Christian observers still saw a silver lining in the unrest. Griffith John, of the London Missionary Society, wrote in 1860, "I fully believe that God is uprooting idolatry in this land through the insurgents, and that he will by means of them, in connection with the foreign missionary, plant Christianity in its stead."[24]

From 1850 until its final suppression in 1864, which was achieved with the help of Western military advisors eager to uphold the Qing dynasty, the insurrection devastated central and southern China, leading to the deaths of an estimated 20 million Chinese. It must have etched in the minds of Chinese officialdom that Christianity could become an ingredient in a revolt against the ruling dynasty just as easily as other religious sects, such as the Red Turban revolt at the end of Mongol rule.

INTO THE HEART OF CHINA

Yet it was in the early years of the Taiping Rebellion that another English missionary arrived in Shanghai. His approach to China would do more than any other foreigner to plant the roots of Christian belief deep inside Chinese society. He was Hudson Taylor (1832–1905), a young man who arrived from Liverpool at the age of twenty-one in Shanghai under the auspices of the Chinese Evangelization Society (CES). At his birth, his parents had prayed, "Grant that he may work for you in China," and even as a boy, Taylor had told his friends, "When I am a man I shall go to China."[25] Taylor was something of an oddball from the outset. He insisted on dressing and eating like a Chinese. And unlike some of the other British and foreign missionaries who had arrived in Shanghai, he disliked the clannish and insular mode of British expatriate life, and sought whenever possible to live in a Chinese area. This alienated him both from the British authorities in Shanghai and from most of his own missionary and trading compatriots.

But Taylor's dream from the outset was to take Christianity well beyond the boundaries of the treaty ports and deep into the heart of inland China. In 1865, with his own contribution of ten pounds, he founded in England the China Inland Mission. Its principles were radical for the day: it would be interdenominational, no formal education was required, unmarried women could become missionaries, Chinese dress would be worn, and the mission authority would be in China, not back in London. "China," he wrote later, "is not to be won by quiet, ease-loving men and women. The stamp of men and women we need is such as will put Jesus, China [and] souls first and at foremost in everything and at every time—even life itself must be secondary."[26]

In 1866, Taylor sailed back to China with his wife, four children, and sixteen young missionaries willing to join the five already in China under Taylor's direction. The CIM, as it became universally known, gradually increased its membership until, by 1895, there were 641 missionaries from many countries, in all of China's provinces except the border regions of Tibet, Inner Mongolia, and Xinjiang.

In one respect, Taylor was unconsciously imitating Ricci, who had sought from the outset, three centuries earlier, to look and behave in public as much like a Chinese as a foreigner ever could. Language was vital, along with an understanding of China's history and culture. But in other ways, Taylor resembled more closely the Dominicans and Franciscans who had irritated the Jesuits by trying to reach out to China's lower classes while Ricci, Schall, Verbiest, and others were doing everything possible to secure the approval of China's ruling literary class.

It was not long before a new generation of Western Protestant missionaries arrived in China determined to replicate, as far as possible, Ricci's earlier accomplishments. James Legge (1815–1897), for example, decided that it would be impossible for Western missionaries to be effective in China until they comprehended the breadth and depth of China's great historical cultural achievement. He thus devoted himself to the translation of the Chinese literary classics that had been required study for centuries for the scholar-gentry examinations. Legge so admired Confucius that he often simply referred to Confucius as "the Sage."

Other missionaries decided that the best way to introduce Christianity to China would be to serve China in ways that the Chinese, even if "pagan," could appreciate as practical and helpful. Peter Parker, an American (1804–1888), started out as a brilliant physician and surgeon in Canton, even treating Chinese officials who were at odds with the Western opium traders. Timothy Richard, a Baptist Welshman (1845–1919), sought in 1880s and 1890s to penetrate the Chinese intelligentsia in the same way as Ricci. Richard devoted himself to exposing educated Chinese not only to Christian ideas, but also to useful general knowledge about the outside world through a Chinese-language magazine, *The Globe Magazine*,[27] which operated first as a weekly, then as a monthly, from 1875 until 1907. He also warmly supported efforts, largely of American Protestant missionaries in the second half of the nineteenth century, to introduce Christian education beyond the elementary and secondary levels and into the universities.

Other missionary pioneers of higher education in China moved Richard's efforts forward. Several young graduates from Yale were deeply involved in China ministry. One of them, Henry Winters Luce (1868–1941), father of Henry Luce, one the founders of *Time* magazine, was a major advocate for the development of higher education in China and for a while served as vice president of Peking University, which grew out of the Yenching University project initiated by Yale alumni in China.

A THIRD VANISHING?

But China's forced exposure to the West ignited sparks of nativist antiforeignism, which surfaced again and again from the late nineteenth century onward until, most recently, the death of Mao Zedong in 1976 and the collapse of the leftist utopian Communism that he had championed at different times since 1949. The worst of such outbreaks was the Boxer Rebellion of 1900, during which the foreign legation quarter in Peking was under siege by rebels for fifty-five days. The rebels struck particularly hard at both Chinese and foreign Christians. Of the 230 Western missionaries killed, 189 were Protestants, and seventy-nine were from the China Inland Mission.

When troops from eight foreign powers (the U.S., Britain, Russia, Japan, Italy, Austria, France, and Germany) rescued China's capital from the Boxers, they imposed huge reparation burdens on the country. To his considerable credit, CIM founder Hudson Taylor rejected any compensation from China for the lives and properties of his missionaries savaged by the Boxers. He wrote afterward, "Should I have a thousand pounds, China can claim them all; should I have a thousand lives, I would not spare one not to give to China."[28] Likewise, the U.S. required that reparations be paid toward educational opportunities for Chinese students.

China's last dynasty, the Qing, was already staggering to its end. When it collapsed after an army mutiny in 1911, the leading revolutionary, and founder of the Republic of China, was Sun Yatsen (1866–1924), a Christian from Guandong Province who had first been exposed to Christianity in an Anglican school in Hawaii after emigrating there in 1878. Sun's political ideas, the Three Principles of the People, were clearly derived from American democratic ideals, and his concept of a republic aimed to produce a society that would be recognized internationally as a political democracy. But he lacked the political skills, military savvy, and indeed ruthlessness to strike down the upsurge of regional warlords and local anarchy that stalked China from the downfall of the Qing in 1911 until Mao Zedong's triumph thirty-eight years later. Sun's death in 1924 made it impossible for him to be associated with the Nationalist Party in the Nationalist-Communist civil war that racked China intermittently for nearly three decades. No doubt that is why Sun, China's first modern political leader and a Christian, is still revered today both by the Communist Party and its former foe, the Nationalists, who retreated to Taiwan in 1949.

Even while Sun still lived, the resentments that had been stirred because of the identification of Christianity with Western humiliation of China in the nineteenth century exploded several times into anti-Christian demonstrations. The New Culture movement, a Chinese intellectual movement that sprang up in 1915, tried to express the frustration of many Chinese over the failure of democratic institutions to establish roots in China even after the overthrow of the imperial system in 1911. Intellectuals like Chen Duxiu, who became the first secretary-general of the Chinese Communist Party at its founding in 1921, embraced science, democracy, social Darwinism, and the abolition of all of the old Confucian ideas that had been central to the imperial system.

The social and political radicalism of Chen Duxiu was invigorated by yet another political upsurge, the May Fourth Movement—named after a demonstration on May 4, 1919,[29] by students in Peking protesting against the anti-Chinese decisions made by the great powers at the Versailles Conference. This new movement, with considerable encouragement from China's Communists, helped form strong anti-Christian movements among intellectuals in China during the 1920s. Demonstrations and physical attacks on missionary compounds and missionaries themselves took place as a backdrop to an emerging clash between China's Communist Party under Mao Zedong and the Nationalist Party under Chiang Kai-shek.

When the Nationalists turned on the Communists in 1927, driving them into the countryside and rural guerrilla war, some Christians in China thought that there would be breathing space for the emergent Chinese national church. Chinese twentieth-century evangelists like John Sung (Song Shangjie), Wang Mingdao, and Watchman Nee, who helped form the foundation of China's twentieth-century Christian growth, began to become prominent just after the anti-Christian movement was approaching its climax in 1925. The following year, as it happened, the number of Protestant missionaries in China reached its highest point ever: 8,325.

As civil war raged in the 1920s and 1930s, Western missionaries continued to operate in China, though under increasing pressures. Some of them were captured and executed by the Communists. Others suffered after the Japanese invaded China in 1937—in 1941, after

Pearl Harbor, all of the missionaries were interned in the areas under Japanese control. (One prominent China missionary who died in internment was Eric Liddell, the hero of the movie *Chariots of Fire*.)

Chiang Kai-shek had publicly declared himself to be a Christian by being baptized in the year 1930, which made him an attractive Chinese leader for many Americans. But after the surrender of the Japanese in 1945, the Communists were too strongly entrenched in China's northern countryside to be dislodged by the well-trained and well-equipped armies of the Kuomintang, the Nationalist Party. The civil war came to an end in 1949 when the Communists swept away all political opposition inside China and Mao Zedong announced the formation of the People's Republic of China atop the Tiananmen gate in Peking (thereafter to be called Beijing) on October 1, 1949.

In little over a year, some ten thousand Protestant and Catholic foreign missionaries were forced to leave China. A number of them were imprisoned and subjected to brainwashing before being expelled, leading, interestingly, to the writing of some of the most remarkable Christian reflections on Communism produced in the twentieth century.[30]

The third major entrance of Christianity to China in its long history, that of Morrison and his Protestant successors after 1807, coincided with the most violent period of expansions into Asia by all of the Western imperialist nations. Gunboats had indirectly enabled missionaries to penetrate the remote fastnesses of China's teeming inland. But the message of their barking cannons deafened many Chinese to the serene sounds of the Gospel. Historian Wolfgang Franke commented on the departure of foreign missionaries in 1949, "The Christian missionaries had to pay a particularly heavy price for the mistakes of their predecessors, and reaped the hatred that had been sown in the past."[31]

At the time of the missionary departure in 1949, Chinese Christians were numbered at approximately 3 million Roman Catholics and three-quarters of a million Protestants. Many of them, particularly Wang Mingdao, Watchman Nee and others, courageously stepped up their evangelistic efforts, especially among China's frightened urban population, even as the Communists began to assert more and more control over national life. But to many Chinese Christians, and certainly to many foreign observers, it seemed that Christianity was going to vanish for a third time in China as the ancient nation stirred under new rulers. The assumption turned out to be wrong, but it took quite a few years before that became clear.

Chapter Three

PATRIARCHS

I TOOK A CAB TO THE WALK-UP apartment on Shanghai's Wu Kang Street and made my way as unobtrusively as possible up three flights of stairs to apartment 301. But the children, uninhibited as children always are, noticed the big-nosed foreigner knocking on the door of the old Chinese couple and commented loudly, "Foreigner! Foreigner!" followed by a peal of giggles. It was 1985 and foreigners were still not as familiar in large Chinese cities as they were to become in the late 1990s.

But the visit was well worth the mockery of Chinese children. For years I had heard about the man I was about to meet. He had become an icon of Chinese Christian courage and saintliness under Communist persecution. Both Chinese Christians and foreign observers of China's religious scene have long considered Wang Mingdao (1900–1991) to be one of the outstanding Chinese Christians of the twentieth century. His impact on the lives of hundreds of other Chinese Christian leaders both before and during his imprisonment had been incalculable. Without the political implications, he was the Nelson Mandela of Chinese Christianity.

Wang was arrested in 1955 and then again in 1958 and held until the very beginning of 1980, a total of twenty-two years and ten months. His crime was straightforward: he was a "counterrevolutionary" because he had refused to attach his church, Beijing's Christian Tabernacle, to the newly established Three Self Patriotic Movement, the communist umbrella organization designed to control all of China's Protestant Christian churches.

His fame was worldwide among evangelical Christians interested in China. In 1980, Ruth Bell Graham—wife of the well-known American evangelist and daughter of an American medical missionary to China, Dr. Lemuel Nelson Bell (1893–1973)—while on a private visit to China, had dropped by to pay her respects to Wang Mingdao just months after his release from labor camp. As I made my way up the stairs, I wondered how Wang had survived the decades-long imprisonment and what he was like now.

As instructed by my contact, I knocked several times and said, "Shushu! Shushu!" ("Uncle! Uncle!") A kindly-looking, white-haired lady answered the door and led me through a small kitchen area into a miniscule living room, about eight feet by twelve, to meet the aging Wang and his wife.

He was a diminutive old man in a Mao suit with a woolen cap on his head. Wearing wire-rimmed eyeglasses and sitting in a chair next to the wall, he was fiddling with an antiquated hearing aid that rested on his chest and occasionally let out strange whistles and shrieks. As we talked he smiled frequently, his jaw coming half open and revealing a mouth almost devoid of teeth. He told me he could still read, but only with great difficulty, and by using a magnifying glass. His wife Debra, a soft-faced lady eight years younger than him, had a gentle expression also, but it was apparent her own health had suffered during fifteen years in a labor camp separate from Wang's. Her right eye was milky and seemed to be sightless. But her mind was sharp, and at times when Wang didn't grasp the question I was asking him in Chinese, she would rephrase it so that he could understand.

We spoke about Wang's imprisonment, his meetings with Mrs. Graham and other foreigners, his attitude toward the Three Self ("a way for the Communist Party to control religion"), and the importance of good leadership in China's churches, which he already knew had begun to grow rapidly in China's countryside. What had been most important to him during his time in prison, I wanted to know? "The Word," he said simply, "the Word."

Then it was time to leave. Ninety minutes of conversation with a foreign visitor he didn't know was enough, and I expressed my thanks for his courtesy and hospitality. Suddenly, he rose to his feet and stood at attention. Then, in a quavering voice, and in English, he began singing the nineteenth-century hymn "Onward, Christian Soldiers." I stood up too, and sang with him.

I knew I had been in the presence of an extraordinary character.

Piecing together his life, which was not difficult to do, helped to explain why.[1]

WANG MINGDAO

Wang was born in Peking in the besieged legation quarter of the city right at the height of the Boxer uprising in July 1900. Tragically, his father, looking out at the rampaging Boxers from within the compound, became so filled with fear for himself and his family that he hanged himself. Wang was brought up by his mother in nearly destitute circumstances, though because of their Christian faith they were able to send him to a Christian elementary school and later a middle school.

Wang became a Christian at fourteen while in middle school, nudged in this direction by a slightly older boy who was already a believer. But his faith, rather than bringing peace and harmony into his life, brought him conflict with his peers. Surrounded by typically rambunctious youths at a school that was nominally, but not very devotedly, Christian, Wang from an early age was deeply offended by brazen and immoral behavior, especially from people claiming to be Christians. He was earnest and sought eagerly to live a Christian life that was in accordance with the Bible.

At the age of twenty he was fired from his teaching job at a Chinese Presbyterian school because he did not consider the Presbyterian doctrine of baptism, wherein baptismal candidates were "sprinkled" by the clergyman while standing upright in the church, the biblical pattern. Wang was convinced that a true baptism required the candidate to be fully immersed in water. He had less than one day's notice to leave the school. Five of the students who agreed with him were also expelled. All six of them, pausing en route back to Peking, were baptized by a Chinese pastor in a stream so icy that the water on Wang's clothes froze into solid ice as he came up out of the stream.

Wang's own Christian ministry started humbly, with him leading a Bible study in a tiny hut in the courtyard of his mother's and sister's home in Peking. His understanding of the Bible and his simple and pious way of life impressed visitors. He began to be asked to speak at Christian conferences in Peking and in different parts of China. By the end of the 1920s he was in great demand as a Christian speaker.

His messages were simple yet deep. The Bible, he insisted, was the only authority for all Christian doctrine and for how a person should live out the Christian life. He was constantly challenging congregations to live out lives of personal virtue. This wasn't an especially popular position. From his very earliest days as a preacher, Wang encountered opposition and derision because of his jeremiads against sin and corruption within the church. It was nevertheless "part of his commission," he wrote in his autobiography, "to call upon people in the churches to repent and forsake their sins."[2] He explained, "I prefer to be attacked by men than to call forth the wrath of God."

He rented a hall to conduct Christian services in Peking, but the crowds wishing to attend soon grew so huge that he was forced to construct a large building to contain the congregations. He dedicated this church, the Christian Tabernacle, on August 1, 1937. Exactly one week later, the invading Japanese army marched full force into that city.

Wang proved to be as stubborn and uncompromising with the invaders as he had been with Christian churches he thought were falling short of high moral standards. When the Japanese tried to force all Chinese Christian churches in the occupied area to join a "North China Christian Federation," a puppet entity that they could control, Wang Mingdao flatly refused to participate. Amazingly, the Japanese didn't arrest him. Though they were harsh toward many Chinese Christian groups—especially the Western missionaries who were interned along with American or British residents after December 7, 1941—the Japanese seemed secretly to admire Wang's inflexible stand. Wang was at an advantage over other Chinese Christians in one respect. Since starting his own independent church in Peking in the 1920s, he had never been connected with any foreign group, above all with any foreign Christian missionary or denominational group. And though he spoke from time to time at missionary conferences, such as those organized by the China Inland Mission, Wang never received any financial support from the British or the Americans.

Throughout his career as a pastor and evangelist, Wang insisted that Chinese churches needed to be completely independent of foreign mission organizations or foreign church denominations. Chinese Christian communities should also support themselves financially, he held, and do their own evangelizing and disciplining of new Christian believers. In effect, long before Communism came to power in China, Wang Mingdao was living out his own Christian version of the so-called Three Self principles (self-support, self-propagation, self-governing) that later became the slogan of the Three Self Patriotic Movement, the "official" Protestant organization claiming to represent all of China's Protestant Christians.

After the defeat of the Japanese by the U.S. in 1945, the Chinese hoped that their country could finally be at peace and repair the deep rifts in their society created by the upheavals of the previous decades: foreign invasion and occupation, famine, warlords, and civil war. Many idealistic Chinese, including many Protestant Christians, believed that, on balance, the Communists might prove to be less corrupt and more effective rulers than the Nationalists, who had intermittently been in power since the imperial Qing dynasty was overthrown in 1911. Indeed, some Protestant seminary students and pastors had been clandestinely recruited into the ranks of the Chinese Communist Party in the 1940s or earlier. Once the Communists defeated the Nationalists in 1949, others, even non-party members, were willing to do the bidding of China's new rulers. Many of them thought that perhaps the

Communists had inherited "the mandate of heaven," that indefinable mantle of moral authority for national rule that each new Chinese dynasty was believed to inherit after the collapse of the preceding one. Others thought that the Communists could be no worse than the corrupt and inept Nationalists who had tried to govern China for two decades. In short, after more than a century of humiliation by foreign powers, of chaos, warlords, and corrupt authoritarian rule, the Communists seemed ready and eager to write a new page in Chinese history. "China has stood up!" Mao Zedong exclaimed atop the Gate of Heavenly Peace, the Tiananmen, on October 1, 1949. It was a heady declaration, and many Protestant Chinese Christians were eager to respond.

There was no national census of Roman Catholic or Protestant believers in China in 1949, but compilations from various sources indicate that the Roman Catholic Church had 3,274,740 baptized members in China in 1949 and the Protestant churches, combined, had about 936,000.[3] Yet these figures told only part of the story of the Christian influence on the country. Catholics and Protestants together had founded a total of 429 middle schools and high schools, sixteen universities, and 538 hospitals. As many as 40 percent of all qualified physicians in China in 1949 may have been trained at missionary-founded medical schools. The cultural influence of such Christians in positions of social prestige and influence was considerable.

On coming to power, therefore, what the Communists needed to accomplish in relation to China's Christian population was a twofold challenge. First, they needed to intimidate into total compliance or cow into silence any prominent Catholic or Protestant Christians leaders who opposed the new regime. Any center of independent civic leadership, and hence potential political opposition, could not be permitted to survive beneath the new "mandate." Second, to avoid totally alienating the entire mass of Christian believers in China while they were still consolidating their power, the Communists needed to co-opt a large portion of the clergy. These were not to be just passive supporters of the new regime, but active enthusiasts. They could be described as "patriotic" because they would be willing to endorse Communist policies as good for China.

When the Communists' Eighth Route Army, later to be renamed the People's Liberation Army, rolled to power across China, these new conquerors were ruthless in their treatment of "class enemies." Landlords were "tried" and denounced in kangaroo courts, and often summarily executed, their peasant tenants rounded up both to participate in the "trial" and to be complicit witnesses of their deaths. In the Communist-controlled areas of north China during the civil war of 1946–1949, "people's courts" were often used to denounce and punish foreign missionaries, especially foreign Roman Catholic priests. An estimated forty foreign Roman Catholics and fifteen to twenty foreign Protestant missionaries were put to death, with or without such "trials" by the Communists, during the first and the second civil wars (1927–1935 and 1945–1949).[4] Once China's military entered the Korean War in October 1950 and began fighting the U.S., any Chinese associated with American Christian or other groups was in danger of being labeled a "running dog of imperialism."

As we shall see in greater detail in a later chapter, the Communists had planned the infiltration and control of Protestant Christian churches carefully and thoroughly. It was more difficult for them to do the same with Roman Catholics, partly because of the global structure of authority inherent in the Church of Rome. In April 1951 a newly established government agency, the Religious Affairs Bureau, at the Communist Party's direction, invited 151 prominent Chinese Protestant leaders to a conference in Beijing to make a complete and public break from foreign Christian organizations. The conference established an institution at first called the Protestant Three Self Reform Movement. That name was changed in 1954 to the Protestant Three Self Patriotic Movement. Its purpose was explicit:

> To thoroughly, permanently, and completely sever all relations with American missions and all other missions, thus realizing self-government, self-support, and self-propagation in the Chinese church.[5]

To advance this program, training sessions for Protestant pastors and seminarians were held all over China to teach "patriotism" (uncritical support for everything said or done by the Communist Party), the meaning of "New China" (Communist Party social and economic policies), and the nature of "imperialism" (wickedness of the West, the U.S. in particular). Part of this reeducation process involved "accusation meetings," where carefully targeted individuals were denounced in public before their peers. Communist investigators also forced people to write arduous autobiographical confessions to expose any personal attitude or action that might be deemed unsympathetic to "New China." It was during this period of mass reeducation all over China that the terms "thought reform" and "brainwashing" first acquired wide currency. The large majority of Protestant clergy in China went along with the process. The price for resistance ranged from public denunciation, arrest, imprisonment, and possibly execution.

But once again, Wang Mingdao was the bold holdout. He refused to join the Three Self movement and resisted the party's efforts to recruit the entire nation into a campaign against the United States. Wang's legendary stubbornness was one explanation for his refusal to join the Three Self Patriotic Movement. In 1949, he had refused to sign a document being broadly circulated among Protestant leaders by sympathizers of the Communists that called Christianity "a tool of imperialism." Wang simply disagreed with it. All his life he had been entirely independent of any foreign mission connection and had carried on a "three self" policy in his own church without any outside pressure. Stoutly continuing his evangelistic meetings in Beijing, especially popular among Beijing's students, Wang had even been brought before an "accusation" meeting in July 1954 without result. No one outside of the Communist Party itself or its various toadies seriously considered Wang a tool of anybody.

For his principled attitude, Wang was first denounced in the official publication of the Three Self Patriotic Movement, *Tian Feng* ("heavenly wind") magazine, and then arrested with his wife Debra in the middle of the night on August 7, 1955. Other members of the Christian Tabernacle were arrested at the same time.

For months, two carefully coached cellmates terrified him with their stories of the tortures that could be inflicted upon stubborn prisoners. Toward the end of the year, he began to break, and started writing confessions to the prison authorities that indicated he was beginning to have serious doubts about his own faith. After promising his persecutors that he would join the TSPM and preach everything they wanted him to preach, he was released in September 1956, along with his wife.

He was a tormented man. Despite his promises to the authorities, he couldn't bring himself to join the TSPM or speak in any church. At the same time, he was convinced that he had completely betrayed Christ. Some stories had him wandering around Beijing muttering, "I am Peter, I am Peter," a reference to Peter's denial of Christ after Christ's arrest (Luke 22:60).

The anguish had an unusual outcome. Wang Mingdao lived for months in constant fear of rearrest and attended the various meetings where his coerced confession was read aloud—including one at the YMCA, which in 1949 had become the springboard for China's Communists in their efforts to control Protestant Christianity in China. He simply could not bring himself to join the Three Self Patriotic Movement, even though it was one of the conditions of his release from prison. The Communists had broken his will and damaged his spirit, but they had not "converted" him.

So, on April 29, 1958, Wang Mingdao and his wife were arrested yet again. This time, Wang was sentenced to life in prison and his wife to fifteen years.

Not long after his arrest, he became seriously ill with pneumonia. After his recuperation in 1961, the authorities approached him to determine if he might now be willing to cooperate with them. But Wang had regained his former pugnacity. He had been deeply ashamed and depressed by his momentary display of weakness. Wang told friends later that it was only when he remembered a particular Old Testament passage (Micah 7:7-9) that he realized the life sentence was actually the Lord's punishment for his own many failings, especially for having succumbed to fear and for writing a false confession. The passage, memorized by him many years earlier, was this:

———

But as for me, I watch in hope for the Lord,
I wait for God my Savior;
my God will hear me.
Do not gloat over me, my enemy!
Though I have fallen, I will rise.
Though I sit in darkness,
The Lord will be my light.
Because I have sinned against him,
I will bear the Lord's wrath,
until he pleads my case
and establishes my right.
He will bring me out into the light;
I will see his righteousness.

———

Wang Mingdao now did something astonishing to the authorities. First orally, then in a long written declaration, he withdrew all of his earlier confessions and denounced them as lies, the result of coercion. He spent the next twenty-two years in prison, with the Cultural Revolution years (1966–1971) being especially brutal. At one point he was handcuffed for four months at a stretch and subjected to daily beatings and humiliation.

His wife Debra was released in 1975 and was allowed to visit him a few times. He himself was only finally released in January 1980. "No Christian Chinese leader in the twentieth century," wrote Hudson Taylor's grandson, James Hudson Taylor III, "has more clearly articulated the power of the Gospel of Jesus Christ, or more poignantly experienced what the Apostle Paul described as 'the fellowship of sharing' in his sufferings."[6]

Due to his more than two decades of incarceration, Wang Mingdao was unable to personally influence the unauthorized Christian communities that began to spring into life. But his phenomenal courage in refusing to buckle under Communist pressure served as a rallying cry to other Chinese Christians leaders.

ALLEN YUAN

Another leader who has acquired an almost legendary reputation for integrity and faithfulness under persecution is Yuan Xiangchen, better known by his English name, Allen Yuan. Today, he is still preaching and baptizing hundreds of converts to Christianity in Beijing each year. Yuan rose to brief prominence in June 1998, when the Chinese authorities decided that none of the 2,000 or so foreign reporters covering President Clinton's visit to China would be permitted to meet with the

Allen Yuan

eighty-three-year-old. "There are two thousand foreign reporters in Beijing," Beijing's police, the Public Security Bureau, told him. "They all want to see you."

Well, maybe not all, but a lot did. Yuan was the closest to a public dissident that any foreigner could meet in China, especially after the purges of China's embryo dissident community that had taken place in the wake of the June 4, 1989 Tiananmen Square crackdown. This survivor of nearly twenty-two years of hard labor in China's prisons had persistently refused to join the Three Self Patriotic Movement even after his return from prison exile in 1979. Many foreigners have visited him, including Billy Graham in 1994. I met Yuan once in the mid-1990s, when friends helped me navigate the narrow alleyways to his home on Xi Jia Dao Street, in Beijing's Xi Cheng district, close to a prominent large white statue of Buddha. In August 1998 I visited him again with another American reporter, Mark O'Keefe, then writing a series for *The Oregonian* newspaper on regime persecution of Christians around the world.

The simple living room of Yuan's home was decorated on one wall by a photograph of Billy Graham. The room itself, just twenty feet by ten, was already crammed around 6:30 at night with twenty-six people who had come to attend one of Yuan's unofficial weekly worship and prayer meetings. "We have a saying in Beijing," he told us. "If you dare to preach, people will believe. In Hong Kong and Taiwan they have everything, but here they have nothing. It is just like the Apostles' time."

Despite his rise to prominence during the Clinton visit in June of 1998, he told us that he had gone ahead on August 1 with his annual baptism of people who had become Christian in his meetings. He and the Christians of his unregistered house church rented Bei Hai Park's swimming pool for two hours. By the end, Yuan at age eighty-four, had baptized 316 people, dunking each one of them fully under water. "We have so many limits on what we can do, but this work now is just like that of the first Christians," he explained. "We have miracles now." While he was talking, more visitors arrived, not just Chinese wanting to join the worship meeting that started at 7:00 P.M., but three Christian missionaries from Norway. "There is a saying," Yuan went on, "that persecution is the growing pain of the church. It is good for the church."

Singing got started shortly after 7:00 P.M., with a number of Chinese hymns and then one familiar to the foreigners attending the meeting: "The Old Rugged Cross." The tune was familiar, but the informal congregation sang it in Chinese. Yuan explained, "This song has great meaning for me because I was in jail for twenty-one years. There was no Bible, no Christian fellowship. Only two hymns encouraged me. One was Psalm 27. The other was 'The Old Rugged Cross.'"

Yuan, fourteen years younger than Wang Mingdao, was greatly influenced in his early years by the defiant old patriarch. Born in 1914 in Anhui Province, Yuan had moved with his family to Peking when he was still a child. Like Wang, he was deeply interested in what might be called "ultimate questions," and for a time investigated Buddhism and Confucianism to see if they provided the answers he was looking for in his own life. But they didn't. Then, one evening in his parents' Peking home, he had an epiphany. "God revealed himself into my heart," he wrote later, "and gave me the faith to believe in Him."[7] About a year later a Pentecostal pastor who had played a major role in a Pentecostal revival in Shandong Province prayed for him. At a Peking prayer meeting that Yuan said was a turning point in his life, he wept uncontrollably, then laughed with joy.

After completing middle school in 1934, Allen Yuan disappointed his parents by choosing to attend Far East Theological Seminary, an evangelical Bible school in Peking. He often attended the church services of Wang Mingdao at the Christian Tabernacle. He never took a regular salary from anyone, and like Wang Mingdao, avoided any financial or administrative ties to foreign missionary groups. During World War II, despite the dangers of provoking the Japanese occupiers, he traveled as a preaching evangelist throughout Hebei Province.

With the war over, he resumed his preaching activities in Beijing in a rented building that had been used during the war by a Japanese Christian pastor. When the Communists cranked up the TSPM and started pressuring Protestant pastors to join, Yuan, like Wang Mingdao, flatly refused. There were three reasons for this. First, he insisted, he had always been completely independent of foreign support or control. Second, he considered that Jesus Christ, and not some political group, ought to be the head of the church. Third, he heartily disliked the theological modernism that characterized the leaders of the TSPM. Because he was younger and less well known than Wang Mingdao, the authorities initially thought he was "redeemable" and not worth arresting in the first phase of the crackdown against TSPM resisters. As political tensions continued to rise in China during the "anti-rightist" political campaign ordered up by Mao, police arrested him at home on the night of April 19, 1958, and kept him in a series of prisons and labor camps for nearly twenty-two years. It was a busy month for police cracking down on Beijing's Christians. Ten days later, they rearrested Wang Mingdao.

Some thirteen of Yuan's twenty-one years in prison were spent in a labor camp in China's chilly northeastern province of Heilongjiang, not far from the Russian border. It was here that Yuan encouraged himself during prisoners' "smoking breaks" by walking back and forth in the camp compound singing "The Old Rugged Cross." Though he very briefly encountered Wang Mingdao in 1959 at a prison event in Beijing, the only other Christians he ever met were four Roman Catholic priests and a young Catholic layman he encountered during preparations for his trial.

Yuan, like Wang Mingdao, was subjected to torture in prison, especially during the Cultural Revolution. Yuan was consigned to a windowless cell uninterruptedly for six months, his belts and buttons removed in case he tried to commit suicide.

On his release in 1979, Yuan resumed leading prayer and worship groups in his home on Zhengyang Street in the Jia Yuan District and continued to refuse to have any connection to the TSPM. Despite frequent visits from Public Security Bureau officials, Yuan refused to register his house church, and steadily continued to preach, to welcome foreign visitors, and to help disciple and baptize growing numbers of new converts from Beijing's student and professional community. In 1999 he moved the mass baptismal service, always scheduled for early August, to a river and lake location in Hebei Province about two hours from Beijing. "If someone really wants to be baptized, we will baptize him," Yuan told me over dinner in a Beijing restaurant in June 2002. "A lot of party members have become believers."

The authorities, of course, were fully aware of Yuan's unauthorized church activities. When he was able to move to a larger, more comfortable apartment in a different section of the city in 2001, they pounced, threatening him with arrest if he allowed foreigners or journalists to visit him. "When foreigners come, the police always ask who they were and what they said," he explained.

Still, Yuan has continued with the out-of-town baptisms. In 2001, the local police showed up at the riverbank, and asked, "Are you Falungong?" When told no, they responded, "Okay, carry on." In 2002, the numbers were down a bit, but the old man, now eighty-eight, his round face creased with a wrinkly smile and his hearing getting worse, seemed as energetic as ever. "Even when we are old we work for Him until one day when He comes back," Yuan said.

SAMUEL LAMB

There is only one other man in China who has matched Allen Yuan in maintaining an unregistered house church while being in the public eye, meeting with foreigners, and staying out of jail. He is Lin Xiangao, better known as Samuel Lamb. Lamb, seventy-eight, was born in Macau the son of a Baptist pastor. He went to primary school

Samuel Lamb

in Guangzhou and lived with his family on Cheung Chau Island, Hong Kong, during the summer months. For a while he studied at Queen's College, Hong Kong, where he attained a high level of English fluency. Lamb's fluent English has enabled him to meet hundreds of visiting journalists, diplomats, pastors, and English-speaking foreign professionals in his humble Guangzhou home and church.

Lamb's story is very similar to that of Wang Mingdao and Allen Yuan. His own problems with the government started with a sixteen-month arrest in September 1955 and then a twenty-year prison term that began in May 1958, within weeks of when Yuan and Wang were rounded up. Though he had half-heartedly joined the Three Self, believing that the organization would not interfere directly with the ministry of his house church congregation in Guangzhou's Dong Shan District, the authorities were looking for a way to arrest him anyway. He was, they charged, a counterrevolutionary, partly because he had met with Wang Mingdao. He was anti-Russian, they supposed, because he had preached a sermon on the Book of Ezekiel, chapters 37 and 38, which speak of an attack on

Israel from the far north. He was indirectly connected to the CIA, they also charged, because his grandfather had worked in America and Lamb himself had cooperated with Western missionaries in the 1940s. The Communist investigators charged that this was tantamount to cooperating with foreigners determined to subvert and enslave Chinese culture.

At first Lamb was held in a prison farm in Guangdong Province. Though the work was very arduous, the southern, subtropical climate and the rich foliage of the area were congenial to Lamb's temperament. This relatively easy period came to an abrupt end when he surreptitiously tried to copy the entire New Testament in his own handwriting from a copy that another prisoner had managed to bring with him into the prison. Interrupted at night by a guard, he was abruptly transferred in 1963 to the Taiyuan Xiyu Coalmine of Shanxi Province, far to the north with more arduous conditions. It was here that he spent the next fifteen years, coupling and uncoupling millions of coal carts on the mine's underground railroad. He seemed miraculously protected when accidents happened, cars came careening down the track out of control, or the locomotive backed up too soon. Other prisoners lost fingers, feet, and even their lives in hideous accidents, but Lamb suffered not a single injury or serious illness.

In 1978, exactly twenty years after his 1958 arrest, Lamb was released in Guangzhou. But the timing was in many ways cruel. His father had died in 1971 and his wife, Li Huiling, whom he had not seen since his second arrest, had died just two years earlier. He had eleven months with his ailing mother before she, too, passed away.

A man of astonishing emotional and mental vigor, Lamb wasted no time in pensive regret over the lost two decades of his life. He started to teach English in Guangzhou in 1980 and within weeks had converted some of his students to form the nucleus of a new house church congregation. As the numbers grew from the dozens to the scores and then to the hundreds, Lamb installed close-circuit TV so the congregation could hear and see his preaching from the nooks and crannies of the tiny row house on Damazhan Street. As more and more new believers began to attend the church, Lamb conducted baptisms—more than one thousand between 1980 and 1990. He organized a tape-duplicating system for his sermons and a private printing press to produce teaching pamphlets in both Chinese and English.

His fame spread: Here was a Chinese house church pastor publicly conducting services several times a week, distributing literature, greeting foreigners visiting Guangzhou, and acting as though restrictions on house churches didn't exist. In January 1986 an official from President Reagan's White House showed up to present Lamb with a pen, a gift from the president. Astronaut Jim Irwin offered greetings in Lamb's church in 1988. Evangelist Billy Graham dropped by to do the same in April 1988.

The authorities noticed all of this, and began to pay Lamb as much attention—of an altogether less pleasant kind—as his foreign supporters. In 1988 he was called in to the Public Security Bureau six times for questioning, on each occasion being threatened with his church's closure or even arrest if he didn't register his church with the Three Self. In February 1990 a task force of about sixty police raided the church and confiscated thousands of books, Bibles, and tapes. They even took away (though they later returned) the Ronald Reagan pen and a Bible that the former president had also presented to Lamb. Summons to interrogation, threats, and another confiscation raid continued in the 1990s.

Throughout all of this, Lamb showed a fortitude that few men far younger would have displayed. "I'll not register even if you arrest me again," he repeatedly told them, "because these laws [requiring registration with the Religious Affairs Bureau and the Three Self] give us no freedom." On one occasion he said, "I'm even prepared to be a martyr." "Oh no," they hastily replied. "We are not the Romans."

Why wouldn't he join the Three Self, they kept demanding to know? Were all of the Three Self pastors false? "It's not that they are all false," said Lamb. "The Three Self includes genuine and false Christians. But we don't want to worship with a mixture of the true and the false."[8]

"Man is snuffed out like a candle," the interrogator commented. "You would do better to live to a ripe old age. You believe there's a God. But where was he when we summoned you yesterday evening?"

"God allowed this to happen."[9]

Lamb is characteristically chirpy in his confrontations with the authorities, and often stumps them with canny references to statements in official Chinese legal documents that nominally authorized house churches to meet privately. He often attributes the seeds of growth to persecution. "The more persecution, the more the church grows," Lamb told me during a visit in the summer of 2002.

Neither the Public Security Bureau nor the Religious Affairs Bureau has called on Lamb in since October 1999. "Arrest me again," he puckishly told them when he went to their offices. But China's Public Security Bureau has had bigger fish to fry than Samuel Lamb. For three years it has been intent on stamping out the Falungong meditation movement. It has also focused on another cult, which pretends to be Christian but has played havoc on China's house church leaders by kidnapping them. This is the Eastern Lightning cult, which believes Jesus has already returned in the form of a middle-aged lady in China's Henan Province (discussed in greater detail in chapter 12).

Lamb may also be just too hot to take into custody. In 1991, *Reader's Digest* ran a story on Lamb, further publicizing his situation. In 1993, the most senior American official to date visited him: assistant secretary of state John Shattuck. With characteristic thoroughness, Lamb noted the date of the visit, along with dozens of other journalists and diplomats who dropped by, in the ever-updated privately printed version of his story, *Samuel Lamb's Testimony*. With a Bible and a pen from Ronald Reagan and a guest book that sports up to 140 journalists and countless diplomats, taking Lamb into custody just might provoke too many people, including various U.S. congressmen, diplomats, and prominent clergy members who have stopped by to pay their respects.

Lamb is known to Chinese house church Christians all over China and to foreign visitors not only for his robust resistance to Communist Party pressure to control his church, but also for the amazing joy and serenity he exudes despite the labor camp ordeal, loss of family, and some nasty health problems. Thus he remains for many Chinese Christians a patriarch who has not only endured and survived great suffering, but someone who has come out of it brimming with Christian evangelistic energy.

MOSES XIE

One of Lamb's patriarch-generation contacts is Moses Xie (Xie Moshan in Chinese), who has over the years helped Lamb print various Christian booklets. Xie was born in 1918, the same year as Billy Graham and, like Wang Mingdao, became a Christian at fourteen and

Moses Xie

was the first convert in his family. Unlike Wang Mingdao, who was a Pekinger to his fingertips, Xie, a balding, slender, but vigorous old man today, was born in Jiangsu Province and spent much of his life there and in Shanghai.

Over dinner at a Beijing restaurant, Xie told me his own story of harsh persecution starting in the 1950s. As director of the Chinese Christian Mission in Shanghai, he adamantly refused to link up with the Three Self. He was arrested in May 1956 and initially imprisoned for

twenty-three years (1956–1979). While Allen Yuan and Samuel Lamb, despite defying the government in the 1980s and 1990s, were not rearrested, Moses Xie was, twice. Each time it was the Shanghai police who picked him up. He spent three months in the Shanghai Detention Center in 1986–1987 for leading Christian meetings, and another three months in 1992 for violating an administrative order introduced in 1982 that prohibited Christian ministers from one part of the country to conduct any pastoral, evangelistic, or teaching activity, in another part of China without authorization.

Xie is still feisty about his twenty-four years of incarceration. In many ways he was treated more harshly than Wang, Yuan, or Lamb. During his initial interrogation after the arrest in 1956, his wrists were handcuffed continuously for a period of 133 days. The cuffs were so tight that they cut directly through his skin into the bone. Guards pulled his hair, kicked him with boots, and day after day tried to force him to abandon his Christian faith. He recalled, "During the torture I would sometimes say, 'Lord, Lord, I am following you so closely. What is the meaning of this?'"

The physical pain and the constant torment drove him to such desperation that he attempted suicide. One night he managed, even with handcuffs, to remove the electrical lightbulb in his cell. He then thrust his fingers and thumbs as deeply as possible into the socket, hoping to be electrocuted. But the current was insufficient to kill him and he fell back down onto the cell floor. "So you're threatening the government by doing that, are you?" the guard shouted at him through the door grating when his screams alerted people to what was happening. His cellmates later told him matter-of-factly that the iron in the cuffs had somehow diverted the power.

Later that night, anguish and contrition flooded his soul. Lying on his wooden cell bed, after his cellmates had sunk back into sleep, he sobbed in prayer. All of a sudden, he heard an audible voice saying to him in Chinese, "My grace is sufficient for you." He says he heard these words, a quotation from the New Testament (Second Letter to the Corinthians 12:9), repeated three times, very clearly. His cellmates were sound asleep, the door and its grating were closed, and it would have been impossible, Xie says, for another prisoner to have spoken this to Xie without a guard interrupting. "It was God's audible voice," Xie insists to this day.[10] "After that incident," Xie said, "God's grace was really strong. When I was beaten after this, I didn't feel the pain."[11]

When the physical torture stopped, Xie had to face other challenges in prison. His sentence was extended for two years because someone overheard him sharing the Gospel with another prisoner.

These were spent in a prison factory in Qinghai Province, notorious for the number of *laogai* (reform through labor) camps. Even though his sentence formally expired in 1978, he was still kept in prison. He finally managed to return to his family in Shanghai after hearing of Deng Xiaoping's order that those over sixty could leave prison if they had completed twenty years.

Suffering followed even after his release. His wife, who had been under constant surveillance while Xie was in prison, decided to leave for the U.S. in 1993. Xie refused to follow despite invitations from several different American Christian groups. "Who will continue the work in China?" he would say in response. Xie and his wife divorced, and he remarried in 1995.

Xie now lives in Beijing and is sometimes visited by foreigners. He has to act with great care to avoid arrest, and to protect the many younger house church leaders he is quietly helping to train.

LI TIANEN

Li Tianen

The last of the patriarchs to be introduced in this chapter, Li Tianen, another Shanghainese, has had the most direct influence on the sudden surge of the house church movement in the Henan Province of central China.

Li, born in Fangcheng County, Henan, in 1928, is a generation younger than Wang Mingdao and Allen Yuan. But he has a direct connection to the nineteenth-century foreign Protestant missionaries: his grandfather was converted by the preaching of Hudson Taylor, the founder of the China Inland Mission.

Li's mother and father were both Christians, but his mother was expelled from her family home when, convinced that the Holy Spirit was telling her to do so, she sold all of the property she had inherited and said she wanted to be a full-time evangelist. This happened when Li was two. Mother and son began to preach the Gospel and rely on local Christians for sustenance. But after the Japanese invasion of north China in 1937, Li's mother died in Shanxi Province when Li was nine years old. His paternal grandparents then brought him up until he entered the Hua Zhong Baptist Theological Institute in Kaifeng in Henan Province.

Though a British missionary invited Li to come to England for a year of theological study before being reassigned to India, Li was inwardly convinced he was supposed to stay in China. During the 1950s he acted as an independent house church evangelist and pastor in the Pudong area of Shanghai (then completely rural, but today the location of Shanghai's booming new downtown business center) for a decade. He says he was not imprisoned by the PSB at the same time as Wang Mingdao, Allen Yuan, Samuel Lamb, and others because they knew that he had no connections to any of the national Christian leaders being targeted by the regime at the time. But in 1960, when Mao's utopian Great Leap Forward experiment was approaching its climax, Li was caught in yet another roundup of potential oppositionists. He was sentenced to ten years in prison.

Li's was assigned to a labor camp in Anhui Province, digging and moving iron ore. Two prisoners were assigned to cell beds next to him to ensure that he didn't move his lips in his bed, and thus pray. If they reported to the prison authorities that he had done so, he was forced to stand against a wall, sometimes in winter, without a shirt, for up to six hours, with his arms and feet splayed out. He says that during these punishment sessions he never felt the cold.

Once, he tumbled thirty feet down from an ore heap and was thought to have died. During this time Li says his soul was flying around the camp and observing what was going on, "like an eagle." "I was dead for more than ninety minutes," he said. Meanwhile, the camp doctor was working on him, trying to see if Li could be resuscitated. He evidently thought not, and was ordering the inmates to prepare a grave when Li suddenly opened his eyes. Seeing he was coming to, the doctor bent over him and asked him who he was.

"I am Li Tianen," he replied right away.

"Do you believe in God?"

"Yes, I do."

"I believe in God now," said the doctor. He could not understand how life had returned to a prisoner who had stopped breathing and had no discernible pulse.

Li Tianen received neither letters nor packages from his family while in prison, and was permitted to see them just once a year for half an hour. His wife struggled to make ends meet doing laundry for neighbors.

After his release in 1970, Li returned to his family in Shanghai. At this point his most productive and important work began. Shortly after his release, a letter arrived from his brother-in-law Gao Yongjiu. Gao was a local Christian worker trying to organize a small but growing group of younger Christians in Henan Province. Would Li Tianen return to his native province to help them out? Li did so, and for the next three years helped train a new generation of China's house church leaders. He traveled from county to county in Henan, both evangelizing and training. None of the young, Cultural Revolution-era converts had any theological background. With Li's help, during the early 1970s, what is probably the largest of all of China's house church Christian networks, the Fangcheng fellowship, named after the county of origin, began to grow rapidly.

But China's national politics was entering yet another new, turbulent period. Mao's designated successor, PLA veteran Lin Biao, had attempted a coup against Mao in September 1971 and died when his plane crashed in Mongolia as he was fleeing China. A nationwide purge against suspected followers of Lin Biao merged with another campaign—orchestrated by Mao's wife Jiang Qing and three of her associates, the "Gang of Four"[12]—to rid China of the leadership of Premier Zhou Enlai and his supporters like Deng Xiaoping. When four thousand Chinese Christian leaders attended an underground

Christian training session in Fangcheng County, Henan Province, in 1974, the authorities got wind of it and eventually arrested almost all of them.

Li Tianen became a prime target and was arrested in 1975. Some of the Christian leaders were sentenced for long periods in prison, but Li was given the death sentence, along with two others. He was transferred to a prison in Zhengzhou, Henan's provincial capital, to be put on death row. The execution date was set for National Day, October 1, 1975. But a major Henan flood occurred, forcing the province's Communist leaders, some of them closely connected to the Gang of Four, to postpone major political events such as political executions. A new execution date was scheduled for the spring of 1976. But once again, unexpected events intervened. When Premier Zhou Enlai died in January 1976, an intense struggle in Henan Province broke out between the pro-Zhou and anti-Zhou forces. Li was spared yet again during the spring and summer.

Throughout his arrest and imprisonment, Li's nemesis had been Fang Tiancai, secretary of the Nanyang City Communist Party. Fang was an ardent supporter of the Gang of Four and eager to score brownie points by decapitating the top leadership of the worrisomely large and growing Christian community in Henan. Fang's own patrons were suddenly arrested in Beijing in October 1976, leaving Gang of Four supporters isolated and defenseless in cities and provinces throughout China. Li was in a death-row cell. Astonishingly, though Fang was not sentenced to death, he was assigned the same cell as the Christian leader he had personally targeted for execution.

"Are you Li Tianen?" Fang asked, kneeling down and trembling on arrival in the cell. Li said he was.

"God in Heaven, you are an awesome power!" Fang exclaimed. Then he went on, "I was ready to execute you three times, but the Jesus you believe in protected you. Marx was not able to save me. Now I believe the Gospel you believe in is real."

Fang listened quietly as Li explained his Christian faith. He seemed worried that neither the Christian God nor Christians themselves would be able to forgive him for persecuting and executing Christians.

"Your sins are great, but God's grace is greater," Li replied. For the next few months he spent time trying to clean up Fang's flesh wounds after prison beatings and to reassure the Communist leader that God could indeed forgive Fang's particular wrongs. Fang was eventually sentenced to fifteen years in prison. Li was released, along with many other Christian leaders, in 1979. All charges against him were dropped. As the two parted, Fang asked Li earnestly to pray for him. To this day, however, Li has no idea whether Fang experienced any awakening of faith in his life.

Released back to Shanghai at the end of 1979, Li was assigned a job cleaning toilets, mopping floors, and removing operating room trash in the Shanghai Municipal Hospital Number Four. He earned 40 yuan (about $8 at the 1980 exchange rate). The PSB had given orders that he not be permitted to resign this position, even though other jobs were available for people of his qualifications at 300 yuan a month. But a sympathetic hospital official decided that the situation was very unfair and sent him to the hospital's deputy chief of personnel. This man, though a PSB official, seemed to agree. Li was allowed to resign on the spot. "It was a miracle," he says today, noting that it was exactly five years to the day he had been given that job.

Li then spent the next few years in the 1980s preaching and teaching not only in the Shanghai area, but also throughout all of the provinces and regions of China except Tibet, Guizhou, and Xinjiang. "I go mostly to the farmland, to cultivate the youngsters," he says today. "I am known as an uncle."

Of all the terms in China bandied about by Christians, none has greater resonance as a term of respect for revered, courageous, seasoned leadership than "uncle."

Chapter Four

UNCLES

WITH 96.5 MILLION PEOPLE living within its boundaries, Henan is China's most populous province.[1] Henan means "south of the river," referring to its location below China's Yellow River. The province has been the heartland of China's civilization for millennia. Henan's cities of Luoyang and Kaifeng are great landmarks of the coming and going of dynasties and of China's great rebellions in the nineteenth century. Americans and other foreigners who can summon up any association at all for Henan province, however, are likely to pick Shaolin Temple, home to a centuries-old order of Buddhist monks who all but invented China's martial arts.

But Henan ought to be as famous for something quite different. For thirty years the province has been the center of one of the most rapidly expanding Christian communities, not just in China but anywhere in the world. Henan is where three of China's largest Christian house church networks in China got started—Fangcheng (network founded by Li Tianen), Tanghe (also called China Gospel Fellowship), and the Born-Again Movement (also more formally called the Word of Life Movement). Henan is also home to one of the most violence-prone, quasi-Christian cults in China, "Eastern Lightning."

Hudson Taylor's China Inland Mission pioneered Christian missionary work in Henan Province in the 1880s. By the 1930s, the work was well advanced. The late David Adeney, a former English CIM missionary who arrived in Henan in the 1930s, described bicycling through the countryside, helping plant new churches in Henan's innumerable villages, and preaching to many of the Christian congregations already established. By 1949 there were at least fifty-five CIM churches in Henan.

There were plenty of other Christian groups too, some of them quite unconnected to Western missionaries. The American Presbyterians were active in the eastern part of the province before 1949, as was the Shandong Pentecostal revival group that had dramatically affected Allen Yuan in 1934. In the 1940s and 1950s, there were a few individual itinerant Chinese preachers who were almost mythical in the austerity and strangeness of their personal lives. One was Zhou Zhizun, also called "Crazy Zhou," a saintly Christian who worked on the Yellow River. In winter, Crazy Zhou only wore a shirt on his upper body. He lived like a homeless man and ate uncooked meat, evangelizing anyone who came within earshot. Another famous local Christian was Ye Naiguang, a mysterious itinerant evangelist who for a time lived in a cave and ate food brought to his cave by a wild puma.

FENGCHENG FELLOWSHIP: "BETHLEHEM OF THE MOVEMENT"

In the 1940s, a captain in the Chinese Nationalist (Guomindang) army, Gao Yongjiu, was converted to Christianity and became a zealous local evangelist in Henan's Fangcheng County. During the first year of the communist occupation of Fangcheng County, he and other Christian groups were largely left alone. Once the Three Self began to assert control over China's Protestants in the 1950s, however, Gao and two other prominent, independent local Christian leaders were targeted at accusation meetings and jailed as counterrevolutionaries for several years. Late in 1966, amidst the Cultural Revolution, Gao, along with other Christian prisoners, was forced to wear a conical dunce's hat and paraded through the streets by Red Guards. It was winter, and he was wearing a thickly padded cotton coat. The Red Guards beat him so hard with sticks that the cotton padding came flying out.

Quan Zhaoquan remembers that period well. A resident of Guan Zhuang village in Yangji Township, in Henan's Fangcheng County, he was the village leader in 1968, a position frequently targeted by Red Guards looking for "capitalist-roaders," as followers of Mao's political target Liu Shaoqi were often called. But Quan was a Christian too, which made him an automatic victim of whatever new campaign was being concocted in China from the late 1960s. Quan was one of a tiny handful of Christians in An Zhuang at that time.

In the summer of 2002, I visited a home in the village. I wanted to learn how the Fangcheng fellowship, now estimated to number in the millions throughout China, had gotten started in this rural corner of Henan. I sat with about ten locals and Christian leaders for several hours in a dirt-floor barn listening to their stories. Chickens wandered in and out on the hot July afternoon, pecking at the watermelon rinds we had discarded. The open-air latrine added its own commentary in periodic wafts. Chen Yurong, a middle-aged lady with hair prematurely white, remembered how her mother in 1968 was paraded through the village streets with a dunce's cap and a placard around her neck reading "cow gods and snake monsters," a favorite Maoist label to humiliate ideological opponents during the Cultural Revolution. Chen Yurong's mother, like other elderly Chinese women of that day, still had bound feet[2] so she frequently stumbled. "At the time, I was ashamed of her," Chen recalled, "but she was very happy. She said, 'I am going to heaven.'"

There were only six Christian believers in this village in the late 1960s, out of a population of close to two hundred. (Today, only three families in a village population of 170 are not Christians.) They began to meet secretly in homes for prayer and worship. Chen Yurong said her younger brother was a Communist Party official in the village who persecuted her fiercely. He had two boys, aged nine and five. One day, they were playing near the village well. Chen, at prayer not far away, felt an intense urge to go there, intuiting that one of her nephews might drown. As she approached, the nine-year-old cried in terror: his younger brother had fallen into the well. "Lord, save this boy! Let me die instead," Chen suddenly shouted out.

Somehow, as other villagers gathered around to see what they could do, the boy spluttered to the surface. Ropes were let down and he was pulled out. "Did you swallow a lot of water?" someone asked anxiously. "No," said the boy. "There was a man in white holding me up." After this, Chen's brother backed off from persecuting his sister.

One villager in 1968 had high blood pressure and went to the local rural medical clinic. Not getting any better after the treatment, he approached the six known Christians in the village. They spent much of the day in prayer and frequently fasted. After the Christians prayed for the sick villager, his blood pressure problem disappeared. He and his four family members became Christian. A sick woman in the village who witnessed this also approached the little prayer band. She also was healed, as was another woman with breast cancer. Very soon, word got around that when the Christians started praying, people rapidly got better. There is, of course, no independent medical confirmation of these suddenly improved physical conditions. The skeptical villagers, however, were convinced by what they were seeing.

It is difficult to investigate the phenomenon of Christianity in China today without hearing stories of miraculous healings. Very often, the people telling the story were the ones healed, so it is a first-hand experience. Other times, those who have become Christian speak of a mother or father, a brother or sister, incurable physically, or even psychologically, who suddenly recovered after being prayed for. These "healing" stories were particularly common during and just after the Cultural Revolution, in the 1970s and early 1980s, when in many parts of China it was still risky to attend any kind of Christian worship service.

Guan Zhuang village, it turns out, was for many years a sort of halfway house, even while the Cultural Revolution was still in progress, for a parade of itinerant evangelists and teachers preaching furtively in China's countryside. The visitors would stay a few days with the Christians, preaching, evangelizing, teaching, and sometimes baptizing new believers. Then they would move on to another village—an underground railroad of clandestine preachers that stretched across Henan and into other provinces.

One of the best known of these visiting evangelists was Li Tianen, the patriarch we met in the last chapter. After his release from labor camp in 1970, Li traveled throughout Henan to train a new generation of Christian leaders. He

Christian villagers in Henan Province

often lived in the home of fellow Christian workers in Fangcheng County, training up to twenty young people at a time, and traveling to other counties and even provinces for additional teaching sessions. It is difficult to overestimate the part Li played in training the next generation of China's

Christian leaders. It was his dedicated training and traveling that helped raise up an entirely new generation of "uncles," the current leaders of China's largest house church networks.

Thousands of Christians were active by 1974, with no fewer than an astonishing four thousand attending a clandestine training session at a village meeting place. The rapidly growing numbers of Christians made Fangcheng County a "problem" county for Henan's party officials. In the 1980s Communist cadres would commonly refer to Fangcheng county as "the Jesus nest" and the whole problem of rapid evangelization in the rural areas as "Christianity fever."

From the early 1980s, Fangcheng and other emerging networks of house church Christians were developing a pattern of evangelism. They would train young—some still teenagers—sometimes rather new Christians for just a few weeks, then send them out in pairs all over China. "The teams are sent to relatives in different parts of China, to preach the Gospel to them first," Zhang Rongliang, one of the fellowship's senior uncles, explained when I first met him,[3] in Zhengzhou in August

1998. "They are told to evangelize everyone. They will not pass anyone on the street or in their journey without sharing the Gospel."[4]

Sometimes, of course, the young evangelists would be reported to the authorities and arrested. They were often jailed, beaten, and tortured. But these experiences didn't seem to dampen their zeal. By the early 1990s, the Fangcheng fellowship had sent evangelistic teams to thirty provinces and municipal regions (Beijing, Shanghai, Chongqing) in China. The number of Christians associated with the network was around 5 million, according to Zhang. In rural communities, some doctors and pharmacists would report the youthful evangelists to the authorities. The physicians complained that medicine sales often declined drastically after large numbers of villagers became Christians.

The structure of the Fangcheng fellowship was necessarily loose because it was nearly impossible to maintain a headquarters in any one location for very long, the risk being too high that the headquarters might be raided. But Fangcheng County remains "the Bethlehem of the movement," says Zhang, and the community where the church started is called "the Mother Church."

ZHANG RONGLIANG

Zhang Rongliang, perhaps one of today's best-known house church uncles in China and for many years a senior leader of the Fangcheng

Zhang Rongliang

fellowship, is one of the uncles who was trained by Li Tianen. Zhang was born in Henan in 1950, in a small rural village called Sun Lu Zhuang in the mountains. His grandfather was a committed Christian and Zhang was much impressed by the old man's kindness. Zhang became a Christian in 1963, before his thirteenth birthday. The isolated rural location of his family provided a reasonably safe location for Christian meetings, but it limited his formal education. Though Zhang is highly intelligent and a good reader, he has only had a few years of elementary education.

Zhang was a diligent rural worker in the commune that was responsible for his family's village, and he was actually admitted into the Communist Party as a member in 1969. His Christian faith was a secret at that time. But in 1974, Zhang Chunqiao, a member of the "Gang of Four," put intense pressure on his political allies around China to rid the country of holdout resisters to the Cultural Revolution. A special focus was placed on Fangcheng's Christian community. Efforts were made to intimidate Christians into openly abandoning their faith. Under this pressure, Zhang was denounced to the authorities by some of the elders in the very fellowship where he had been worshiping. Zhang's Communist superiors, who liked him and recognized his leadership potential, tried hard to persuade him to abandon his faith under questioning—as a small minority of other arrestees had done—and therefore go free. But Zhang rejected their efforts and was beaten by Public Security Bureau officers. With Zhang's hands handcuffed behind his back, the police used sticks to pummel him on his head and on various parts of his body. But he refused to deny his faith or to reveal the identity and whereabouts of other Christians.

Charged with indulging in "counterrevolution under the guise of religion," Zhang was sentenced in 1974 to seven years in the Xi Hua labor camp in Henan Province. Once in the camp, however, he became even more active in his Christian preaching. He was put in charge of a work team in the labor camp farm and asked to recruit from new prisoner arrivals those he wanted on his team. Criminal gangs in the camp tended to recruit fellow criminals, and "counterrevolutionaries" were obviously more comfortable working with their own. When in 1975 newcomer Feng Jianguo announced his name and his own crime as "counterrevolution under the guise of religion," Zhang immediately signed Feng up for his team. "Are you brother Feng?" he whispered quietly to Feng later in the evening. The two men had known of each other in Henan's Christian circles but had never become acquainted. "Come and make your bed in my cell," Zhang warmly told Feng, and the two of them were fast friends for three years.

They also continued their Christian activism, secretly setting up new churches in the countryside around the prison camp. Zhang was in charge of pigs and Feng worked in the prison apple orchard. They were permitted some measure of freedom to interact with local peasants, so they planted churches as well as apple trees.

Like those of so many such "uncles," Zhang's faith and leadership skills were honed in the labor camp. By the time he was released in 1980, he was acknowledged to be one of the most gifted and seasoned leaders in the Fangcheng network. Zhang is an engaging, informal man of medium height and thick, dark, sometimes uncombed hair. He laughs easily, and has the rare skill of defusing tense personal situations and complex administrative issues. He loves to sit informally on the floor or on a bed, his legs folded behind him, his cell phone constantly ringing. His wife doesn't see him for weeks at a time when he is on the move. He encourages his son, Zhang Zimin, thirty, to spend as much time with him as possible. Zimin is learning the ropes of being a house church pastor.

Zhang Rongliang can also lose his temper a bit too easily. Some in the Fangcheng movement have criticized his lack of formal education and a comprehensive knowledge of the Bible. Zhang's loyalty to old friends and coworkers in China's house church movement has helped keep afloat organizational relationships that might otherwise have foundered. At the same time, it has rendered himself vulnerable to charges of cronyism by rising, younger house church leaders within Fangcheng.

But it is hard to think of any house church leader in China who has been more visionary or entrepreneurial in evangelizing not only his own country but anywhere in the world. Michael Yu (not his real name) is a U.S.-educated Chinese who has worked full-time in a southern city to support house church groups. Yu has met with Zhang and all of the major leaders, and says simply, "Zhang is the most influential Christian leader today in the church in China. Of the leaders of the five main groups, he has been the most mature, the wisest, the most tolerant. He has a strong influence on all of the people. He is the person all the leaders look up to."[5]

TANGHE FELLOWSHIP

Feng Jianguo, Zhang's former cellmate and still a close friend, is the most respected senior leader of the second of the big Henan networks, the China Gospel Fellowship, often more casually called the Tanghe Fellowship after yet another county in Henan. The Tanghe fellowship, though it has had other problems—notably the kidnapping of thirty-four of its leaders in 2002 by the Eastern Lightning cult—appears to have had a more harmonious leadership system. According to Tanghe people, one difference is that while Fangcheng tended to think of itself as a church with unified principles, the Tanghe, coming from a part of Henan with a greater variety of Christian traditions before 1949, thinks of itself as a loose-knit fellowship.

Both the Tanghe and Fangcheng were moved by the introduction into Henan of Pentecostal patterns of worship and prayer starting in 1988 by Reverend Dennis Balcombe, an American pastor of an independent Hong Kong Pentecostal church, Revival Christian Church, in Kowloon.

Originally from Bakersfield, California, Balcombe had arrived in Hong Kong in 1967 at the age of twenty-four on R and R from Vietnam. Two years later, he returned as a resident missionary, quickly learned both Cantonese, the southern Chinese dialect, and Mandarin, and set about building up a church primarily of Hong Kong Chinese and focusing on the needs of Christians inside China. Balcombe himself in the early 1980s made regular trips into Guangzhou, quite legally, to teach English at one of the many commercial English-language schools springing up. He used some of his time there both to coordinate the importation of Bibles into China and to get to know the Fangcheng house church leaders who had been assigned the task of taking the train regularly from Zhengzhou to Guangzhou to fetch the imported Bibles.

This growing mutual trust between Balcombe—and later other foreign pastors and teachers as well—and the Fangcheng leadership was to play an important role in the development of the whole house church movement in China. From the late 1980s, as a direct result of Balcombe's teaching, the *majority* of China's major house church movements—particularly Fangcheng, Tanghe, and two smaller movements that grew up in Anhui Province—became Charismatic in their theology. They embrace practices of prayer and worship that involve speaking in tongues, healing, prophecy, and other spiritual gifts familiar to Christians of the time of the Apostle Paul. There are an estimated 450 million Charismatic or Pentecostal Christians globally, making Pentecostalism the second-largest movement in Christianity after Roman Catholicism. Pentecostals, however, are not organized in one group but scattered throughout different Pentecostal denominations, throughout existing mainstream Protestant denominations, and, indeed, throughout large parts of the Roman Catholic community worldwide.

FENG JIANGUO

Feng Jianguo, seventy-six, speaks warmly of Zhang Rongliang, "He is very intelligent and knows a lot more than me." But Feng has the advantage that age, in and of itself, so often confers upon leaders in China.

Feng was born into a Christian family but didn't consciously become a believer until he was eleven—around the time the Japanese were invading China. He attended a high school that had been established by American Presbyterians in Tanghe County. Feng was not targeted by the Three Self during the 1950s because he was not then very well known as an independent Christian leader, though he suf-

Feng Jianguo, senior "uncle" of Tanghe fellowship, and his assistant

fered as so many of his brethren did during the Cultural Revolution. He was first rounded up in the anti-Christian movement launched in Henan in 1975, a year after Zhang Rongliang was arrested. The charges against him under the catchall of "counterrevolution" included: reviving and nurturing old and new Christian believers, proclaiming that Chairman Mao was an idol, and wanting everyone to bow their heads to Jesus and worship Him.

On his release in 1980, Feng maintained close contact with Zhang, but Tanghe was already developing along its own lines. Tanghe had become very active even before Feng's release from prison in 1980. One reason is that thousands of Christians who had been arrested in the 1950s, either because of opposing the Three Self or because they were caught up in the anti-rightist campaign of 1957–1958, were released in the 1978–1980 period, just as Deng Xiaoping was consolidating his hold on power and Mao's anti-religious policies were being reversed. These older pastors and church leaders, many of them well trained in theology school before 1949, were able to take teaching and leadership positions among the growing community of young believers.

Xing Liaoyuan, thirty-nine, a sort of "uncle in the making," was converted in 1978 at the age of fourteen and is today one of the top leaders in Tanghe. In July 2002 he described the early days of the Tanghe network:

> We didn't have Bibles. The Bibles that did exist were hand-made copies, because so many printed copies had been burned by the Red Guards. People with disease came to church and they were healed. You could assume that when people said, "I believe in Jesus!" they suddenly got healed. Some people who were sick said they heard a voice or something, went to church, and were healed. We had dreams, visions, revelations from God. We called this period the "three-shedding period." We shed blood in persecution, we shed tears in our prayers, and we shed nasal mucus because we wept for such long periods of time.[6]

For several months in late 1993 and early 1994 they collected donations from their network all over China. People sold chickens, or handed over money they had been saving for their marriage. Then on March 5–6, 1994, Tanghe had a large meeting at which they commissioned seventy young evangelists to be sent to twenty-two of China's thirty provinces. Each "missionary" was given 1,500 yuan (about $200 in 1994) and told to report back exactly six months later, on October 10, 1994.

All of the "missionaries" were single, some still teenagers. The expedition was extremely successful. Two young teenage missionaries started independent house churches in the Inner Mongolian Autonomous

Region during the six-month mission trip that now number 100,000 people. No one died in the great six-month expedition, and there were only two, short-term arrests in Hunan Province. On October 10, 1994, the missionaries gathered to tell their stories to the fellow members of the Tanghe congregations that had sent them out. "We had simultaneous meetings in five different locations in Henan," Xing explained, and continued,

> It was a testimony meeting. We had given the missionaries one-way tickets. We told them, "You can't fail. If you are not successful in planting churches, nobody will give you money to come back." When we heard their testimonies, everybody was crying. They wore out their shoes, they were rejected by people. They lived in ditches and in forests. Some of them lived with pigs. In the meeting, God showed his love to us. We were joyful because they all came back alive.[7]

A few weeks after hearing Xing's description of this great expedition movement I found one of the original seventy missionaries. To protect her identity, she asked to be referred to as "Sister Ruth." She was now twenty-nine, and so had been twenty-one when the teams left. Ruth had received a few short training sessions before leaving and was not an experienced evangelist. She was, she nevertheless insisted, "mentally prepared."

She needed to be. She and her two teammates, another woman, and a man, both in their thirties, were sent off to China's far north, to Heilongjiang Province. On arrival, they stayed the night on a farm in the house of a contact from Henan Province. Two older women on the farm were trying to organize a small house church with about fifteen participants. One of the women hosts was disappointed that the newcomers were so young. "A pastor should be an older person," she insisted. She told them they could stay one night but must then depart. The three of them got down on their knees and prayed a long time before going to bed. The next day, the older woman had changed her mind and permitted them to stay.

After their host heard them preach and teach, she decided their theology was orthodox and wholeheartedly cooperated with them. They taught lessons about the Second Coming of Christ (a subject that until quite recently was not permitted to be preached in any Three Self churches), the Great Commission (Christ's command to his disciples to evangelize the world, in Matthew 28:19, another theme not popular with the TSPM), and tithe giving (giving one-tenth of one's income to Christian work). Then they began to evangelize the nearby countryside, each team member going in a different direction but taking along a local who was part of the existing house church.

They also prayed for healings. One cause for a breakthrough in the church growth, Ruth reported, came when a woman arrived with a stomach cyst that seemed to be moving about her body even as they prayed. "It was obviously a demonic spirit," Ruth said, "because the woman was thrown to the ground and then started jumping around all over the meeting place." When, after a long time of prayer, nothing seemed to be happening, some of the local Christians began drifting toward the door. The woman with the cyst then bellowed at them, "You're scared, aren't you?" The locals instantly fled.

Finally, according to Sister Ruth, after more prayer, the cyst/demon left the woman's body. The newcomers' successful spiritual battle created a sensation and the local church they started grew exponentially. After several weeks they couldn't fit all the new Christians into the private residence they were using as a makeshift church. The overflow crowd had to sit in the adjoining truck garage.

Such activities weren't popular in two quarters, the farm's Communist Party secretary and his helpers, who became suspicious of all the comings and goings, and the local Three Self church, whose members started to drift away when word got around that the youngsters were teaching a really powerful version of Christianity. Worried about possible investigations and arrests, the three of them split the church they were building up into three separate groups, with each of the missionaries in charge of one of the groups.

By the time the three left in October to return to Tanghe, in Henan, the three new churches had 300–400 members. By 2002, the number had risen to nearly 5,000. "The period 1994–1996 were the three greatest years of Christian growth," Ruth said, speaking of the Tanghe experience. In 1997 the government intensified persecution of all unregistered Christian groups, and several of the Tanghe leaders were arrested. Feng Jianguo himself was arrested in 1997 and got a one-year sentence for holding unauthorized Christian meetings. He was arrested again in August 1999, along with Zhang, leaders from the Anhui network, and others. But Feng had established an efficient leadership structure, which worked well when top leaders were arrested. The network has separate departments for education, literature, administration, pastoral work, worship, Sunday school, and missions.

In October 1999, there was a renewed burst of evangelistic zeal in Tanghe that led to another wave of missionaries. This time, Tanghe accepted volunteers, married couples who agreed to migrate to large and medium-sized cities within China and to areas where China's ethnic minorities lived. Another forty couples were sent out in 2001. By 2002, there were ninety-eight Tanghe couples who had migrated and 120 single missionaries who had settled into every single province of China to work with them. That evangelistic fervor is not limited to preaching the Gospel in China. Tanghe leaders visited Chita in Russia in 2002 in order to evangelize Chinese workers who have migrated to Russian border areas and, as we will see later, the network has extensive plans for missionary work outside of China's borders.

THE BORN-AGAIN MOVEMENT

Like Zhang Rongliang, Xu Yongze had also been a disciple of Li Tianen and later became the leader of a Christian group in 1977. By the late 1990s, Xu's group had became the core of possibly the largest house church groups in China, and certainly the most controversial— the Born-Again Movement, more formerly known as the Word of Life Movement.

PETER XU

Peter Xu, as he is also widely known outside China, was born on October 6, 1940, in Henan Province. The first to come to faith in his family were his grandparents, who prayed when he was born (his father was away from home at the time) that he might become a dedicated Christian leader. In fact, according to Xu's younger sister, Xu Yongling, Xu had a vision of God at the age of five and, by six said he had a desire to preach the Gospel. This sense was quickened when a Swedish missionary, about to leave China with all of the foreign missionaries in 1950, said to him, "Who will take care of the church in

Peter Xu

China?" He meant, of course, what would happen to China's Christians with the Communists in power?

Xu went to the Three Self church in Datong, Shanxi Province, where he was studying mechanical engineering in a vocational school. He started a reading club in the school's spare time, trying to interest his fellow students in reading the Bible and learning about Christianity. But when a campaign called the "Four Cleans" cranked into gear in 1963 (three years before the Cultural Revolution), the cadres questioned Xu intensively for a nonstop period of forty days, at one point forcing him to remain standing for seventeen hours. Despite suspicions about him, Xu didn't face serious threats until he was put under house arrest during the Cultural Revolution in November 1967. As pressures grew and there was danger that he might be arrested, taken away, or worse, he and his wife fled town by night and returned to his parents' house in Hubei Province. But he could not remain there for long because the Datong authorities pursued him energetically as a "counterrevolutionary."

Xu began to earn a living delivering construction materials, still preaching clandestinely in his spare time. He came to know Li Tianen and, according to his sister, was eyewitness to many miraculous healings. By 1978 he had begun to emerge as a powerful Christian leader and preacher in Henan in his own right, with an emphasis rather different from that of Zhang Rongliang, Feng Jianguo, and others. Xu thought that, in the excitement about all of the healing miracles apparently taking place, China's house church networks were not doing enough to disciple and develop solid Christian lives among the new converts. Xu focused on building up a network of Christians that, in his view, were really attentive to a repentant, moral lifestyle. The Born-Again Movement began to emerge as a powerful evangelical group in the 1980s.

It grew with enormous rapidity, for Xu's followers were constantly reminded of their duty to increase their evangelistic efforts. They were also encouraged, more and more, to do something else: to engage in spiritual retreats where they were exhorted to repent their sins. Before long, it became normative at such retreats for everyone to weep as evidence of the work of the Holy Spirit in their lives. I interviewed Xu in California in the fall of 2002, and his sister Yongling in Beijing in August 1998. Both insist that weeping was not considered a theological requirement of Christian salvation. But enough lower-level leaders of the Born-Again Movement emphasized the weeping requirement to convinced outsiders that weeping had acquired a sort of theological value. The group became known throughout China as "the Weepers." Even the patriarch Samuel Lamb, Guangzhou's house church leader, well aware of the persecution the Born-Again Movement had suffered, said flatly in 2002, "Xu Yongce is a cult." By the mid-1990s, the Three Self and China's Public Security Bureau had officially labeled the Weepers a cult, and a nationwide effort was begun to discredit them and to arrest Xu.

Xu is not considered a cult leader by another patriarch, Li Tianen, or by some of his fellow uncles. Zhang Rongliang respects him greatly and has worked closely with Xu at a time when the house church uncles are trying to build national unity and cohesion into the house church movement. By general consensus, none of the networks had any sense of propriety about their activities in China until the early 1980s, when contacts with foreign Christian groups grew rapidly and differences over both doctrine and financial management became quite intense. Some Chinese Christians openly say that China's house churches began forming into "denominations" in the early 1980s. That is probably an exaggeration, but it reflects worries that a once united community of Christian believers, assailed by vicious government crackdowns for two decades, is now focusing on matters that divide—rather than unite—its members.

FINDING COMMON GROUND

By the mid-1990s, there was a pressure among several of the movements—particularly Fangcheng and Xu's Born Again—for the leaders to find common ground. Leaders of the different networks and movements met several times between 1996 and 2000 to try to work out their differences in ideology and personality. Just as in Roman times, during the early days of the church in the Mediterranean, real differences over theology were a larger impediment in the way of unity than personality clashes.

At the first meeting, held in Henan in 1996, there were representatives from Fangcheng, Tanghe, the Born Again, and the two large networks from Anhui Province (referred to respectively as Lixin and Yinshang). Also present were segments of the "Little Flock" network that had grown out of the ministry of Watchman Nee, now commonly referred to as "the Shouters." The "Shouters" got their nickname from the habit of encouraging their congregations to shout at times of worship, or when threatened, "Jesus is Lord!" The Shouters acquired their bad theological reputation in the 1980s when American-based adherents of the group arrived in China in large numbers with the teachings of Witness Lee, a former associate of Watchman Nee who had developed an unorthodox view of the Trinity. The Chinese authorities had labeled them an "evil religion" (similar to, but not quite the same as, the English concept "cult") in the 1980s and persecuted them harshly. The presence of the Shouters was deeply troublesome for some of the groups present, especially the more Charismatic Fangcheng, Tanghe, and Anhui leaders. The Shouters were eventually banned from all of the unity meetings.

A UNITED APPEAL

In August 1998, about a dozen representatives of the groups (excluding the Shouters, but including representatives from the Wenzhou house churches) gathered in a safe house on the outskirts of Zhengzhou, capital of Henan. Zhang Rongliang was instrumental in organizing the gathering. Zhang has been one of the most active advocates of the meetings, having a far broader concept of what constitutes an acceptable and orthodox version of Christianity than many of the other network leaders. He also invited two American reporters to witness the meeting. Mark O'Keefe, reporter for *The Oregonian*, was one of the two, and I was the other.

We were delivered to the safe house in a van with blinds on the side window from a hotel in Zhengzhou and spent the entire day with the group, watching them worship, eating lunch with them, photographing them and peppering them with questions about the house churches in China. Only one participant refused to be photographed, Xu Yongling, whose brother, Peter Xu, was serving a three-year prison sentence at the time.

At the end of the day, Zhang handed us a handwritten copy of an important historical document that he and the other house church leaders wanted to have published in the West and then transmitted in various forms back to China. It was the "United Appeal of the Various Branches of the Chinese House Church" (see Appendix for full text) and was completed (though not formally signed) in Zhengzhou on August 22, 1998. The brief document called on China's government "to admit God's power" and stop persecuting house church members, to release from prison Christians from various denominational groups who had been caught up in the government's crackdown on unregistered churches, to change the definition of a "cult" from meaning simply any Christian group that didn't register with the Three Self to something closer to the acceptable definition in most of the rest of the world, to stop attacking the house churches, and to stop insisting that China's Christians could only be represented by the Three Self. Particularly interesting was the third paragraph, dealing with the estimated numbers of Christians in China. This read,

> There are approximately 10 million believers in the Three Self church but eighty million believers in the home churches in the House Church. The House Church represents the mainstream of Christianity in China. Therefore, the government should face reality as it is. If Taiwan with its population of 22 million cannot represent China but the Mainland can with its population of 1.2 billion, so the Three Self Church cannot represent the Christian Church in China. The Three Self church is only one branch. Moreover, in many spiritual matters there is serious deviation in the Three Self church. The government should clearly understand this.[8]

The complaint by the United Appeal about "deviation" (meaning the liberal theology associated with the Three Self) was interesting because of the document's expressed annoyance with the government's tendency to label as a "cult" any Christian group that wouldn't go along with the Three Self organization or theology. In fact, the second item in the appeal sticks up boldly for the Shouters, rebuking the government for using this term in reference to the Local Church started by Watchman Nee:

> We call on the legal authorities to release unconditionally all House Church Christians presently serving in labor reform camps. These include Presbyterians (who believe that if one is saved once, he or she is always saved), the Charismatic Church, the Local Church (incorrectly called the "Shouters' Sect"), the Way of Life Church (also called the Full Gospel Church) [the Born-Again Movement], the Little Flock Church, the Pentecostal Church, Lutherans who do not attend the Three Self churches, and the Baptist Church. They should be released from prison if they are orthodox Christians—as recognized by Christian churches internationally—and have been imprisoned for the sake of the Gospel.[9]

It is revealing that the house church leaders acknowledge the emergence of Chinese equivalents of some mainstream North American and European Protestant denominations in this partial list.

On his return to the U.S., Mark O'Keefe faxed the United Appeal to the headquarters of the Three Self in Shanghai. Then, like any good reporter, he called up the Three Self to see if they had received it and if they had any comment. Received it, yes, they told him. Comment? No, they said. Perhaps they thought that if they pretended the house churches didn't exist, the problem might simply go away.

A Christian Constitution?

In November 1998, an even more significant document came out after two days of intense conversation, which itself climaxed nearly two years of discussion among a significant group of the house church leaders (with Zhang, of course, at the center). The issue was: What can we agree on as the basis of the Christian faith? The document then released, signed by representatives of four networks (Fangcheng, Tanghe, Born Again, and Anhui), was called the "Confession of Faith" (see Appendix for full text). It instantly received widespread recognition in China among the various house church movements, and even among some Three Self pastors dissatisfied with the official theology of that organization. The midwife of this document, in one sense, was an American, Dr. Jonathan Chao, founder and president of China Ministries International and director of Christianity and China Research Center, Taipei, Taiwan, who had been born in China and spent the decades since the 1970s traveling between China, Hong Kong, the U.S., and Taiwan, studying China's Christian situation at the grassroots. At the request of the house churches, Chao, a theologian by academic training, helped them to formulate their theology and training curriculum.

The Confession is historical in several respects. First, it emphatically demonstrated that the mainstream house church networks were theologically orthodox and had not taken on strange or heretical interpretations of Christian doctrine. Second, the Confession explicitly addressed some of the real cult doctrines that have sprung up in

China, especially those of the Eastern Lightning. Third, the document trod with great skill and tact around two potentially thorny issues among evangelical Christian groups all over the world. One is the Charismatic interpretation of prayer life and worship. Another is the doctrine of the end times and the Second Coming of Christ.

The preamble to the Confession has the ring of the opening sentences of the U.S. Constitution. It begins:

> In order to arrive at a common standard of faith among house churches in China, in order to establish a common basis for developing unity among fellow churches in China and overseas, in order to let the government and the Chinese public understand the positions of our faith, and in order to distinguish ourselves from heresies and cults...[10]

The following segments of the Confession amount to a classic restatement of Protestant Christian theology, but also display remarkable flexibility on how Christians might view some of the potentially more controversial issues like the Charismatic experience or the Second Coming of Christ. On the role of the Holy Spirit, for example, the Confession showed that the house churches do not accept the teaching of dispensational Protestants (notably certain Fundamentalist Baptist churches in the U.S.) that the gifts of the Holy Spirit (speaking in tongues, for example) died out at the end of the first century.

On the other hand, the Confession also refutes the assertions of some Pentecostal traditions that a person is not "saved" if he does not speak in tongues:

> We do not believe in the cessation of signs and miracles or the termination of the gifts of the Holy Spirit after the apostolic period. We do not forbid the speaking of tongues and we do not impose on people to speak in tongues; nor do we insist that speaking in tongues is evidence of being saved.[11]

Yet the Confession is firmly premillennialist in its view of the Second Coming of Christ.[12] Though it shies away from any statement about the Rapture or the Tribulation, it unambiguously asserts that when

Christ returns, He will inaugurate a reign of one thousand years, together with the "saints," i.e., those Christians who have been chosen to reign with him for the Millennium because of their suffering for the faith while on earth. There is no doubt that the premillennialist view of the Second Coming is indeed the one most widely held by China's house church Christians. As for the Three Self, it has shown extreme reluctance to address in any clear way the matter of Christ's return. After all, if Christ does return, then Marxism-Leninism will turn out to be a false doctrine.

The core group of house church leaders working toward unity at first called themselves the Sinim Fellowship. The word Sinim comes from the Bible's Book of Isaiah (chapter 49, verse 12) and has been interpreted by many Bible scholars for several decades as referring to China. Even after the Confession of Faith, unity did not come easily. Sinim met from time to time in different parts of China, often with different numbers of representatives from the component groups, sometimes with outsiders like Dr. Jonathan Chao. What quickly became obvious was that Zhang Rongliang had a more tolerant understanding of what constituted orthodox Christian belief than some of the other leaders. By early 2002, the Shouters had been definitively banished from Sinim, and because Xu Yongze was no longer in China, so was the Born-Again Movement, whose leadership had fallen into turmoil after Xu's departure. The name was changed from Sinim to Shen Zhou, an ancient Chinese term for China that has been resurrected in a Christian reinterpretation of China's past, as we shall see later.

Some of the uncles, meanwhile, managed in the period 2000–2002 to travel outside of China: to Jerusalem, to the U.S., to Hong Kong (since 1997 under Chinese sovereignty, but still considered an "international" destination for Chinese travelers), to Singapore. They spoke at conferences, prayed with Christians from scores of different countries around the world, and plotted mission strategy for China for the next few decades. They argued among themselves, reconciled, and struggled over how to relate to each other and to each other's movements. Touchingly, old friendships hammered out on the anvil of intense persecution and imprisonment in the 1970s survived. Zhang remained in close touch with Xu in the U.S. Xu's son, in the Philippines for several years, was on good terms with other uncles inside China.

China's uncles are not really patriarchs yet, and they might never become so. But they are heroic personalities in the passage of China's Christendom from a beleaguered remnant to an assertive minority.

Chapter Five

AUNTS, NEPHEWS, AND NIECES

ON A VISIT TO WENZHOU, some 150 miles down the Chinese coast from Shanghai, in the province of Zhejiang, my taxi and I were a half hour from the center of town. The Santana, a made-in-China version of a Volkswagen, took an unexpected lurch off the main road on the western side of the city and the Ou Jiang River, and pulled up at a three-story building. It was clearly a church, with a sloping roof, a tower at one end, and a cross at the top of the tower. Constructed of stone, it was hardly "underground." Yet it was a house church, with no connection to the officially sanctioned Protestant organizations in China—the Three Self Patriotic Movement (TSPM).

The pastor wasn't around, but I thought I ought to at least to peer through the nearest window into the building and see if anything was going on. There was something going on. As the cabdriver remained at the wheel of the car, the engine idling, and country singer Deborah Allen's 1994 "My Baby" thumping through the half-open front window, I saw about fifteen women stretched out on the floor, in prone position, praying in high-volume anguish. It was an intercessory prayer meeting of the church.

Fifteen women. No men. It underlined what I had heard for years from the church in China and was to hear repeatedly in my three-and-a-half-month visit with Christians in China: 80 percent of China's Protestant Christian house church members are women. The figure is approximately the same in the churches affiliated with the China Christian Council and the Three Self.

WOMEN OF THE CHURCH

I always ask for an explanation of this numerical imbalance and always receive the same posy of responses: In China men are more interested in making money, more interested in their careers. In China women are more willing to ask questions, more serious about life, more open and vulnerable about their personal thoughts.

I had no way to confirm this, and the anecdotal evidence didn't really support these explanations. I would not have put the gender imbalance as high as 80 percent, on the basis of what I saw at house church gatherings and underground seminaries. Still, no one from any quarter, official or unofficial, disputed the 80 percent figure I was given.

What *is* clear is that the 80 percent female composition of China's Christian community as a whole is not reflected at the leadership level of the house churches. I met several "patriarchs." I met one elderly lady evangelist in Beijing who might have qualified as a "matriarch." But I never met a single female leader of China's house church who was referred to as "auntie." I was unaware of the extraordinary talent and courage among China's female Christians. That is, until I met "Sister Ding."

SISTER DING

The term "sister," here, has no connotation of a cloistered community in China, because there are few if any such places either for men or for women among China's Christian community. But if "sister" carries with it the ring of classic authority, intelligence, spiritual wisdom, and even glamour, the sort of cachet that Roman Catholic TV art expert Sister Wendy carries, then Sister Ding certainly has it.

I first met her in Wuhan in 1999. The "uncle" who introduced her said that she was the "Madeleine Albright" of China's house church. By that, he meant that she was extremely intelligent, well versed in world events, something of a strategic planner, and, of course, a woman. (If that first meeting had taken place in the year 2001 or 2002, he would perhaps have said the "Condoleezza Rice" of the Chinese house church.) Taller than most Chinese women, slim, handsome, shorthaired, and with a ready smile, she would have been striking in any professional environment. Within just a few minutes of

conversation she was demonstrating to the two American reporters that she possessed vivid narrative skills, a keen analytical mind, obvious charm, and dazzling self-confidence. She was used to being a leader and she was also used to having everyone around her know that she was good at it. By

Ding Hei, leader in Fangcheng fellowship, and Miao Zitong

the end of the evening, I thought the comparison to the U.S. secretary of state of that hour—and this is not said disrespectfully—flattering to Madeleine Albright.

Sister Ding, or sometimes Ding Hei (Hei being a given name she adopted later in life), had been born Ding Xiuling in June 1961 in a village in Fangcheng County, Henan. Her father was a leading cadre of the village, and certainly not a Christian. Her mother had become a believer after she had secretly visited a house church, asked for prayer, and had a serious eye problem healed. Ding's mother began taking her daughter to church, and the rapidly growing girl was exposed to Christian teaching as a preteenager. By her own account, what brought her to faith was an old lady telling her, quite simply, "If you believe in Jesus, you will go to heaven. If you don't, you will go to hell." Of her own accord, Ding became a believer at the age of thirteen and was baptized in 1974.

Her newfound faith, combined with a deep seriousness about life, had almost immediate consequences in the middle school she was attending in Fangcheng County. As far as she knew, she was the only Christian among all the students, and there was only one teacher that Ding knew to be a Christian. Within six months, forty of her classmates had become Christian, meeting secretly after school, burying their book bags in the ground so that no one would notice that school kids were attending a Christian gathering. The classmates would greet each other as they passed in school corridors not with words, which would have given them away to the teachers, but with eye movements.

While Ding was still in middle school, the intense persecution of 1974–1975 broke out, and the Henan provincial authorities began "struggling" against Fangcheng's chief "uncle," Zhang Rongliang, who had just been arrested. "Struggling," in this case, meant the televised trial of Zhang shown to schools all over Henan Province on closed-circuit TV. Classroom lectures denouncing the accused and "superstition" accompanied the TV coverage. Ding felt that when the court was reciting the criticisms of Zhang ("counterrevolutionary under the guise of religion"), the authorities were actually criticizing her. She hated the process and the TV sessions in school. Whenever she got home from school, she would try to find some space away from her family and practice "preaching."

During a one-month period in 1976, while in prayer, Ding began to feel that God was showing her things, in a sort of mental picture, that were directly related to what she thought he might be leading her to do in life. She had no Bible of her own, so had to spend precious spare-time hours hand-copying the Bible of a fellow Christian in the village. At many of the prayer meetings held secretly by this handful of Christians of the village, the believers would earnestly pray for God to bring them Bibles. One day, in such a prayer gathering, Ding suddenly found herself seized by an inner conviction that one day the Bibles would be available to the group in great numbers. "Some day, everyone will have a Bible," she told the small circle of believers confidently at a late-night meeting. Her mother, when Ding told this story, dismissed the whole thing as fantasy. "Very few people at all have a Bible now," she told Ding, "so it is impossible for everyone to have a Bible." Ding's visions began to come true sixteen years later in Guangzhou.

In the mid-1970s, the still beleaguered Christians of Henan Province focused a great deal on miracles, visions, and God's supernatural intervention in difficult circumstances. The ordinary villagers often thought the local Christians were out of their minds. The believers would sometimes gather for prayer late at night by the riverbank. The women would often be weeping out loud as they prayed, leading some locals to wonder if the group wasn't just a little bit hysterical. When rumors of these late-night prayer sessions reached Ding's father, with the suggestion that his own daughter was involved, he was both embarrassed and furious. He rummaged through the house to locate some of Ding's copied scriptures and tore them up. Ding says that he would beat her if he found that she was planning to go out to a late-night meeting. If she went anyway, he would beat her on her return. Sometimes he dragged her around the house by her braids. Ding was rescued from the worst rages of her father by her grandfather, who adored her and rebuked his son for beating his own daughter. "Let her pray," the old man said. "If she prays for something and doesn't get it, she'll just stop praying."

More and more frequently, Ding would be asked to speak at house church gatherings in her village and nearby. Though she was still a teenager, her reputation as a powerful and dynamic speaker began to spread even among the long-established preachers. One of them, Gao Yongjiu, the brother-in-law of Li Tianen (and the same man who had invited Li back to Henan from Shanghai in 1970), came to a nearby house church for a three-day meeting of Bible teaching, and sent a co-worker to invite Ding to attend. Her father, naturally, refused to permit her to leave the house. But she felt compelled to go anyway, went out the front door, and while on the road simply prayed, "Lord, show me a miracle. My father is almost certain to beat me again when I get back. Let it not happen this time. It will be an encouragement from you that you want me to continue preaching the Gospel."

When she returned, her father, for some reason, left her alone and let her go quietly to her room. On another occasion Ding feared that if she tried to enter the house after her father had locked the door, he would once again beat her. Fearfully, she pulled the door and it opened by itself. In the morning, even her father was surprised to learn that she had entered the locked house unassisted.

Still, the intense conflict at home continued. On the one hand, Ding felt that God was calling her to be a full-time Christian worker. On the other hand, her father and her uncle were adamantly opposed to this. Her uncle recognized Ding's intelligence and thought she should train as a Chinese herb doctor. He gave her a medical book and asked her to start memorizing it. When she failed to complete the memorization, her uncle also beat her. To add even more pressure, Ding was now twenty, in the full bloom of her young womanhood, and her father was pressuring her to get married.

One night in prayer, Ding had a picture in her mind of an egg lying on the table with its shell broken. A small chick was picking its way out. "God has trained you," her mother said on hearing of this picture. "You can now fly. You can leave."

Ding began to cry, realizing that her mother, as the only other Christian in the family, would come under increased pressure if Ding were no longer around as buffer. But her mother stoically prepared a small bag of extra clothes, wrapped together some Christian books, and told her daughter that it was time to leave. Ding ran away that night.

She never again came home to live. After staying the remainder of the night at the home of one of the local Christians, who collected some 320 yuan (about $53 at the time) for her, she walked more than thirty miles over the mountain to Guai He, where Zhong Rongliang lived with his wife and young son. He had been released from labor camp the year before and had already begun organizing different house church groups throughout Fangcheng County. Ding wrote a note to her father: "Your daughter doesn't exist. Please don't try to find me." Her father, the village leader, lost face—he couldn't explain his daughter's disappearance to his colleagues or neighbors.

Ding stayed with Zhang's family for six years, until 1987. By running away from home and joining up with Zhang Rongliang's family, she became the first Fangcheng full-time worker volunteering outside her own locality. It was a period of volcanic growth for the church in Fangcheng County, Henan as a whole, and many other parts of China.

It was also a period when, for the first time, the Fangcheng Christians decided to defy openly the local party authorities. In a remarkably brazen move, on October 1, 1981 (China's national day) Zhang, Ding, and several other leading evangelists and teachers arranged an all-day meeting for 400–500 young evangelists in a village called Yangji Datian in Yangji Township. They even slaughtered a sheep for a large midday meal.

The PSB and the United Front Work Department of the local government, which oversees the Religious Affairs Bureau, got wind of the event and showed up with about forty officers and officials, surrounding the meeting area with police cars. A UFWD official approached the meeting place, which was being guarded by five young Christians with sticks, just in case hooligans wanted to break up the gathering. Could he address the whole gathering, the official asked? Zhang Rongliang agreed, but first asked if the whole group could worship. When the Christians began to sing Psalm 146 ("Do not put your trust in princes, in mortal men, who cannot save"), the official, whose name was Wen, became nervous, and started to smoke. A young evangelist shouted at him to stop because this was a place of worship. Ding saw Wen continuing to fidget nervously and brought him a glass of water.

When the singing was over and Wen took the microphone on the platform, he told them that it was illegal for the group to be meeting for religious purposes in a place not approved by the government. "Now you must all go home."

"No, we won't," Zhang said. "We are going to continue. Our meeting is scheduled to continue until the end of the day."

Confused and still a bit frightened, Wen descended from the platform and went to rejoin the other UFWD officials and PSB officers. The meeting broke at noon for lunch and the Christians began to eat the roasted sheep. But they didn't invite the PSB to join them, which infuriated the watching officials. When the meeting came to an end, the police moved in and began arresting people. They had heard about Ding, and they noticed the prominent role she was already playing among local Christian communities. But Ding had cannily changed her clothes with another Christian woman who resembled her and managed to get away in the confusion. Zhang also escaped. "This was a turning point in the history of the Fangcheng church," explained Wu Baixin, a Henan intellectual who has studied closely the Christian developments in the province.[1] "The church moved from being underground to open meetings in front of the police. The evangelists became very bold. They traveled far and wide telling people to have nothing to do with the Three Self." The police themselves were surprised to discover that most of the Christians were not old people, as they had expected from encounters in the 1960s, but dedicated young men and women.

In 1982, Ding and other Fangcheng leaders began taking turns traveling to Guangzhou to pick up Bibles brought in by Hong Kong Chinese and foreign Christians (the program was called "Donkeys for Jesus" and was organized by Dennis Balcombe). Ding and Zhang Rongliang came to know Balcombe well during those years. In the 1980s, Balcombe and his church coworkers supervised Bible deliveries in Guangzhou and began to share with the Fangcheng workers the Charismatic teachings that characterized the Chinese Revival Church in Hong Kong. Balcombe showed Ding, Zhang, and others from Fancheng and Tanghe videotapes of the effect on Christian believers in his own church and elsewhere of accepting, as from God, an experience with the Holy Spirit that usually led to speaking in tongues, prophecy, and various gifts of healing. Ding became Charismatic in her theology and worship practice in the late 1980s, as did Feng Jianguo of the Tanghe fellowship, after praying with Balcombe and others in Guangzhou. Feng, the old prison cellmate of Zhang Rongliang, formally introduced Balcombe to the Fangcheng fellowship. But it was Ding who arranged for Balcombe's first visit to Henan in the summer of 1988.

In 1983, the year when Beijing's authorities launched a political campaign against "spiritual pollution"—a code word for cracking down on the same social manifestations, like religious belief, that had been suppressed during the Cultural Revolution—the Christians of Henan became easy targets for arrest, long prison terms, and even execution by the authorities. At one stage of the campaign, an all-points arrest warrant for Zhang Rongliang, Ding, and several others gave local PSB units the authority, if they chose, to shoot the wanted Christians on sight. The Fangcheng leaders went around wondering where they should be buried. For Zhang it was easy: not far from his home. But it was a dilemma for Ding, since her own family had disowned her. "We'll take your body and bury it in an unmarked grave," her fellow Christians told her.

The authorities in Henan had become aware of the rising star Ding's leadership, not just within the Fangcheng network but throughout China, and they also knew about her contacts with Balcombe in Guangzhou. On October 12, 1989, Ding was arrested at the Xu Chang railroad station in Henan. The police interrogated her 123 times before sentencing her to three years of "reeducation through labor" at the Shi Balihe labor camp in the suburbs of Zhengzhou. The interrogators from Nanyang, Henan's second largest city, were especially interested in knowing more about the Henan church's ties to Balcombe, because he was an American.

Ding flatly refused to provide any details, in line with a principle accepted as the norm for almost all of the house church groups in China. Despite threats, beatings, and torture, China's house church Christians have by and large been extraordinarily consistent in not reporting any details of their meetings or the identity and whereabouts of fellow Christians. The prison experience was formative for Ding, as indeed it was for so many Chinese believers, but in a rather unusual way. "It was during my time in prison," Ding told me when we first met in 1998, "that the Holy Spirit taught me the most."

What Ding learned in prison went well beyond the usual Christian injunctions to be patient in suffering and faithful under persecution. Ding and the prison authorities discovered that she was an astonishingly gifted leader and administrator. Though she was the only one of 800 female labor camp inmates to be serving a sentence for "counterrevolution," within forty days of her arrival she had been promoted to cell-block leader for 189 prisoners. This was itself a violation of prison regulations because new inmates were not normally permitted to assume any leadership responsibilities in the camp. But Ding was put in charge of discipline, health, sanitation, and prison work projects. "God just gave me ideas of management," she said later.

They must have been effective, for she became a legend of good management among the nine women's labor camps throughout Henan Province. Even a decade after her release, she was being phoned by the province's prison officials asking for advice on how to solve various disciplinary problems in Henan's prison system. She had, in a sense, to cooperate with the authorities in helping prevent escapes. But a natural competitive spirit helped her to organize the camp to win province-wide labor production contests that were rewarded by provincial authorities with material and financial gifts to the camp. Ding was instrumental in exhorting the prisoners to work hard enough to meet the production goals, and the prisoners followed her because she fought fiercely for basic privileges: better food, better rest periods, better medical treatment.

Ding shared her faith with many of the prisoners, and they came to rely on her leadership. In one incident, which she described as a "miracle," she told the prisoners under her charge to take a break from working on a brick wall and sit down at a distance on the grass because it was such a pleasant day. Just then an explosion in a chemical factory next to the prison destroyed the wall where the prisoners had been working. The prison officials were frightened, but not a single prisoner was hurt. Ding recalled, "One of the officials grabbed my hand and said, 'Your God is truly a great god.'"

Ding was so helpful in maintaining discipline, improving morale, and raising production levels that the authorities, deeply grateful, released her months ahead of her schedule, in March 1992. She was arrested again briefly in 1993 for leading an unauthorized meeting, but escaped in time to attend her own wedding in late May 1993 to Zhang Gangzhu, a younger factory worker and a devout Christian introduced to her by Zhang Rongliang. A year later, Ding had a daughter, their only child to date.

Ding continued to have run-ins with the authorities, sometimes being picked up for a few days, then released after questioning, sometimes escaping from custody in the confusion frequently surrounding police raids on Christian meetings. Her dynamic speaking style, her vision, and especially her leadership skills led her in the 1990s to become one of the nine members of the headquarters leadership team of Fangcheng. In the late 1990s and during 2000–2002 Ding helped set up twenty-four-hour intercessory prayer chains involving more than 2 million Christian women all over China. She also traveled to the U.S., Jerusalem, and Southeast Asia to speak at Christian conferences.

But her prominence and her closeness to Zhang Rongliang led to criticism and suspicion. Was this just a brother-sister partnership in Christian work, some people asked, or was there something more to it? She agonized several times whether she should leave the Fangcheng leadership team altogether in order to put an end to the gossip. Late in 2002, Ding and her husband took a two-year sabbatical to spend more time with each other and with their daughter. Wu Baixin, who came to know Ding very well in the 1990s, said of her, "She has a spirit of Deborah (the heroine in the Old Testament Book of Judges who helped conquer Israel's enemies)." In fact, Deborah is her given Christian name. Michael Yu, a house church worker who came to know Zhang well, was similarly effusive. "Sister Ding is a tremendous source of history," he said. "She has amazing testimonies. Whenever she speaks at a meeting, people's testimonies are directed to her."

Ding is unquestionably the most gifted and intelligent of all the women leaders in the Chinese house church movement, and I suspect she is smarter than most of the "uncles." China's house churches for the most part don't share the same deep theological reservations about women in Christian leadership as some Protestant groups—the Southern Baptists in the U.S., for example. Women have simply played too important a role in the continuity of the church in China. In the nineteenth century, for example, Chinese "Bible women" and "colporteurs" (people who literally carried scriptures to different locations) did magnificent work in bringing scriptures to different Christian communities and in maintaining a continuity of Christian presence. However, China's strong cultural inhibition makes it very difficult for women to assume leadership positions within their Christian community. There are exceptions (notably, within the Three Self part of the church, as it happens), but they are rare.

SISTER RUTH'S "SONGS OF CAANAN"

Warmhearted and generous, Ding over the years became good friends with a younger woman who has become something of the Fanny Crosby[2] of China, a genuine legend among China's Christians. She is Lu Xiaomin, or "Sister Ruth," to use her selected Christian name. Most people in China simply refer to her by her Chinese given name, Xiaomin.

Born in Fangcheng County in 1970 into a family of the Hui minority, China's largest Muslim community, Xiaomin had no connections to Christianity. Unlike Ding, Xiaomin was only an average student in school. She completed elementary school but had to quit middle school because of sickness. The only book available to her in her parents'

Lu Xiaomin, prolific
Christian songwriter

home was a Chinese dictionary, which she perused avidly.

Once she left school, Xiaomin helped the family in agricultural work, in particular, picking cotton. One day, in the cotton fields, her aunt, also of Hui descent, and thus originally of Muslim background, but now a Christian, began sharing her faith. Xiaomin responded, and joined a house church fellowship near her home in 1989. She was just nineteen. The real change in her life occurred the following year, when she attended a house church service in a nearby village, where her sister lived. There, just a year or two earlier, Dennis Balcombe had come from Hong Kong to preach and teach about the Holy Spirit. Balcombe had laid hands on many people in this church, and many of them had come into a new Holy Spirit experience. Xiaomin found the atmosphere lively and the worship strangely moving.

One evening, after attending one of the worship sessions, she returned to her family's simple home but couldn't fall asleep. "A song came into my mind," she explained when I caught up with her in the autumn of 2000 in Guangzhou. Xiaomin was surprised at the ease with which the song had come into her mind. Neither she nor anyone in the family had ever studied music. But since she was very shy, she sang the song only to a young girl in the village. When the girl in the village sang the song to her parents, who were Christians, they started asking about Xiaomin. When they heard the story of how Xiaomin had composed the song, they told their daughter that this was the inspiration of the Holy Spirit. Some of the other elders in the church were skeptical. After all, Xiaomin hadn't even finished middle school, much less taken any music lessons.

Then a young Christian showed up in the village with a tape recorder and taped Xiaomin's first twenty-three songs. Another Christian, who knew how to render the melodies in the Chinese numerical mode, wrote out the words and the melodies. They simply called the music "Collection of Songs." Soon all of the Christians in the nearby villages were singing them. When traveling evangelists came through, they picked up the songs and the music, and began to spread Xiaomin's hymns all over China. Fangcheng's leaders began to find that, whenever they met with Xiaomin, the modest young woman would often have songs that seemed to speak directly of the dilemmas they were facing. "So many times when the leaders were at a low point in their lives, on hearing the songs they began to cry and get encouraged," Xiaomin recalled. In other places, people reported that when Xiaomin's songs were sung people sometimes healed.

Xiaomin went on composing, averaging a new song every two or three days. The collection grew, as did knowledge of the songs across the whole of China. In 1992 police raided a meeting she was attending in Henan Province and detained her and other Christians for more than two months. Xiaomin, as was usual in a Chinese police station, was slapped around for a few minutes after her arrest, though she says she was not beaten as roughly as some of the other women who were arrested. She had composed fifty songs before her arrest, and continued to write more songs from the Fangcheng County jail. Released after sixty-seven days, she had composed fourteen new songs. She was sharing a cell with four Christian women and seven other women being held on criminal charges. By the time they were released, all of her cellmates had become Christian.

When I first met Xiaomin in 2000, she had about 732 songs in her collection. She gave me tapes of herself singing the last dozen or so. When I interviewed her again in Beijing in June of 2002, the number was up to 863 and still growing. A VCD had been made and was being sold not only in house churches, but also in Three Self churches. The Three Self, however, couldn't let this phenomenon pass without some sort of snippy comment. After all, she hadn't made any appearance in a Three Self church. So in 1999 the organization's magazine *Tian Feng* criticized some of the songs. The magazine took special issue with song number 195, "Lord, have mercy on China, hold back your anger," which it took to imply that China as a nation had collectively angered God. That didn't fit in with the Three Self's notion of using Christianity to serve socialism.

I have heard Sister Ruth's songs sung all over China and even in overseas Chinese Christian communities. In early 2003 I heard many Chinese Christians singing "It is 5:00 A.M. in China" in a church in Fairfax County, Virginia, just fifteen miles from the White House.

The music has been professionally recorded, too. Yuan Zhiming, a leading Chinese intellectual exiled to the U.S., needed background music for a TV documentary he was preparing about Christianity in China. He traveled all the way to Moscow to hire an orchestra and choir to sing a selection of Xiaomin's collection. Timothy Su, one of

China's top conductors and a Christian, put together another CD using a professional orchestra and choir in Beijing. The collection is now known as "Songs of Canaan."

Xiaomin is profoundly modest about what she has done and her quiet demeanor contrasts markedly with her fame inside China. With a long, oval face like many Hui people, she keeps her hair long and parted in the middle. She dresses simply and lacks the sense of energy that her good friend Sister Ding invariably projects. On the third floor of a fast-food restaurant in Beijing she spoke openly about the challenge of keeping her family together and traveling to different parts of China for at least half of every month. Some of her songs have grown out of struggles in her own marriage. "Many Christian brothers and sisters have been so kind to me, but relations with my husband have sometimes been very difficult." Her husband, an oil worker whom she married in 1993, is a Christian but not entirely comfortable with her fame and travels.

Xiaomin's son, nine, is also a believer, but has been mocked for his faith at school. "When he comes home from school he sometimes asks me, 'Mama, why do the boys in school persecute me?' I told him to memorize Matthew, chapter 5 [the Sermon on the Mount], 'Blessed are those who are persecuted for the sake of righteousness.' "

Like virtually every house church Christian in China, Xiaomin has a passion for mission work outside of China and says the greatest task for China's Christians is to take the Gospel to Arabia. "Arabia is the vision of the Chinese church," she said. "For me I have three times had a vision of preaching to black people in Africa. We are all sure that, when God's time comes, he will open the door for us to travel overseas as missionaries."

IN CHINA'S CITIES:
URBAN PROFESSIONAL CHRISTIANS

Xiaomin's songs may not have made it to Arabia yet, but they are sung from Harbin in China's far north, to Guangzhou in the south, from Gansu Province in China's West, to Shanghai, China's urban center on the Yangtze River. In Beijing her songs are sung in the prayer meetings and Bible studies of many urban professionals.

Mary Li

"We do 'Songs of Canaan' a lot," said Mary Li (not her real name), a young U.S.-trained Internet expert who leads a group of four families in a Beijing house church. "These songs are so good because they are so indigenous. They fit so well into the culture and the life of the church."

Mary, like many urban Christians, constitutes a bridge not only between the house church and the Three Self, but also between the established city dwellers and the "floating population" of rural migrants who have become squatters in all of China's major urban areas. In Beijing, this group is estimated to be close to 3 million in number.

Mary also goes to the Gangwashi Three Self church on Beijing's Xisi South Street every Thursday evening, and leads music ministry there. It is always packed, and if you are an ordinary churchgoer and are not at the church by 6:30 P.M., you can't even enter the main congregational hall for the 7:00 P.M. midweek meeting. There are some five thousand worshipers filling out every square inch of both the main church hall and the courtyard outside. Mary thinks a great deal about the "floating population." She says, "I don't think most Chinese Christians in the cities realizes that the 'floating population' is even there. The city people have this attitude about the countryside. They joke about them having a different mentality and attitude." She and a handful of fellow members of her house church reach out to no fewer than seven "floating population" Christian groups scattered around Beijing. But she has to be very careful. "We were doing worship songs and realized it wasn't safe," she said. Neighbors could hear them sing and might have reported an unauthorized Christian gathering to the Public Security Bureau.

Mary's educational level gives her plenty of connections in Beijing's upwardly mobile professional community. She has been to some house church groups in China's capital where every participant owns a car, a highly unusual concentration of wealth in China. She knows a Christian from China Central Television who leads a house church group in his home. "Chinese society is supposed to be Confucian," she says, "but because of modernity I don't think people believe in anything. When I was little, family values and marriage commitment were still greatly valued. But these days you see a big difference. There is really a new moral standard. For a while it was fashionable to have affairs. That is why there is so much divorce going on. I think it is so sad."

Mary, an attractive, elegantly dressed young woman of twenty-seven with short hair and a self-confident air, says she and her friends worry about dating. "There are just no guys out there who are strong believers," she says. "We want to marry Western-minded, strong Christian brothers. This is a common problem everywhere you go in China. The Three Self has a teaching that if you are a Christian and marry someone you respect, it is fine. But a lot of Christian women are compromising with the world. Often they know it is a bad decision and they don't tell you about their husband's lack of Christian belief until they get married."

Mary's Chinese company does business with European corporations. In 2001 when the company had a big meeting with an energy company from Finland, a Finnish woman asked about Mary's Christmas plans. "Do you go to church?" asked the Finn. She was surprised that a Chinese would want to go to church at all and said that she, like many Europeans of her age group, had never even attended a Christian church service. She accepted Mary's invitation to visit the Gangwashi Three Self church for the Christmas service. "There are more Christians in China than in Europe, it seems," said Mary, almost sadly. "I run into a lot of European business people. Externally, they are professional, but if you get away from that they are totally bad, especially the men." One Finnish man made a move on Mary at a social gathering for their joint venture and was greatly surprised when she turned him down. European and American men often consider China a bachelor's paradise because of the easy availability of attractive Chinese women.

Helen Wong

Large numbers of Chinese in the nation's cities are influenced by the innumerable foreign experts and teachers who are devout Christians and who have come to China largely in order to share their faith. Take Helen Wong (not her real name), for example. She first met a woman from Canada who was teaching English at the Beijing university where Helen was studying to obtain a B.A. in marketing. The Canadian woman told the class, in a discussion about religion in the West, that Jesus was a real person. Most of her classmates laughed, but not Helen. She went privately to the teacher and asked her to explain.

A little later, Helen met two young American teachers. In a Beijing McDonald's, one of them told her how he had become a Christian. Both of them were studying Chinese at Beijing Normal University and Helen asked them to pray for her, even though she had still not come to any faith of her own. She eventually did come to Christian faith in 2000, the year she was baptized in a bathtub in a Chinese home. Now she shares an apartment with two other young Chinese Christian women who were introduced to her by another foreign teacher. She is part of a house church group with about ten to fifteen people, four-fifths of whom are women. "Not many men are believers," she explains. "They are too ambitious." The group meets on Sundays and Fridays, and sometimes on Tuesdays as well, for singing, worship, prayer, and preaching. Mary wants to marry a Christian man, but she is prepared meanwhile to date non-Christian men. "Most of them don't have any problem with the fact that I am a Christian," she explains, adding, revealingly, "Many people think that if you are a woman and a student from a major university in Beijing, you are likely to be a Christian. But most of the girls in our fellowship have decided for the time being not to get married."

Benjamin Chen

A few weeks later, I was talking to young house church members in Shanghai. Benjamin Chen (not his real name) was a rising young executive of a product marketing company. He had first heard about Christianity from his English teacher at the Shanghai college he attended. Then he spent some time in Switzerland acquiring advanced business training. On his return to Shanghai he joined a small house church group of about thirty people that met in three private apartments. There were foreigners there: Singaporeans, Korean students studying Chinese, and Taiwanese business executives. The age group was quite varied, which suited Benjamin fine.

Benjamin had discovered that a few of the younger people in the group liked to join him for evangelizing trips into the countryside of Shandong Province. He said he found the experience of meeting Christians in the heart of the countryside invigorating. Reflecting on all this, he said, "In the villages the people have a lot of time to read the Bible. Christianity is about a personal relationship with God. In the Three Self churches no one will tell you that. But in the villages people can have a good faith relationship. Back here, in Shanghai and other cities, we are all very busy, under intense job pressure. We miss things."

Richard Lu

Over in the south of Beijing, a few nights later, I sat down over coffee with Richard Lu (again, not his real name), a young executive in his twenties working for a major Western financial management corporation. Both Richard's parents had attended Beijing's elite Qinghua University, where Richard himself was an undergraduate. They believed, like many earlier Chinese intellectuals, that science could save China. But in his first year Richard came across a book in Chinese called *The Bible Story*, which explained the contents of the Old and New Testaments and made the point that the Bible had originally been the center point of Western civilization. Then, in conversation with an American teacher, he was surprised to learn that most people in the U.S., a scientific superpower, believed in God.

Richard discussed some of his university conversations with his father, who wasn't a believer in any religion but held that it was very important for a person to be a good person. "Don't leave anyone an excuse for people to attack you for wrong behavior," his father sternly warned Richard. Richard himself was only too aware that he was tempted in many different directions. He was also conscious of the teachings he received in elementary and middle school that depicted Western missionaries as complicit in imperialist efforts to subdue China.

Conscious of the conflict between his desire to be good and his inability to obey his father's advice to bank on his own strength, Richard came to the Christian faith sometime in his senior year. "I told my parents about it and they laughed at me," he said. "They told me it was a waste of time." After Richard told the American teacher that he had become a Christian, the American agreed to baptize him in the bathtub in his apartment. His life began to change very quickly. He said even his parents noticed that, while Richard had been something of a wild teenager before going to college, he now seemed compliant and polite. Following his own conversion, Richard said that his mother became a believer, largely because Richard's sister, studying in Poland, had also become a Christian.

Upon joining the foreign corporation, Richard was careful to keep his faith to himself. Richard was intimidated when his Chinese boss mocked him for going to Bible study every Friday evening. He currently meets every week with a small group of about a dozen people, mostly in the twenty-five-to thirty-age group, but included one older lady of sixty-seven. The group meets on Saturday afternoon in a friend's house, shares a meal, and then sings Christian songs and prayer. Four-fifths of the group, predictably, is made up of women members.

Richard has also started dating one of the women in the group. "We are the first couple in the group to begin dating after becoming Christians," he explained, more clumsily than he probably realized. "Neither of us believes in romance at all. We are both serious and logical." Richard said his goal is to turn the modest-sized group into an "evangelizing" church. One difficulty, he says, is that his generation of new Christians doesn't have an older generation of Christians they know of who could counsel them and help them grow in their new-found faith.

A MISSING LINK

The age gap among Christians is obviously a problem in China's cities, where there are large numbers of younger believers but not a tradition, as in the Henan countryside, for example, of older "uncles" and "aunties" with decades of experience. There is no one with the time and energy to nurture these young believers.

In Guangzhou I sat in on a prayer meeting of some thirty-five young people—the male-female ratio was actually close to fifty-fifty—who had gathered furtively on a weekday after the evening meal. They sang a few Chinese worship choruses and listened to a young man (not much older than themselves) give a teaching on the need for Christians not to be distracted by problems in the world around them. As they were preparing to complete their evening's prayers, they realized that the four Americans with me were seasoned members of a strong American church in Virginia. They gathered eagerly around the visiting Americans, who had been told carefully not to speak even to each other while entering the apartment stairwell for fears that neighbors might report the foreign visitors and bring the police into the building to investigate. The Americans, from a Charismatic church, were eager to help the young Chinese Christians and prayed intently with them for nearly an hour.

The Chinese opened up to the foreigners about all kinds of personal problems: chronic headaches, conflicts with family members, opposition at work, frightening dreams at night, anxiety about finding a good job. The Americans appeared genuinely thrilled that they were meeting with Christians in a country where it is dangerous to be found in an unauthorized Christian gathering. The young Chinese believers seemed equally delighted that experienced, middle-aged foreign Christians could offer them a sense of continuity with an older generation.

Michael Yu, the American-educated overseer of several house churches in Guangzhou, commented on this afterward. He said there is a huge need for education on the most basic aspects of living a Christian life, because there are so many new believers in the cities. In the past, he said, he has invited many of the experienced, older leaders of the countryside networks to teach services. But the great demand for their time from all over China has been a huge strain on their family relationships. Some of the experienced teachers were breaking apart from their own families because of the long separation required by their travels and teachings.

Yu said he estimated that there were some 50,000–60,000 active Christians in Guangzhou, not a large number for an urban population of around 6.5 million. The community tended to worship in house churches, but, Yu said, there was a lot of crossover traffic; many house church members also liked the convenience of openly attending a more traditional style of church on a Sunday. Yu is running his own training of young house church leaders in Guangzhou. He is showing them the principles and methods of forming Christian cell groups of about a dozen people, methods that had been developed in evangelical churches in Bogotá, Colombia.

Chapter Six

SEMINARIES: TRAINING A NEW GENERATION

LOOKING OUT THE WINDOWS of the small van—tinted so that villagers or nosy PSB officers wouldn't notice the long-nosed foreigner heading far off the beaten track into the heart of rural China—I saw that we were passing through communities still bearing the painted slogans of the Cultural Revolution: "Raise high the banner of Chairman Mao's Thought!" "Repudiate Lin Biao and Confucius!" and "Long Live Chairman Mao!" There were also signs of China's burgeoning consumer wealth: stores selling boom boxes or stylish electric fans. But by and large we were entering deeper and deeper into the heart of ancient China, Hudson Taylor's "inland China" of more than a century earlier.

The hills became steeper and the bamboo forests more lush. Finally, we pulled off the road onto a concrete private drive heading farther up into the forest. A stream of crystal-clear water tumbled down parallel to the driveway, providing a refreshing backdrop to the cicadas and circling birds as we stepped out of the van. We had reached the end of the concrete strip and would be making the rest of our journey by foot.

A small posse of young men and women greeted us with smiles and led us farther into the woods. The pathway had been cleverly reinforced by stone slabs, into something close to a staircase that ran alongside the stream, making it easy to climb the hill. The bamboo clusters grew thicker and the undergrowth along the pathway lusher. It began to resemble the fabulous bamboo landscape in the movie *Crouching Tiger, Hidden Dragon* in which the hero, Li Mubai, played by Chow Yun-Fat, appears to float lyrically from one bamboo tree to another as though gravity were a mere afterthought.

After about half a mile of a steady climb, made delightful by the twists, turns, and gurgles of the accompanying stream, we reached our destination: a sturdy two-story house with a concrete face looking over the bucolic valley and filled with activity.

GETTING AWAY FROM IT ALL

Emmanuel Seminary is home for six months at a time, sometimes longer, to thirty-one young men and thirty-seven young women, ranging in age from eighteen to twenty-six, sent to it by more than eighty house church congregations in the area and by Protestant Christian communities in ten other Chinese provinces.

It was midday when we arrived, and the students were having their lunch break. They had been served their food—green vegetables, rice, and a simple beef dish—in metal bowls and were now, chopsticks flying, chatting and laughing, devouring it while standing around circular tables on the second floor patio overlooking the valley. Most of the ten full-time teaching staff were having their own meal of the same food at sit-down tables closer to the kitchen. The four of us visitors joined them for the remains of the lunch.

I was soon introduced to the seminary's president, a thoughtful-looking Chinese man in his fifties. The building, he explained, was owned by a local Chinese currently living in Holland. The owner was himself a Christian and had made it available to the seminary. All of the local villagers were also Christians. This ensured that electricity bills were paid and food purchased in such a way as not to arouse suspicion by the authorities. The seminary president, whom I'll call Chen, said that the students and staff consumed more than 1,000 kilograms of rice every month. Students were not permitted to leave the seminary except for a family emergency or when embarking on a daily trip to the market to buy fresh vegetables.

The seminary had been in operation, Chen said, for five years. It seemed to be well planned and well run. The dormitory rooms on the third floor were clean and neat, the students' mosquito nets and bedding rolled tidily to the sidewalls. About six students shared each room, the boys in rooms at one end of the corridor and the girls at the other end.

The midday meal over, it was time for the students to have a brief nap, a welcoming break from the day's tight and demanding schedule. Chen described the daily activities:

5:40 A.M.	*Wake up and personal devotions*
5:40-6:40	*Toiletries*
6:40-7:30	*Scripture reading*
7:30-8:00	*Breakfast*
8:00-8:30	*Learning new worship songs*
8:30-9:00	*English lesson*
9:00-11:00	*Morning study sessions*
11:00	*Lunch and a nap*
1:00-2:00 P.M.	*Congregational prayer*
2:00-2:30	*Praise and worship session*
2:30-3:00	*English lesson*
3:00-5:00	*Afternoon study sessions*
5:00-5:30	*Evening meal*
5:30-6:30	*Washing clothes, private time*
6:30-7:00	*Praise and worship session*
7:00-9:00	*Evening study sessions*
9:00-10:00	*Toiletries, private time, lights out*

Chen explained that the six daily hours of study for the first three months covered Christian theology basics such as salvation, the church, and the Holy Spirit. The sessions on the Holy Spirit would often be taught by house church "uncles," Chen said, because the theology of the seminary was Charismatic. Other courses on church history, the history of world mission, and other topics would be taught by the resident staffers, each of whom had long been a full-time church worker.

I used the remaining part of the midday naptime to wander into a small vegetable field above the building both to admire the incredible view and to get a sense of the compact logistics of the seminary. By the time I returned, the afternoon worship session was well under way and the sixty-eight students were singing a series of worship songs with zest. The boys sat on rattan matting on the left side of the main assembly room, which took up all of the ground floor of the building and opened to the outside patio. The girls sat on the right, in neat rows of five or six like the boys. On a slightly raised platform at the front of the room one of the students was keeping time and approximating the various melodies on a Yamaha electric keyboard. One by one, each of the rows, first the boys, then the girls, then the boys again, would scramble up to the platform, face the rest of the students, and lead everyone in worship. The clapping of hands or the waving of arms appeared genuinely enthusiastic. I watched carefully and surreptitiously to see if any of the students seemed bored or put upon, but I found nothing.

All of the students seemed to know the songs by heart. There were no song sheets or overhead projectors. The process seemed second nature to them as they got up and took their seats again without direction. Each of the rows, with five or six students in it, was led by a previously agreed-upon student, who would start up a song without introduction or explanation, expecting all the students to join in, which they always did. "China, China, rise up, rise up to share the Gospel because God loves you," was one of the songs. Because I was there, they sang it twice, the second time with the words, "America, America, rise up to share the Gospel." At the back of the room, three of the women teachers were dancing in worship, waving their hands and clapping in time with the music, evidently as excited as the students were. The song was one of the many in the seminary repertoire that had been written by Lu Xiaomin, the prolific songwriter.

At the scheduled English-language session, I was asked to speak, which I did, my English translated by my accompanying interpreter. What would they like me to speak about? I asked. "Tell us about Jerusalem, both historically, as it was in the Old Testament, then at the time of Christ, and today," said president Chen. It was an easy enough topic because I had lived in Jerusalem for two years in the 1980s, had presided over a *Time* magazine cover story on the city, had taught university courses on the Arab-Israeli issue, and had been back to the city many times. All of the students listened raptly, asking questions not only about the city and about Israel, but also about America's Middle East policy. They did not appear to be very up-to-date on the news, but they asked intelligent questions—for example, wanting to know whether the White House supported the idea of a Palestinian state.

Chen told me that I was not the first foreigner to visit, being preceded, among others, by two Americans from a church that has often helped in the teaching of China's new generation of ministers. A few Korean and overseas Chinese visitors had also dropped by for some teaching sessions. Many of China's better-known "uncles" and "aunts" had come through the seminary as well—Zhang Rongliang and Ding Hei among them—to teach or tell stories of their often hazardous lives.

The staff at Emmanuel totaled twenty-six, including teachers, kitchen help, and others. At a ratio of six to four, female to male, it was more balanced than China's church as a whole. The students would attend the seminary for six months at one go, then leave for three months of practical training, then sometimes return for another six-month period. Each one of them is committed to full-time Christian ministry in the house churches, and all had been selected from a competitive process because there were many more applicants than places available. Two of the students from the summer crop of 2002 were scheduled to fly to Singapore to learn more about Christian ministry at one of the many thriving evangelical Protestant churches there.

"God's grace is so great; I want to pay it back. I want to preach the Gospel," said Wang Ailan, twenty-three, one of the women students.

Xu Daoye, a young man of eighteen, said that at fifteen he had wanted to kill. Then he had a personal faith encounter that turned his life around. His father was a deacon in a house church and his mother was in charge of pastoral ministry there also.

I asked Zhu Xiaoguang, twenty, what he most liked about the seminary. He replied. "I like the physical environment. You can really get to know people well." Didn't he find it just a bit claustrophobic being crammed in so closely to nearly seventy other students? "No," he replied, "I can take a walk into the hills." Of all the classes, Zhu most liked learning English. Where did he think he would be in ten years? "My country is quite poor," he said. "My father wants me to go overseas to study." Wang Ailan said she thought she'd probably be married by then.

Xu Daoye said that a few months earlier one of the teachers had asked the students to write down what each most wanted to get from the time they all spent in this seminary. Xu had written, "I think what I want most from this school is to have an abundant life. Now I am getting some. When I meet God I want to have him say, 'Well done, good and faithful servant [a scripture verse from the Gospel of Matthew, chapter 25, verse 21].'" Wang said, "I want to serve the Lord all my life, not half my life." Chen, the seminary president, added, "Most of the young people have a burden not just for China but for the whole world. Some of them have a burden in prayer to preach the Gospel in Jerusalem."

I wondered if the prolonged isolation from families was a challenge to both students and teachers, marooned as everyone was on this remote hilltop. One of the students privately told me that being unable to write to his family—the letters might be traced back to the seminary—was a burden, but from time to time he made surreptitious calls to home on his mobile phone. I also couldn't help wondering about the male-female tensions and excitement. Here were sixty-eight young men and women at the height of their youthful masculinity and femininity crammed so closely together you wouldn't have to extend your arm fully to "reach out and touch someone." How did the seminary handle the potential hurricanes of mutual attraction and romantic yearnings?

Chen became quite serious. Dating or flirting of any kind, he said, was strictly prohibited on campus. It would be grounds for immediate expulsion. Then how, I all but blurted out, would these fine young people ever be expected to find a marriage partner? Chen's response was more calmly expressed than my question had been. "Those who go out on full-time commitment," he said, "will be introduced to their future spouse by the church." Hmm. A sort of ecclesiastically arranged marriage. That might not be very appealing to most young American churchgoers, but I didn't detect a brewing rebellion on the male-female issue among any of the young people I talked to. In fact, a system of semi-arranged marriages exists in Christian communities in several Third World countries. The difference between this system and systems in many countries is that the youngsters involved have the choice of saying no to the proposed spouse partner.[1]

The students all appeared excited that a foreigner had shown up to look at the school and write about it. All of them seemed to brim with optimism about China's spiritual future. China, they seemed convinced, would in just a few years be largely Christianized. Zhu explained, "We believe there will come a time when most of China will become Christian. We all believe that before the 2008 Olympic Games [in Beijing] there will be a revival in China. God chose Tiananmen Square for us to worship the Lord. Not only Tiananmen, but the sports stadiums themselves."

How could this be, I asked, since China's government was still resolutely opposed to full freedom of religion? "God will change the hearts of the leaders by then," Zhu replied with great conviction.

It struck me as almost astonishing that, as Chinese society plunged ever more giddily into the ups and downs of an entrepreneurial and consumer-based lifestyle, sixty-eight talented young people from several of China's provinces would voluntarily detach themselves from it all for a near-monastic six-month apprenticeship as impecunious Bible students. But as I was to discover, Emmanuel Seminary was only one among hundreds of such underground Protestant Christian centers across the whole of China.

URBAN SEMINARIES

Emmanuel, it turned out, was unique only in its verdant isolation from the rest of China. Hundreds of other seminaries dotted rural and urban communities throughout the country. A few weeks later, I visited an underground seminary in a major city in China's southwest. It was one of four apartments being used as seminary colleges. This time, besides having to be in a van with tinted windows, I also had to duck my head down as we drove into the apartment complex. Even Chinese visitors might be closely scrutinized if they were not recognized locals, and too many unanticipated arrivals could trigger a police search at any moment.

This urban seminary had been established with the support of an American para-church group that for several years has tried to help China's house churches with administration, finances, curriculum development, and training materials. An American called Bob (not his real name) lived in the city and helped coordinate the seminary's development. Bob knew most of the house church "uncles" quite well, and over a period of time had established a basis of trust with them. A Chinese woman, who was married to an American and had become a Christian just before attending a college in the U.S., assisted Bob. She was using her considerable knowledge of the city to help organize the seminaries. Bob, whom I had first met in Hong Kong, helped arrange my visit to this urban seminary.

In the city as a whole, about 240 full-time men and women students were scattered throughout five apartments to receive seminary training. Some of them were preparing to go out of China as missionaries to the Muslim world and were awaiting the arrival of teachers of Arabic, Urdu, Indonesian, and several other languages besides English. The particular apartment I visited was right in the heart of town and sprawled up and down four stories. Thirty students and four teachers lived on the premises, but, surprisingly, it did not give the impression of being densely populated. The largest of the rooms, presumably the original living area of the apartment, was the main classroom, and had room for all thirty students to sit at tables and listen to a lecture.

The teachers were assigned to the seminary directly from the major house church networks and all seemed to have had enormous practical experience as evangelists, pastors, and seminary organizers in other parts of China. It was quite nerve-racking for them much of the time. The city PSB had already visited the apartment once, demanding to know why there were so many out-of-towners present. The teachers explained that the students were learning English, which was true, and tried to give the impression that this was just one of the many private English-language cramming schools that have mushroomed throughout China as more and more Chinese sought to study in the U.S.

But it didn't seem to me a very convincing story. There were none of the usual landmarks of overseas English-language schools: no travel posters of Stratford-on-Avon, no New York skyline illustrations, no chalked-up English phrases or vocabulary lists on the blackboards. I suggested that they at least make an effort to clothe the seminary in the appurtenances of an English-language sweatshop. But I don't think I convinced the teachers. "If the PSB comes, we won't open the door right away," one teacher explained. "We'll move the religious books and Bibles into the landlady's own room." Well, what happens if the PSB don't politely wait until all of the Christian pedagogical materials are schlepped from classroom to landlady's bedroom? What if they unceremoniously push their way in? "We have English textbooks," she countered, "but they already suspect we are a Christian school because they saw the dorms, the cooking equipment, and so forth."

Okay. So the apartment was already under suspicion. Perhaps it was also under constant surveillance. I looked at my watch. We had been there less than half an hour.

The students, as was the case in Emmanuel Seminary, were from all over China, eleven provinces in all. One was from as far away as Gansu Province, not far from Xinjiang. "If I told you I did not miss my family," he confessed, "that would not be true. But we didn't dare call home because there is a good chance that the phone will be tapped."

There have been internal problems, too, in the five apartments serving as seminaries. In one of them a male student had to be sent home because he had fallen in love with a girl student and wasn't willing to go along with the ban on dating and fraternizing within the seminary. In another instance, seven students were found to have contracted hepatitis. They had to leave to avoid infecting the others.

The rigid isolation within an urban setting is more restrictive on the students than in the coastal hills at Emmanuel. If you are tired of your roommates, you can't just go for a walk; you can't leave the building at all. The students are permitted to go out in small, escorted groups, but they have to be inordinately careful about what they say to strangers they run into in the city. "My biggest frustration," said Paul Yang, twenty-four, from Henan Province, "is that I am being trained to preach the Gospel, but when I meet people I can't tell them anything about it. Of course, one of the greatest benefits is that I am being taught the truth every day. I can see a bigger picture. My vision has been enlarged. I have this faith that the day will come when China will become a Christian country. I think one day God will open the door for China so that Chinese can go overseas to share the Gospel."

One of Paul's teachers, Mark, thirty, also from Henan, had been part of the great 1994 Tanghe six-month evangelistic outreach across China. He had been in charge of a one-year school in Henan and said he thought that the Tanghe network alone had around sixty seminaries all over China. All of the other groups together, he said, might have as many as two hundred.

Of all the seminary teachers we met, Mark seemed most aware of the security risks involved in these underground institutes of learning. According to Mark, one of the Henan seminaries had been raided in September 2000, and one student, Liu Haitao, just twenty-one, died from police beatings. He was, in effect, a Christian martyr. Though there have been many other Chinese martyrs, students undertaking their studies at these seminaries do not seem to fully anticipate this possibility.

The estimate of some two hundred underground seminaries for the four main house church networks (Fangcheng, Tanghe, Born Again, and Anhui) may be close, but it is probably significantly less than the total number of seminaries actually operating in China. We met a Korean-American who had taught for a year at an underground seminary in Beijing and had to jump every few months from one residence to another in order to keep a step ahead of the authorities. This particular seminary was unusual in two respects. It was organized and financed by Korean Christians, and it encouraged graduates from the Three Self seminaries to attend. The Korean American who taught there said that his speaking on the topic of reconciliation had led to a softening of animosities between house church students and Three Self graduates. This, in turn, had precipitated the attendance of low-level Three Self clergy at the Beijing Forum (to be discussed in chapter 10).

The Korean-led seminary in Beijing had never been harassed by the authorities, but a Wenzhou student who had studied there said he believed the authorities might have had something to do with a car wreck in which the top Korean leader of the seminary died in Beijing in 2002. My Korean-American contact disagreed but he was aware of an argument in Beijing between the municipal PSB and the central government. The municipal authorities had enacted draconian restrictive measures on religious activity in the city, in part to crack down on illegal demonstrations by Falungong meditation practitioners against the government in Tiananmen Square. But the central government PSB, according to him, was more worried about a serious negative foreign reaction if the police became too violent in stemming the various Christian activities in the city. The central government, it seems, was aware that the Christians were not "cults" and thus potentially less dangerous to the regime than Falungong.

PROFESSOR JI TAI

In a hotel in Shanghai I talked with a former Nanjing Theological Seminary professor who may know more about China's underground seminary activity than anyone else. He is Ji Tai, a Swiss-trained Christian intellectual who was moving rapidly up the ranks of the Three Self through his position as associate dean at the Nanjing Theological Seminary until he was fired in 2000.

Ji Tai was for a few years a protégé of Bishop Ding Guangxun, president of the Nanjing Theologocal Seminary and secretary-general of the Three Self. He was born in Wuxi, Jiangsu Province, in 1958, to a cotton mill worker father and a teacher mother. At seventeen, Ji Tai was sent to the countryside. Three years later, he returned to Wuxi and got a job in the same factory where his father was working. But his interest in classical Western literature started Ji Tai on a search that led him eventually to the Christian faith.

Ji's father, though a worker, had read widely and had managed to conceal a Bible in his home during the Cultural Revolution. Ji Tai for some reason was eager to read it, but when he did, he didn't really understand it. Then he started going to the city's Three Self church, where he met an older man, a serious and committed Christian believer. This man spoke to Ji Tai about sin and the Cross and gave him a basic understanding of Christianity. Ji Tai became a believer in 1980.

Three years later, he learned that Nanjing Theological Seminary was accepting applications to study there. Though his father was not happy about this—it would mean the loss of his cotton factory job of 60 yuan (about U.S. $12 in 1983) a month, Ji Tai took the examinations, and was accepted as one of forty from a total of four hundred applicants. After spending 1983–1987 in the seminary, he took a year off to help pastor a small, rural Three Self church. The congregation loved his easy, pastoral, and unpretentious manner. Ji Tai, still a bachelor, happily slept in the church premises but loved to meet with the many devout churchgoers who would show up on Sunday mornings as early as 5:00 A.M., seeking prayer or counsel.

Ji Tai did not lose touch with his mentors in Nanjing, including Bishop Ding. In 1988, seeing promise in the intelligent young man, the Nanjing Seminary authorities arranged for Ji Tai to study language and theology in Germany. He started in Munich, and later moved to Heidelberg and Stuttgart, where he studied biblical Hebrew and Greek. "The theology was quite liberal," he said of his first few months in Munich, "but I had a chance to live with genuine Christian brothers and sisters." Ji Tai also helped an overseas Chinese pastor who ministered to the Chinese Christian population in the city.

I asked Ji Tai why the Nanjing authorities had risked sending him for studies in Europe. "Ding Guangxun's strategy," he said bluntly, "was to make use of evangelicals [as a public relations venture], including my teacher, Wang Weifan. His purpose was to bear witness for the Chinese Community Party, not for Jesus Christ." Whether accurate or not, that blunt judgment was to characterize Ji Tai's relations with Ding from henceforth, and ultimately would lead to his decisive break with Nanjing.

He returned from Germany in 1991 and immediately began to teach homiletics (the art of preaching) at Nanjing. Though the position was comfortable and not especially demanding, Ji Tai was restless. He was formally ordained in 1992 at a ceremony involving several pastors, candidates, and Bishop Ding himself. But his heart seemed to be with the simple rural believers he had come to know and love during his one-year pastoral interlude between the seminary and going to Europe. Gradually, rural churches—TSPM, not house churches—wanted him to come and preach to them and baptize their new Christians. "Most of the seminary professors," he explained, "never went to these rural areas. I did a lot of baptisms. In Anhui Province, I baptized more than three hundred people from morning to afternoon."

Ji Tai's rural excursions began to attract negative attention. Some of the professors were angry that he, rather than they, was constantly being invited to teach and preach. Others, including Ding, felt that Ji Tai was pushing the envelope of acceptable TSPM pastoral activity. Ding, then president of the seminary, didn't say anything directly to Ji Tai, but the seminary authorities drew up regulations restricting the number of times in an academic term a professor would be permitted to leave campus for pastoral work.

The decisive clash with Ding broke out in 1998, when Ding began pushing hard to spread his "Reconstruction Theology" in the seminary and in the Three Self churches as a whole. Ding's "Reconstruction Theology" was heavily political, an effort to squeeze Chinese Protestant Christianity into a format compatible with building socialism. Ji Tai wrote three articles in Chinese and foreign theological journals unequivocally criticizing "Reconstruction Theology," which angered

Ding. Ji Tai explained: "My main point was that we have to make a difference between politics and religion. I said in my articles that they are not the same thing. My point was that we cannot use political criteria to judge religion. I also said religion is not simply political ethics, i.e., just 'serve the people' [a slogan first coined and popularized by Mao Zedong]."

The Nanjing authorities wanted to kick Ji Tai out, but by the late 1990s it was hard to do so on purely "theological" grounds. They found an easier pretext when, during a police raid, Ji Tai was found teaching at an underground seminary in Shanghai. In June 2000, he was expelled from the seminary for "illegal religious activities" and opposition to the educational policy of the seminary. The second charge was related to his reluctance to show up at the weekly political study course required of all teachers at the seminary.

Aware that he had broken a strong Three Self taboo—reaching out to the house churches—Ji Tai knew that his future with the Three Self was finished. He decided to concentrate on instructing in underground seminaries in the Shanghai area as well as in other parts of China. Shanghai alone, he estimates, has close to one hundred underground seminaries. He thinks the number for all of China may be closer to one thousand. While conducting his teaching he also serves as a teacher and pastor to a house church group that includes not only house church leaders but also members of the clergy from the Three Self who are disenchanted with Ding's "Reconstruction Theology" that has been forced upon them. Working in and around Shanghai has given Ji Tai an opportunity to meet with a new generation of Shanghai students from mainstream universities who are turning to Christianity. "There are more and more university students in Shanghai who are becoming Christian," he says. "I know this will play a big role in China's future."

TRAINING A NEW GENERATION

Zhang Rongliang, a natural leader in any environment, once explained to a visiting British Christian writer about where he had received his training. "Chinese prison is my seminary," he said. "Police handcuffs and the electric nightstick is our equipment. That is God's special training for the Gospel."

Well, that may have been adequate—it may have been the only possible training—while China's Christians were still feeling their way out of decades of isolation and intense persecution in the 1980s. But by the mid-1990s, the training of a new generation of pastors and leaders had become an urgent necessity. The chief problem, of course, was that because the government continued to demand that house churches register with the authorities and through them with the Three Self, all of the training had to be done underground. Church and para-church groups in the U.S., Hong Kong, Taiwan, and Korea helped in various ways to respond to the need, providing material, financial support, and quite often gifted volunteer teachers for short-term sessions. And the underground seminaries have also helped to train new leaders for China's fast-growing Christian community.

What needs to be explained is: why did the Three Self demand the submission of all Protestant Christian activity in China to itself? Was Three Self simply a conscious stooge of the Chinese Communist Party from its inception, its leadership heavily compromised by a theology that it was almost a version of Marxism? Or did the Three Self do what limited good it could to protect at least the external forms of Christianity in China for more than five decades as China's domestic policies lurched from one extreme to another under Mao Zedong?

Chapter Seven

EARLY YEARS OF THE "STATE CHURCH"

IT'S JUST AFTER 9:00 A.M. on a Sunday morning in Beijing, the courtyard at 57 Nan Da Jie is already packed with people. This is the location of one of Beijing's five authorized Protestant churches. It is familiarly called Gangwashi, meaning "Pottery and Jar Market." The main Sunday morning service starts at 9:30 A.M., but if prospective congregants are not in the main sanctuary half an hour earlier they won't be able to get into the church. In the courtyard, the sermon by Pastor Zhang Suchang is being played on closed-circuit TV sets. About two hundred men and women, mostly in their twenties and thirties, are listening intently, many of them taking notes as they follow Zhang's remarks. Ushers politely guide latecomers like me into recesses of the courtyard where we can stand leaning against a wall. A rooster minces its way along the courtyard wall, crowing occasionally. From the open windows of an adjacent building emerge the sounds of what seems to be a choir practicing.

Gangwashi is a Three Self church. Or as Three Self officials would prefer to put it, since they claim there is no such thing as a "Three Self church," it is a church affiliated with the China Christian Council, the organizational twin of the Three Self Patriotic Movement, authorized by the government to operate Protestant church services across the country. Gangwashi is one of the four "open" churches in Beijing to which Chinese and foreigners can freely go. In cities throughout China, as well as in rural areas, some 13,000 churches are recognized by the Three Self and thus permitted to operate. According to estimates by Three Self officials, these churches serve about 15 million Protestant believers—some Three Self officials privately say it is closer to 20 million—and are led by an authorized clergy ever fewer in number, around 3,000.

For most foreigners visiting China, these churches are as close to public Christian activity in China as they will ever get. It is often quite impressive. In Shanghai's International Church, foreigners who attend Sunday services can be provided with headsets for simultaneous translation in English. In both Shanghai and Beijing the open churches have robed choirs of men and women who sing with great skill and gusto. Chinese Bibles can be openly purchased at Three Self churches, and many of the churches have Christian bookstores where Chinese translations of other devotional literature are also available. A popular one is *Streams in the Desert*, by American missionary Mrs. Charles E. Cowman (1870-1960), who served as a missionary in both China and Japan in the first two decades of the twentieth century.

The churches are almost always packed to capacity. Mary Li, the Beijing professional we met in chapter 5, often attends Thursday evening youth meetings at the Gangwashi. She says as many as 500 young people are there on any Thursday evening. The Three Self church in Haidian District, which serves the city's largest university community, is similarly packed every Sunday. This shouldn't be surprising. Four open churches for all of the Protestants of Beijing, a city of 12 million, are hardly adequate. What is important is that any Chinese, young or old can attend a Three Self church and learn about Christianity. [1]

Most Three Self churches teach a Christianity that is orthodox, evangelical, and different from house church communities only in that there is unlikely to be any Charismatic expression—e.g., praying in tongues, joyful hand-waving, or even dancing. It is also unlikely that a worshiper in a Three Self church will ever hear a sermon on the Second

Coming of Christ. Despite the fact that the Three Self is basically a state church (the pastors receive salaries from the state and all activities are closely monitored by state authorities), the overwhelming majority of its clergy are evangelical in their faith. They believe Christians must make a specific personal faith commitment and not just wander into a church because it's the done thing or because their parents did. They also believe that it is a matter of eternal significance whether people come to faith. Chinese evangelicals from Three Self churches are as eager as evangelicals all over the world that all human beings should hear and receive the Christian message.

Sometimes, the evangelicalism of pastors becomes a problem for the government. A few years ago, at Chongwenmen church, Beijing's other large Three Self church, the pastor was removed because he was considered too evangelical, despite the anger expressed by an overwhelming majority of the church membership. A Christian community that is vibrant with growth and enthusiasm is still deeply threatening to some Three Self officials and the Religious Affairs Bureau apparatchiks. In Guangzhou's Dong Shan Church, on Tangjin Street in the Dongshan District, a youth meeting that gathered on a weekly basis in one of the church's smaller meeting rooms was not permitted to meet in the larger and otherwise empty sanctuary despite the fact that it was bursting at the seams in the smaller meeting room.

But Gangwashi is firmly, almost defiantly evangelical. In addition to the Sunday morning services, there are Thursday evening youth services, which are crowded with young people. Becky Neufeld, who lived in Beijing for many years before returning to the U.S., attended the Thursday evening services several times. She describes the atmosphere as "an old Youth for Christ rally [Youth for Christ was the evangelical ministry to young people for which the young Billy Graham was an international evangelist in the 1940s]." There are prayers and testimonies. "A few months ago," she said, "the senior pastor, an elderly man, announced, 'We need to pray for more people, that this church will reach out to the city. We want to pray that everyone in Beijing knows Jesus and that Jesus will be known in the whole country and that China will be a country from which the Gospel is spreading to the rest of the world.'" That's as evangelical as you can get and virtually echoes what all of the house church leaders would say.

CATERING TO THE SURGE OF INTEREST

All over China, there is unmistakable evidence that the Three Self churches are doing their best to keep up with the surge of interest in Christianity. In some local areas, even the authorities are cooperative. Kim-kwong Chan, a scholar and member of the Hong Kong Christian Council, was formally granted unusual access to study remote regions of China where Christianity is changing local cultures. In Yunnan's Lancan Lahu autonomous county, within the province's Simao prefecture, local officials for years wrung their hands at the opium addiction that was widespread in many of the villages. The county is close to the infamous "Golden Triangle" area of Myanmar, Thailand, and China, where for decades regional warlords have presided over a lucrative opium business.

Though opium smoking and growing are strictly prohibited in China and punishable by imprisonment (in the 1950s, the death penalty was routinely meted out by the Communists, who sought to eradicate one of the worst social evils in China), there are always strong incentives for the villagers to grow it. For one thing, opium cultivation yields a much higher income than regular crops. For another, opium creates a vicious economic cycle that is hard to break. As more villagers became addicts, family income would go down and family sicknesses would increase. The area's ethnic Lahu minority, traditionally belonging to a polytheistic and animistic religion that relied heavily on sacrifices to the ruling spirits, would normally sacrifice their own livestock in hopes of appeasing the spirits causing an illness or misfortune. Within a short period of time, these families would impoverish themselves.

In 1992, according to Chan's investigation, Christianity was introduced to the village by traveling house church evangelists.

Before long, local officials noted that Christian families were becoming wealthier than the Lahus, who continued their traditional religious practices. In addition, opium addiction went down and several notorious crime-gang villagers converted to Christianity and changed their ways. Thus the officials encouraged the locals to heed the Christian message. By 1998, according to Chan, fifty-eight Christian families and more than two hundred villagers, out of a total village population of 234, were taking Christian instruction. At the end of 1999, the Village Administrative Committee and the Religious Affairs Committee, along with the administrative committee of the local church, sent a letter to Religious Affairs Bureaus and the Minority Affairs Bureaus of the county and the prefecture, requesting money to help repair the leaking tarpaulin roof of a church the village had built the previous year. The letter said, in part,

> During the past two years, all of these new Christians experienced lifestyle improvements. For example, Mr. Li Muguo and his family had slaughtered two pigs and two oxen to send the evil spirits away and had no animals left. Two years after they converted to the Christian faith, they have three oxen and four pigs.[2]

Summing up her research on the impact of Christianity on China's border regions, Chan writes, "There are ethnic minorities who have adopted Christianity as an ethnic identity. Christian influence has transformed their culture. One example is the Lisu minority, living in Yunnan province."[3]

Chan discovered that pragmatic-minded local officials didn't object to the Christianization of any community if it was an "official" Christian group and if the social behavior of that community improved, which was almost always the case when significant numbers become Christian. In effect, Chinese officials at the local levels can be less hung up about what ordinary people believe than the nationally based officials whose job it is to regulate religious practice in China. Grassroots Chinese officials in some of the minority areas are actually favorable toward Christian evangelization.

Where the Three Self churches are allowed to do what churches in most parts of the world do—counseling and encouraging for church members, visiting and praying for the sick, operating orphanages and homes for the elderly, or explaining Christianity to anyone interested in it—they generally do it very well. Much of it is accomplished through the Amity Foundation, a nonprofit institution established in 1985 to enable North American and European churches and private individuals to fund a broad variety of social and cultural projects in China, many of them administered by Three Self churches in different parts of the country. The Amity Foundation has an annual budget of $5 million, of which 25 percent comes from the U.S. and Canada, 51 percent from Europe, 15 percent from Hong Kong, Macau, and Taiwan, and only 2.5 percent from China itself. Much of its support from the U.S. comes from mainline Protestant groups like the Lutheran World Federation, and the Church World Service, the global service arm of the National Council of Churches of Christ in the U.S.

AMITY FOUNDATION

Amity is an organizational oddity, a sort of government-approved NGO. Its projects include: bringing dozens of foreign teachers of English to China every year in order to improve the teaching skills of Chinese teachers of English, improving the teaching skills of Chinese rural schoolteachers in areas like math and science, preventing blindness by training cataract eye workers, instructing in basic health care, and assisting church-initiated social programs. An unusual Amity project is helping fund the Nanjing Center for Legal Aid, a charitable legal organization that fights cases, and sometimes wins them, for Chinese workers caught up in the vortex of a highly competitive entrepreneurial system that lacks due process under the rule of law and the most elementary labor rights. The Amity website (*www.amityfoundation.org*), available in both English and Chinese, has this blurb on the legal aid program:

What do you do if you have a labor accident and your boss is unwilling to pay for hospital fees, let alone compensation? Your husband beats you—what are your legal options of dealing with the problem? Can you sue your grown-up children for support? What if your brand new imported hifi-equipment turns out to be a fake?[4]

This reads more like a Manhattan-based American workers'-rights organization than something from China. It reveals just how far Chinese society has moved away from the regimentation and economic and cultural poverty of the 1970s. Amity official Zhang Liwei, assistant to the secretary-general at the Hankow Road headquarters of Amity in Nanjing says he is "not yet" a Christian. He says of Amity, "We are a non-church body, an NGO even though we were started by Chinese Christians. We want to contribute to the modernization of China and to make Christian involvement in social work more widely known. We also want to work more with foreigners."

Although a non-church body, Amity has done something quite significant for Christians in China. The Amity Printing Press, started in 1987 with considerable support from American Christian organizations, has been printing the Bible in Chinese for a quarter of a century and has already produced more than 30 million copies in both the standard, simplified character Union Version (1919) and in seven Chinese minority languages, including Lagu, Miao, and Yi. "Several government officials want to have a copy of the Bible," says Zhang. "I think that this is an effort to look at Christianity in depth from a spiritual point of view."

As mentioned earlier, while Bibles are indeed available for sale at Three Self churches in at least seventy locations throughout the country, house church leaders repeatedly tell me that it is not possible in most places for one person to purchase several copies at a time. House church Christians wanting a Bible may have to travel a hundred miles or more in order to obtain one. In some cases, Christians have been asked to indicate their names and addresses before being allowed to purchase Bibles. Bibles are also not available in ordinary Chinese bookstores, even though copies of the Koran and of Buddhist scriptures are.

BISHOP DING GUANGXUN

Nanjing, where Amity is based, has for half a century been the powerhouse of the Three Self, even though the national headquarters are in Shanghai. Nanjing is home to a state Church that is almost reflexively submissive to the Communist government. More important, it is home to China's most easily recognized Christian in international circles, Bishop Ding Guangxun (also known, in the old, Wade-Giles Romanization of Chinese, as K. H. Ting). Ding has been the president of the Nanjing Theological Seminary for the past half-century. Though he was officially slated to retire at eighty-five, Ding, now eighty-eight, shows no signs of slowing down. Ding is also honorary chairman of the China Christian Council and secretary general of its twin, the Three Self Patriotic Movement. The two groups together are often referred to as the *lianghui* ("two organizations") in Chinese, indicating that their functions overlap.

Ding Guangxun is in some ways an enigmatic figure, and a very controversial one. In a recent biography of Wang Mingdao, the author opens his account with a conversation between a Western reporter and a "wizened Beijing Christian" at some unspecified moment in the recent past. The Beijing Christian says to the reporter,

"Understand two men, and you will understand Chinese Christianity."

"Which two?" asked the reporter.

"Wang Mingdao and K. H. Ting!"[5]

AN ENIGMA

At eighty-eight Ding is still a real lightning rod. According to the overwhelming majority of the house church leaders and their flocks, he is not even a Christian, but a Marxist who has betrayed the Christian church repeatedly to the Communist authorities in the government. To his admirers, he is a man who has acted vigorously to give

Chinese Christianity a certain amount of "civic space" in a nation from which religion as a whole was all but expelled in the 1950s and 1960s as China's radical politics lurched from one extreme to the next.

Ding's critics are certainly outspoken. One of the veteran Henan Christians puts it quite bluntly. He snorted, "I don't think he is a real Christian. Many facts proved that Mr. Ding is a Communist Party member. When Premier Zhao Ziyang was in power he talked with Ding. He said, 'Ding, Comrade Ding, how should we govern Christians?' A lot of local Communist Party secretaries had asked Premier Zhao how to deal with the Christians because there were too many of them. Ding replied, 'You are unable to suppress them. I advise you to bring the underground church above ground. When they are public we can destroy them.' Ding has no faith at all. He does not believe that Jesus Christ came in the flesh, or resurrected, or that Jesus Christ will return. He doesn't emphasize the Cross, or atonement by the blood of Jesus Christ. Ding emphasizes the government can save people. Just talk about Jesus' love. Ding is not a Christian. He is the government's controller of religion. How can he be a Christian?" Many similar judgments of Ding can be heard from the house churches in China.

In person, Ding looks like a kindly man, a Chinese version of a nineteenth-century Anglican prelate from Anthony Trollope's Barchester novels. He has a cherubic smile, an impressive pasture of white hair swept straight back from his forehead, and, at least in public, a gentle and modest disposition. He never raises his voice, speaks graceful and fluent English, and can at times be critical both of himself, the Three Self, and the authorities in control of religion in China. He has performed acts of personal kindness to both Chinese and foreign Christians. In Beijing, a Chinese Christian woodcarver was finding it impossible to locate premises where he could legally sell his fine biblical scenes carved in bas-relief. Ding made some phone calls and worked the problem out. The current American clergywoman of the English-language Congregation of the Good Shepherd in Beijing, a Christian worship locale favored by English-speaking Christians of more liturgical background, is Reverend Ellyn McInnis. McInnis had studied for the priesthood at a seminary in the U.S., but it was Ding who personally made arrangements for her ordination in China.

Ding has occasionally spoken out on behalf of Christian communities in China to the state authorities. In 1988, when the Guangdong provincial government passed a law requiring all Christian church organizations to register with the authorities or face disbandment, the obvious target was Samuel Lamb. Ding wrote a long letter to the Religious Affairs Bureau in Beijing supporting Lamb's refusal to register. "As long as Lin does not oppose the party or socialism, does not do anything illegal and does not 'cooperate with the infiltration of anti-China forces' he has the right to run his house church."[6] When the Religious Affairs Bureau authorities were mobilizing their harsh campaign in Wenzhou in the summer of 2002 to close down children's Sunday schools in various churches, John Pomfret reported in the *Washington Post,* four Wenzhou pastors met with Ding to protest and Ding in response wrote an official letter to the Chinese People's Political Consultative Conference pointing out that it was "impossible to defend" keeping children under the age of eighteen from entering a church. Ding's letter evidently resulted in the release from detention of pastor Chen Guogang, who had started Sunday school in Wenzhou's open churches in the 1990s.[7]

There is no question that Ding, though an Anglican bishop and China's most internationally prominent Christian spokesman, has been exceedingly uncomfortable with the notion of Christian evangelism—the nonstop goal of the house churches for several decades—from the very beginning of his very long career in China's Three Self. I had a chance to question the bishop during a trip of his to New York in 1979. Well aware that the Three Self churches—which were only just coming back into operation after the repression of the Cultural Revolution—were constantly being cracked down upon if any of their members tried to spread the Gospel by open evangelism, I asked Ding, "Why can't Chinese Christians evangelize openly, wherever they want? Why must it only be on church premises?"

"Where else would it be?" he asked, a bit surprised by this.

"Well, on the street, for example, or in a bus station."

"A bus station!" he snorted, conveying a Trollopian Anglican divine's indignation that any respectable person would ever want to discuss religious faith in such a disreputable place as a bus station. For a moment I was transported to that transcendent moment in the Oscar Wilde play *The Importance of Being Earnest* when Lady Bracknell is told that Jack Worthing, aspiring to marry Lady Bracknell's daughter Gwendolyn, can't really explain his social origins because he was discovered as an infant in a handbag at London's Victoria Station. In what must be one of the English theater's great moments of expostulatory humor, Lady Bracknell trills back in indignation, "A handbag!" Bishop Ding on the Chinese house churches' desire to evangelize his country from "A bus station!" was equally indignant.

COMMUNIST OR CHRISITAN?

Ding's highly controversial role in China's church goes far beyond his personal Anglican mannerisms. The suspicion that Ding may never have been a real Christian believer but rather a secret member of China's Communist Party goes back decades, to the very beginning of Ding's national prominence.

Ding was born into a Christian family in Beijing in 1915, grew up there and later in Shanghai, and in the 1930s was a student at Shanghai's prestigious St. John's University. China had been drawn into full-scale war by Japan's invasion of June 1937, and Shanghai's students were filled with outrage at this latest episode in China's national humiliation. Communist cells operated among students on campuses throughout Shanghai. Communist Party members were most certainly secretly ensconced on the campus of St. John's. It's likely that Ding knew of them. It's certainly possible that he became a secret party member in his twenties while still at St. John's University, but the party records are still, six decades later, sealed and unavailable for public scrutiny. Chinese academics in Shanghai will tell you privately that Ding was almost certainly a Communist Party member by the 1940s.

Pastors and officials of China's Three Self who were also secret Communist Party members were fairly common, a phenomenon that came into the open during the Cultural Revolution. The pastor of Shanghai's International Church, Li Chuwen, a leading Three Self official, was targeted by the Red Guards in 1966. At a key moment in the proceedings, no doubt to forestall really nasty punishment, Li showed the Red Guards proof of his Communist Party membership. He was spared any further harassment. After the Cultural Revolution he moved from one part of the Communist bureaucracy to another, first in Shanghai and then on the Hong Kong branch of the New China News Agency in the early 1980s. (The NCNA in Hong Kong served as an unofficial Chinese embassy in Hong Kong while it was still governed by the British.)

During an interview in Nanjing in the autumn of 2002, Bishop Ding flatly denied to me that he had ever been a member of China's Communist Party, not even as a clandestine member such as Li Chuwen.

What is known is that during 1947–1949 Ding was a graduate student at Union Theological Seminary in New York, then already a mecca for Chinese Christians and inclined to the modernist (the 1930s version of today's "liberal") theological viewpoint. Several Chinese Protestants who were to play leading roles in adapting China's Protestant Christianity to Communism spent time at Union Theological Seminary.

Y. T. WU

The most significant of these was Bishop Ding's mentor, Y. T. Wu (Wu Yaozong) (1893–1971). Wu was born into a non-Christian family in Guangdong Province and didn't have any interest in Christianity until he was twenty and studying at the Customs College in Peking. An American missionary baptized him in 1918. Two years later he was appointed secretary of the student division of the Beijing YMCA. This organization was to become the foundation point of all his major career turns.

In 1924 Wu, then thirty-one, arrived in the U.S. to begin his own studies at Union Theological Seminary in New York. He then moved to Columbia University, and in 1927 received an M.A. with a thesis entitled "William James' Doctrine of Religious Belief."

The seminary in the 1920s was a bastion of the Modernists who were battling the Fundamentalists for control of America's mainline Protestant denominations. The Fundamentalists had come into prominence with the publication of a series of pamphlets from 1915 onwards called *The Fundamentals*. These booklets defended one by one traditional Christian beliefs such as the inerrancy of the Bible, the Incarnation, the Virgin Birth, the physical Resurrection of Jesus, the "substitutionary atonement" (the concept that Jesus died as a sacrifice to ward off God's judgment on men for the sins of the whole world), and the Second Coming of Christ. The Modernists—who would call themselves theological "liberals" or "progressives" today—tended to disbelieve anything supernatural in the Bible and thought that Christian doctrines should be contextualized with the knowledge of history, culture, and the discoveries of modern science.

Wu wholeheartedly adopted modernism as the basis for his own Christian worldview. His skepticism of the supernatural prepared him for the evolution of his Christian thinking in the 1930s. In 1937, he openly supported the Chinese Communists (who had been intermittently at war with the Nationalists, or Guomindang, since 1923) and joined the Communist-organized Chinese Defense Alliance. Quite possibly, Wu at some point also joined the Communist Party as a clandestine member. According to George N. Patterson, a former Christian missionary in Tibet who had access in Hong Kong to a high-level Chinese defector from the Religious Affairs Bureau in the 1960s, both Y. T. Wu and Zhao Puchu, who became the secretary-general of the Chinese Buddhist Association, were secret members of the Chinese Communist Party, and were from the 1940s under the orders of the Communist Party authorities in Beijing.[8]

Even if Wu had not been a party member, he manifested in both his pronouncements and his actions a clear belief that Marxism-Leninism—which he called "Communism"—was the future destiny not just of China but of all humanity. In 1948 Wu wrote an article, "The Present-Day Tragedy of Christianity," in the *Tian Feng* magazine (which he himself had founded in 1942). In it, Wu castigated Christianity for its identification with capitalism, arguing that the

Christian religion's primary value was as "a rational faith to supply the driving force of doing good."[9] The true principles of Christianity, according to Wu, were revealed in social progress, and more explicitly, the tide of revolution now sweeping across China. Wu insisted elsewhere, "Since Communism is practicing what Christianity merely professes, Christians have no right to stress the points on which they differ from the Communists, until they are similarly practicing their beliefs."[10]

The Communists were poised to take over China, but they hadn't yet done so. There was widespread outrage at Wu's lavish praise for the incoming regime and for his wholesale embrace of the Communist worldview. Wu was forced for a season to resign from *Tian Feng*. But he continued his use of Protestant Christianity to assist the new regime in consolidating authority over the country.

Mao had perfected the "united front" tactic as a device to identify supporters of Communist revolution, to target resisters, and to win over the undecided. The Communist Party had—still has—a department specifically responsible for controlling and directing all parts of society, including religion, that do not naturally belong in the political arena. It is called the United Front Work Department. Since 1949, the UFWD has developed the regime's concepts of how to cope with religion in China. Since 1951, the UFWD's policy has been carried out by the Religious Affairs Bureau.

To understand how China's "state church" is handled by the regime today is to observe how Communism's state power, with guidance and cheering from Y. T. Wu, and later Bishop Ding, managed in the 1950s to isolate and remove potential Protestant opponents of Communist dictatorship, and to intimidate everyone else.

In 1949 Wu, whose official position was still the director of the Shanghai-based Christian press of the YMCA, "Associated Press" (no connection to the well-known U.S. news organization), traveled overseas to attend Communist-organized "peace conferences"; one took place in Prague in 1948 and another in Paris in 1949. Prague came under the control of the Communists in 1948 after an internal putsch in Czechoslovakia. By September 1949, Wu was back in Beijing. Just a month before Mao Zedong proclaimed the triumph of the People's Republic of China in Tiananmen Square, October 1, 1949, Wu attended a Communist-organized conference in the capital, the Chinese People's Political Negotiation Conference, along with four other Chinese who were designated to represent Christianity.

Wu had gone through a gradual evolution in his thinking between his time in New York in 1937—when, though a Modernist, he was under the influence of Reinhold Niebuhr, the moderate German theologian who had left Nazi Germany in 1933—and the Communist revolution in China of 1949. In July 1951, *Tian Feng* published Wu's "Autobiographical Confession," a model of the required expression of conversion to the Communist viewpoint after a person had gone through a "reeducation" process. In his "confession," Wu admitted that he had been an "anti-Communist" in his early Christian years. But now, he said, little more than a year after Communist control of China, he had seen with his "own eyes the great accomplishments of the Communist Party in the construction of the New China." He added, "This not only greatly increases my faith in and admiration of the Communist Party, but also leads me to express on behalf of the Chinese people and myself an unbounded affection for the party."[11]

The Communists, Wu asserted, had taught him the true meaning of Christ's commandment "Love your enemies" (a Bible reference to Matthew's Gospel, chapter 5, verse 44). After all, he explained, they had shown it was necessary not to turn the other cheek to what was wrong, but to move against it. They had done so, he said, by attacking the Japanese invaders of China, yet they had treated Japanese prisoners of war with kindness. Pacifism, despite Wu's earlier support of it, was "an imperialist opiate to keep oppressed peoples quiet." The most urgent problem for China and the whole world, he now thought, was how to destroy imperialism. He deemed imperialism to be "the world's deadliest enemy." He said that it "must be destroyed before the people of the world can obtain true peace, freedom, and prosperity." The "world's only road to safety," he was sure, was "communism, and the socialism and new democracy that form the foundation of socialism."[12] As regards to Christianity, "the Communist Party," he insisted, "has shown me that the whole of organized Christianity has a class nature."[13]

Wu made it quite explicit that he now accepted materialism as the true philosophy of life. He never explained how he could be a Christian, which the Communists defined as "idealist" and at the same time a "materialist," whose premise is radically opposed to the presuppositions of religion.

"In the past thirty years," he wrote, "I have experienced two major changes in my thought. First, my conversion to Christianity—from religious skepticism to faith. Secondly, my acceptance of the antireligion philosophy of materialism, and blending it with religious belief."[14]

Wu is a classic example of someone who started with one set of faith beliefs (a Modernist version of Christianity that denied true supernatural realities in Christianity such as the physical Resurrection of Jesus and the Virgin Birth), and was led by a real-life challenge to his views (the chaos, injustice, and violence of China in the 1930s and 1940s) to a belief in a completely new set of metaphysical attitudes (Communism). From the late 1930s, Wu was fully willing to cooperate with the Communists in every possible way. He had met Zhou Enlai, Mao Zedong's top lieutenant, in 1943, establishing a connection that was to play a crucial role in Wu's subsequent construction of the Three Self movement. Zhou had been also involved in helping develop the "Christian Manifesto."

THE CHRISTIAN MANIFESTO

In May 1950, Y. T. Wu had three long meetings within eleven days with Zhou, who was to emerge both as China's new premier and as its most skillful diplomat. Zhou and Wu both understood that a full-scale assault on Christianity as a religion would backfire domestically and cause outrage abroad. Zhou grasped that part of the united front policy would require, in a sense, redefining Christianity as a faith. Wu comprehended the doctrinal challenges to do so. The only acceptable Protestant Christianity for China, Wu grasped, would be one defined as being against "the imperialists"—i.e., against the U.S.—in favor of the "New China," the Soviet Union, and everything the Communist

Party deemed necessary to acquire and strengthen national control. In July 1950, a new Christian document was published that became known as "The Christian Manifesto." This brief statement, only one thousand Chinese characters in length, spelled out with brutal bluntness the tasks Chinese Protestants would have to undertake. The manifesto required its signatories to acknowledge that during the 140 years of Protestant missionary presence in China, "Christianity consciously or unconsciously, directly or indirectly, became related with imperialism."[15] It went on in the section headed "The Task in General" to say,

> Christian churches and organizations [must] give thoroughgoing support to the "Common Political Platform" [of the Communist Party] and under the leadership of the government oppose imperialism, feudalism, and bureaucratic capitalism, and take part in the effort to build an independent, democratic, peaceful, unified, prosperous, and powerful New China.[16]

In the following section, headlined "Fundamental Aims," the manifesto made it clear that Protestant Christian churches must also be fully engaged in a constant political propaganda campaign to further Communist control of the country:

> Christian churches and organizations in China should exert their utmost efforts, and employ effective methods, to make people in the churches everywhere recognize clearly the evils that have been wrought in China by imperialism; recognize the fact that in the past imperialism has made use of Christianity; purge imperialistic influences from Christianity itself; and be vigilant against imperialism, and especially American imperialism, in its plot to use religion in fostering the growth of reactionary forces.[17]

There was no mistaking the full implications of the manifesto: the only acceptable version of Protestant Christianity in China under Communist control would be a radical leftist version that was completely

Modernist on issues that the Fundamentalists and Evangelicals disagreed about not as matters of political judgment but as differences central to Christian orthodoxy. An article in *Tian Feng* magazine entitled, "How to Hold an Accusation Meeting," illustrates the brutal political pro-Communist tactic of Y. T. Wu and his acolytes. The meetings must be very carefully prepared in advance, the article stressed, with all of the "evidence" against the target Christian meticulously planned and organized. This would be followed by a good-cop-bad-cop routine. "The order of arrangement of the accusers is very important; they should be arranged as follows: first high tension, then moderate, then another high tension, etc.; only then can the accusation meeting be a success."[18]

The manipulative cynicism of this recipe for coercive intimidation of fellow Christians is breathtaking. If a Christian pastor or leader were opposed to the manifesto, then he was not "patriotic" and could be humiliated in a public "accusation meeting" until he changed his tune. None of the Three Self's current leadership, all of whom were rising up through the ranks of the organization in the 1950s, has ever shown the slightest embarrassment at being associated with this crude treatment against their fellow Christians.

The "Christian Manifesto" was originally made public in July 1950. By September, the Korean War was well under way. China's Communist propaganda against the "American imperialists" grew in its shrillness. To not support China's "New Democracy" was to be an enemy of China and a "counterrevolutionary." Within two years it was reported that some 400,000 Chinese Protestant Christians, about half the entire Protestant population of China, had signed the manifesto. That figure is quite artificial. In some areas of China, some Lutheran church analysts later argued, more Lutherans supposedly signed the manifesto than actually were known to exist.[19]

THE THREE SELF IS FORMED

By October 1950 with China having now entered the Korean War directly against the U.S. on the side of North Korea, the political climate in the country favored institutional steps to formalize the new direction of Chinese Christian Protestantism. The biennial meeting of the Chinese National Christian Council, the highest formal gathering of Chinese Protestant leaders, formally adopted the manifesto and began to establish the Three Self. The organization was officially launched in April 1951, when the newly created Religious Affairs Bureau, set up by the UFWD, summoned 151 Chinese Protestant leaders to a "Conference on Dealing with Christian Institutions Formerly Receiving American Aid." Senior Communist Party official Lu Dingyi, chairman of the Cultural Education and Religious Bureaus of the Government Administrative Council, in a speech to the delegates made it quite clear what the meeting's goal was: to expunge from Chinese Protestantism any influence or thought pattern that might be considered to have derived from "imperialist" missionary presence and cultural influence. Lu said,

> The goal of the struggle is to wipe out the influences of the past more than a hundred years of imperialistic cultural aggression toward our country. In this struggle it is necessary for patriotic Christians from the various religious groups to unite with the government in common effort under the supervision of the People's Government led by the Chinese Communist Party.[20]

Christian organizations in China were instructed to eliminate all links with fellow Christian groups in the West. The conference voted "to thoroughly, permanently, and completely sever all relations with American missions and all other missions, thus realizing self-government, self-support, and self-propagation in the Chinese church."[21] Henceforth, the organization authorized by the Religious Affairs Bureau to preside over Chinese Protestantism and implement all of these directives would be the Three Self Reform Movement. One of the twenty-five-member preparatory council members was Li Chuwen, the Protestant pastor unmasked by Red Guards during the Cultural Revolution as a secret party member. Another was Zhao Fusan, who was ordained as an Anglican priest in China and subsequently rose to a high position in the China Christian Council before defecting in Paris after the Tiananmen massacre of June 4, 1989.

Because of stringent opposition by small Christian groups like the Little Flock, which had never had any ties to Western churches, to the use of the word "reform"—which implied "theological reform"—in the name of a Christian organization, Y. T. Wu and other leaders relented. The organization was renamed the Protestant Three Self Patriotic Movement in 1954.

As the military conflict between Chinese and American forces in Korea intensified, so did the political campaigns in China, including the campaign for ideological reformulation of Chinese Protestantism. At the National Conference on Religious Work in 1954, the new Religious Affairs Bureau director Ho Zhenxiang made it clear that Christian theology itself could now be modified and altered at will by the authorities. Calling the process "infusing Marxist-Leninist thought into the positive doctrines of religion," Ho declared,

> The positive values of patriotism should take the place of negative religious propaganda. We Communists can accept as reasonable certain parts of the Bible, which Christians use, but we must also pay attention to the doctrines that they preach. If we infuse those doctrines with our Marxist-Leninist thought, then they will have positive influence and can serve our cause.[22]

Ho made it clear that the parts of the Bible he objected to were the Ten Commandments, anything supernatural, and anything about the the days leading up to the Second Coming of Christ.[23]

During July and part of August 1954, the Three Self held another national conference. Once again, *Tian Feng* magazine announced the objectives. "The goal of self-propagation," an editorial insisted, "is not the unification or modification of belief, but the thoroughgoing eradication of vestiges of imperialist thought and the bringing of preaching into harmony with the true Gospel of Jesus Christ."[24]

Protestant Christianity in China, under the new management by Y. T. Wu, was reformed to be hostile to the U.S., the West, and the global Christian missionary movement as a whole. From the beginning of the 1950s, Chinese propaganda movies relentlessly depicted foreign—and particularly American—missionaries as unscrupulous vultures picking away at the economy, the national integrity, and the cultural heritage of China.

DING AT THE HELM

Ding says that at the Prague peace conference in 1948, Y. T. Wu approached him and asked him to return to China to work in reshaping Chinese Protestantism. After his sojourn at Union Theological Seminary, Ding had moved to Geneva to become regional secretary for the World Student Christian Federation. He finally returned to China in 1951, too late to be in at the start of the Three Self, but not too late to rise rapidly. It would not have been difficult for him, had he been unhappy with the Communist regime in China, to remain overseas indefinitely. Many other Chinese Christian leaders did not return to China until much later, after the Cultural Revolution. But Ding apparently saw in Communism something deeply satisfying at an emotional and philosophical level, and he was fully prepared to take on anyone who didn't want to cooperate with the Three Self.

In 1953 he was made president of Nanjing Theological Seminary, and two years later he was ordained bishop of Zhejiang. At forty, he was the youngest Chinese ever to be ordained an Anglican bishop. Ding was certainly on the fast track.

Discrediting Wang Mingdao

Ding now stepped forward to be the Three Self church's principal propagandist attacking Wang Mingdao. Recall that Wang had not retreated an inch from his positions, despite official editorializing against him and the "accusation" meeting of 1954. He continued to defy the Three Self and was unmistakably a thorn in the side of China's Communist regime. Yet because he had on principal studiously avoided overseas church connections during his career as a pastor and evangelist, it was difficult to pin him down as not "patriotic."

Difficult, but not impossible. Bishop Ding became the Communist Party's hatchet man to discredit Wang Mingdao from 1954. On the Communist Party and Three Self side, the battle was fought through the pages of *Tian Feng* magazine. Wang responded in his sermons at the Christian Tabernacle, through his Christian periodical, *Spiritual Food Quarterly*, and by privately printed pamphlets.

Wang's position was always couched in terms of faith and theology. His conviction that Christian clergy ought not to be involved at an organizational level in the political process was the foundation for his defense. While Wu, Ding, and others saw the struggle as a way for the Communist Party to control Chinese society, including religion, Wang perceived the new pressures from the Three Self as a Modernist threat against his own espousal of traditional core Christianity. Wang was deeply suspicious of the way in which the Modernists were trying to ram their theology down the throats of China's Protestant Christians under the guise of "patriotic" Christianity.

The most important document in this period—during which Beijing was trying to decide what to do about Wang—was Wang's own pamphlet, "We, Because of Faith." In it, he takes on Wu, H. H. Cui, general secretary of the Church of Christ in China and a strong supporter of the Three Self, and Ding. The pamphlet spends no time at all on political issues, above all on the "patriotic" and "anti-imperialist" themes being drummed up constantly by the Three Self. Instead, Wang argues from the outset that the contention between him and the Three Self leadership is purely over the Christian faith itself. To be fair to his opponents, he quotes them verbatim and at considerable length, and then rebuts their arguments.

For Wang, the only importance of Three Self is that it is wholeheartedly on the side of Modernism in the Modernist-versus-Fundamentalist debate. Wang, as he reminds his opponents and his readers, had taken on the Modernists years earlier. In a 1939 article called "How Long Halt Ye Between Two Opinions?" Wu assigned Modernists the term "The Party of Unbelievers." In the 1955 pamphlet, Wang repeats the same points, starting off with an attack on Y. T. Wu. Wang charges Wu with being a member of "The Party of Unbelievers" because Wu, in a book called *Darkness and Light,* had explicitly rejected all of the fundamental points of faith held dear by Wang and those of Fundamentalist or Evangelical persuasion within Chinese Protestantism. The Modernist, Wang noted, rejected all of the following doctrines: the inerrancy of the Bible, the Virgin Birth, the substitutionary atonement (the traditional Christian belief "that Jesus' death on the Cross was a sacrifice to ransom man from sin"), the physical Resurrection of Christ, the Second Coming of Christ.[25]

Wang encapsulated his argument this way: "As a matter of fact, Fundamentalism must oppose Modernists because Modernists with their lips confess faith in the Bible and Christ but in reality they completely overturn the Bible and the Christ of the Bible.... If I call them a party of unbelievers, am I maligning them or offending them?"[26] "These people," he continued, "have no faith; they do not believe in Jesus; they are not Christians. Masquerading as Christians, they mix with church people and spread some kind of ambiguous, false doctrine to lead astray true believers and corrupt their faith."[27] Wang quoted Cui in a 1955 *Tian Feng* article, when Cui referred to "the doctrines of Incarnation, Virgin Birth, Resurrection, Trinity, Last Judgment, Second Coming, etc.," as "irrational and mysterious beliefs, which cannot be understood." Cui had categorically added, "I cannot accept such beliefs."[28]

With Ding, Wang took a different tack. Not explicitly describing himself as a Modernist, Ding wanted to discredit Wang on political grounds. He accused Wang of belonging to "a small minority in the church who are creating division. Just when imperialism wants us to be split, then we give evidence we are split. What do you think of that?"[29]

Wang retorted in his pamphlet, "Mr. Ding seems to have found some proof of connection between imperialism and division in the Church, but does not make clear what that proof is." Then, referring to Y. T. Wu's argument that 1922 was the high-point of the Modernist-Fundamentalist squabble in the U.S., Wang sardonically asks Ding, "I wonder whether Mr. Ding has investigated to see whether this controversy was influenced or exploited by imperialism."[30]

Referring again to the core historical Christian doctrines of the Incarnation, Virgin Birth, and Resurrection, and the Modernist unwillingness to accept them literally, Wang emphatically asserted, "These are all serious theological differences, and because of these differences I cannot unite with these other people. Moreover, in the name of my Lord Jesus Christ I shall fight against them." Ding, Wang added, wanted to "give a bad political name to true believers. I am not being dogmatic; if we read carefully Mr. Ting's [Ding] statement a few times over we can easily see what he is driving at."[31]

Wang was correct: Ding was trying to put a counterrevolutionary label on Wang. As the dispute dragged on into the summer of 1955, Ding became more pointed in his accusations. Wang's use of the Bible, he said, "was purely politically motivated." Moreover, in Ding's spin of the situation, the only reason Wang didn't want to join the Three Self was because he did "not want to be against imperialism."

DING SPEAKS UP

Despite his invective against Wang, and Wang's characterization of him, Ding was probably not a full-blooded Modernist. When Mao Zedong initiated a brief period of cultural liberalization in 1956, called "The Hundred Flowers" movement, Ding emerged in June 1957 from relative obscurity to make an important address to the Nanjing students. It was subsequently published in the August 1957 issue of the *Seminary Review* under the title "Christian Theism."[32] Rather courageously, Ding stood up for theism, i.e., belief in God, taking on the Marxist-Leninist ideologists with whom he had seemed to be in complete political agreement earlier in the decade. One commentator has described the talk as "a brilliant defense of theism against the Marxist position."[33]

"We Christians," Ding said in the address, "do not think it is satisfactory classification to call all shades of thought either materialistic or idealist. It is a hopeless [over]simplification of the facts."[34] Ding reproduced the eighteenth-century Deist "pocket watch" metaphor—the idea that if you came across a watch in the desert and had never seen one before you would have to assume that an intelligent mind had created it—to encourage his students to continue their Christian beliefs in a regime that was now determined to suppress all religious ways of thinking. He said, "The universe is more complicated than a wristwatch, and its workings much more exact. How could it [the wristwatch] possibly be the result of an accidental concurrence of phenomena, without a mind or intelligence behind it? We cannot deny that behind the manifestations of nature there must be a mind, an intelligence, a purpose."[35]

Ding's speech came just under the wire, on June 12, 1957. Four days earlier, an editorial in the *People's Daily* had effectively announced the end of the Hundred Flowers campaign and this period of relatively free speech. The editorial fired the first shot in what was to become a ruthless suppression of all criticism—and a crackdown on all who had spoken out against the regime just a few months earlier. It was the beginning of what would become "the anti-rightist campaign." Suddenly, those who had put their heads up to criticize any aspect of the regime or its thinking became the targets.

One of those who had criticized the Communists was Reverend Marcus Cheng, who made a forthright speech at the People's Political Consultative Conference in Beijing in March 1957, at the height of the giddy freedom of speech. Cheng, an evangelical *and* a supporter of the Three Self, had made pro-theism comments almost identical to those uttered by Ding three months later.[36] But while Cheng was summoned to Beijing and publicly denounced at a meeting of the standing committee of the Three Self in late 1957. Ding was untouched. This suggested to many observers that Ding had protectors high up within the party.

The anti-rightist campaign that started in 1957 segued into the Great Leap Forward of 1958, by far the most radical economic and social experiment that Mao had attempted so far. Churches all over China were being closed down. In Beijing, the number of operating churches was cut from sixty-five to four. In Shanghai two hundred congregations were reduced to twenty-three. All over China, hundreds of thousands of intellectuals, including many Christians, were rounded up and assigned to labor camps for two decades or more.

Ding survived in Nanjing, even though the student body of Nanjing Seminary had declined to twenty-four in 1964 from about eighty-five in 1960. The last seminary class of that decade graduated in the spring of 1966. By then, however, Mao Zedong's nastiest bout of chaos was just getting under way: the Cultural Revolution.

Chapter Eight

AFTER THE CULTURAL REVOLUTION

DING'S ROLE IN THE CULTURAL REVOLUTION is still highly controversial. According to his own account, he had but four hours', notice to leave his Nanjing home before it was occupied and ransacked by the Red Guards. Nanjing Seminary became one of the headquarters of the city's Red Guard units. According to neighbors of Ding who are no longer in China, when Red Guard units began to rummage through Ding's home, his son Stephen, then a very young man, frantic to stop them, told them that Ding had high leadership connections with the central government. One neighbor claims that the Red Guards actually found Ding's Communist Party membership card, going back to the 1930s. Many Chinese from a variety of backgrounds who have known Ding well assert emphatically that he has been a secret party member for decades.

Ding did suffer the indignity of removal from his academic and Three Self positions—by 1966 he was secretary-general of the organization—and from the general upheavals that most educated Chinese experienced during the Cultural Revolution. But many Chinese say that Ding, along with other highly favored members of China's cultural and scientific elite, was protected from serious mistreatment at the order of Premier Zhou Enlai. In one version, Ding was "spirited away" to a safe location at a critical stage of the Cultural Revolution. Ding has never complained of beatings, public humiliations, or similar abuses during the Cultural Revolution, even though other officials and pastors of the Three Self were maliciously mistreated.

China's Red Guard destructiveness reached one of its climaxes in August 1966, when statues of Buddha were smashed across China and crosses, statues, icons, crucifixes, and decorations were torn down from Christian churches. By 1970, order had been restored by the People's Liberation Army in most of China and both city and countryside were being governed by a new institution, "Provisional Revolutionary Committees."[1] Ding Guangxun emerged as a *de facto* spokesman of Protestant Christianity at a time when there were no functioning Protestant or Catholic churches. In an interview with a visiting Canadian Protestant clergyman in early 1970s, Ding seemed almost elated that not a single church was functioning in China. It had forced Christians, he said, to meet in each other's homes, just as in the days of the early Christian church. Ding even claimed to have held informal devotional meetings and Bible studies at his home.

THE CHURCH REOPENS

Such revolutionary romanticism was short-lived. After the arrest of the Gang of Four in October 1976, it was only a matter of time before the state and party structures for controlling China's society would reemerge from the limbo of the Cultural Revolution. In 1978 the first Three Self church opened in Ningbo, Zhejiang Province. In January 1979, the Religious Affairs Bureau, which had also been closed down during the Cultural Revolution, resumed operations.

Ding visited New York in September 1979 and preached a sermon at Riverside Church. His sermon, in fact, was entirely orthodox and not "liberal" in any theological sense. "I might as well begin by saying," he began his sermon, "there is nothing strikingly new to tell you about man as sinner and about man standing in need of Christ's salvation."[2]

In March 1980, the standing committee of the Three Self had a meeting in Shanghai. There was great tension at this meeting, partly because some of the restored officials had cravenly submitted to Red Guard intimidation and renounced their Christian beliefs during the Cultural Revolution. One Three Self delegate demanded, "Can these people who openly renounced their faith and criticized Christianity be restored to their positions in the Three Self? Should they be allowed to preach again?"[3]

Throughout 1980, churches that had been closed or turned into factories and warehouses throughout China began to reopen under the auspices of the Three Self. At the October conference in Nanjing, the China Christian Council was formed, with Bishop Ding elected as president. The October 1980 meeting was significant, because it designated the China Christian Council to handle such church affairs as organization, theological education, and delegations that were to go overseas. Technically, today the China Christian Council arranges admission to China's seminaries, determines who is to be ordained, and assigns pastors to different churches. But there is such overlap between the Three Self and the CCC that the two organizations are often jointly referred to as the *liang hui* (two organizations).

Almost immediately, the *liang hui* was confronted with the question of how to cope with the rural house churches, which had flourished and grown dramatically during the Cultural Revolution, especially in the uncertain three years following Deng Xiaoping's restoration to power in 1978. The Religious Affairs Bureau issued a "three designates" decree in 1982: Christian pastors would not be permitted to preach outside an area specifically designated for their activity, or in a location that was not designated a church, or to any community not assembled under Three Self auspices. This decree was aimed at cracking down on the burgeoning evangelism taking place across provincial lines. In March 1982, in Yunnan Province, an even more restrictive decree, entitled "Regarding Normal Religious Activity," was handed down: "all ministerial activities and religious meetings of every church must be held within the church building."[4]

DOCUMENT NUMBER 19

A far more important official statement of Communist Party doctrine on religion emerged in March 1982 as one of the key documents from the Third Plenum of the Eleventh Central Committee, the watershed 1978 party gathering that confirmed Deng Xiaoping's return to power and China's new policy of engagement with the outside world. Document Number 19 was at once a historical reprise of China's national policy on religion since 1949, a restatement of Communist Party views of religion, and an effort to analyze the religious situation in China after more than a decade of disengagement by state agencies.

Document Number 19 starts off with the usual Marxist axiom that religion "is a historical phenomenon pertaining to a definite period in the development of human society," and that "it will eventually disappear from human history."[5] There had been, the document continues, "many twists and turns in the party's work with regard to the religious question," but the task right now was "to oppose 'leftist' erroneous tendencies," while resisting a temptation "to just let things slide along."[6] The document continued, "We Communists are atheists and must unremittingly propagate atheism." At the same time, the document conceded, it would be "fruitless and extremely harmful to use simple coercion in dealing with the peoples' ideological and spiritual questions."[7] Thus the government authorities should ensure that,

> All normal religious activities held in places so designated, as well as those which, according to religious custom, take place in believers' homes—Buddha worship, scripture chanting—incense burning, prayer, Bible study, preaching, Mass, baptism, initiation as a monk or a nun, fasting, celebration of religious festivals, extreme unction, funerals, etc.—are all to be conducted by religious organizations and religious believers themselves, under protection of law and without interference from any quarter.[8]

This sounded reasonable, except that there was no definition of what "normal" religious activities meant in the Christian context. True, a hodgepodge of religious activity seemed to have been designated as "legal." But then came a clincher, suggesting that one of the prime reasons for Document Number 19 was to cope with China's burgeoning house churches. "As for Protestants gathering in homes for worship services, in principle this should not be allowed," but a tagline added, "yet this prohibition should not be too rigidly enforced."[9] An old prohibition against "preaching religion" outside of a church, mosque, or temple also appeared in the document. "In like manner," the document warned, "no religious organization or believer should propagate or preach religion outside places designated for religious services, nor propagate theism, nor hand out religious tracts or other religious reading matter which has not been approved for publication by the responsible government department."[10] So much for bus stations.

Document Number 19 was riddled with obvious internal contradictions. How, for example, can one freely have a "Bible study" in a private home and yet be prevented from talking about God (the prohibition on propagating theism), not to mention singing a Christian hymn or two? Imagine the scene: Comrade Wang, whose wife has been talking to him about the Bible, decides to attend a Bible study in Brother Li's home. All of this is legal. Then, as they read Genesis 1:1, "In the beginning, God created the heavens and the earth," Comrade Wang puts his hand up.

"Who or what is God?" he asks.

"Sorry, Comrade Wang," Brother Li replies, "I can't tell you about God in this house. We must go to the church before I can tell you who God is. Otherwise I will be breaking the law."

And what would not enforcing the prohibition against Protestant worship services in private homes "too rigidly" mean? Should the prohibition perhaps be enforced every other day of the week, or perhaps there should be gradations of "warnings" against it: first, a "mild warning," then a "moderate warning," then a "strict warning," and finally a "warning against impending arrest"?

Document Number 19 reflected the inability of the Communist Party to reconcile its need for final control over all aspects of civic life in China with a need to provide a freer climate in order to persuade the outside world that China's "open door" policy did indeed offer a measure of personal freedom.

CONTACT WITH THE OUTSIDE

While the Communist Party struggled with these confusing categories, the CCC itself started to reengage with the Protestant world outside China. In 1983, the then archbishop of Canterbury, Reverend Robert Runcie, was Ding's guest during a visit to China. The timing was not auspicious. In an apparent last-gasp effort of leftists to reverse the economic, social, and cultural changes that Deng Xiaoping and the reformers had started, a nasty new political campaign was introduced. Its purpose? To combat "spiritual pollution." During the very week that Runcie was in Beijing, the *People's Daily*, the official organ of the Communist Party, announced some of the targets of the campaign. They included "pornography and religion."

Ding, at a joint press conference with the archbishop, expressed ignorance of this official party objective, even though he presumably had read the *People's Daily*. He declared his satisfaction that so many churches were now being reopened across China. Among the foreign correspondents attending the press conference, I decided to ask a why-is-the-emperor-not-wearing-any-clothes question. I reminded the bishop that he had, about a decade earlier, waxed eloquent on the closing of China's churches as a means of bringing China's Christians back into a condition reminiscent of the first-century church. How could he explain the total reversal of this point of view today, I asked?

"The policy changed," was Ding's brusque response. Translation: It had been the policy of the Communist Party to keep churches closed during the Cultural Revolution, and now it was the policy to keep them open. The implication of Ding's response was that his primary duty was to implement the policy of the Communist Party, whichever way it flipped and flopped, regardless of its impact upon China's Christian communities.

The 1983 campaign in China against "spiritual pollution" had a devastating impact on China's house churches, resulting in many arrests, beatings, and imprisonments. But Deng Xiaoping quickly realized that the campaign was doing great harm to China's image as a country that was picking itself up from Maoist radicalism. Some foreign observers even believed that China was heading toward another Cultural Revolution. The campaign spluttered to a halt after a few months. By the second half of the 1980s, the political pendulum in China was swinging rapidly back to a more moderate, even reformist, position.

Reverend Billy Graham visited China in April 1988. He was not only hosted by Bishop Ding, chairman of the CCC, but was also received by Li Peng, China's then premier, in the party's elite Beijing compound of Zhongnanhai. Graham was not permitted to conduct any evangelistic "crusades," but he was able to speak openly about his faith in churches throughout Beijing and elsewhere. His aides also privately secured approval for him to have a meeting in Shanghai with the aging Wang Mingdao. They were unable, however, to prevent the arrest of Xu Yongze, a prominent house church teacher and evangelist, on his way to meet with Graham at a Beijing hotel.

There is no way of determining whether Graham had any direct impact upon Bishop Ding, but it's possible that Graham's visit to China, in and of itself, triggered some movement within Protestant Christian officialdom. In March 1988, a former Three Self pastor wrote a letter to friends outside of China expressing widespread discontent among the rank and file of the "open" Protestant churches in China. He wrote,

> The vast majority of the preachers and believers in the "open" churches have long ago lost all confidence in the Three Self, and are halfhearted. Many pretend to agree with it, but secretly oppose and resist it. Since 1979 many apostates and people who betrayed the Lord and their brethren have been appointed pastors. This has aroused strong dissatisfaction among the great number of good Christians and cries of discontent are heard everywhere.[11]

The letter also indicated that many lower-level Three Self pastors had become (presumably in secret) members of the Communist Party in the 1950s.[12]

A Changed Man?

In November 1988, Ding seemed to have taken this sentiment to heart. In the official academic journal of the Nanjing Theological Seminary, *The Jinling Review,* Ding expressed repentance for his support of hard-line leftist policies in the past. He had already told some Three Self pastors early in 1987 that Hu Yaobang, the party secretary-general at the time, wanted a new, and presumably much more liberal, version of Document Number 19. Ding also revealed that he had held talks with Yan Mingfu, the head of the United Front Work Department—the party organ in charge of the Religious Affairs Bureau. Yan had told Ding that it was "not good if the church is in the hands of unbelievers," an acknowledgment that the RAB was indeed run by atheists and secularists.[13]

Ding also told the pastors that he was dissatisfied with the government policy of trying to close down all house church meetings. Late in 1987, Ding, in a letter to the RAB, protested the threat of the Guangdong provincial authorities to close down Samuel Lamb's church. Toward the end of the long letter, Ding brought up problems that many outside observers had constantly complained about to him and to other Three Self leaders during visits to China: the ongoing harassment of house churches across the country. Ding had steadfastly denied in public, and especially in front of foreigners, that any such persecution was taking place. But in his letter to the RAB, he said that there were large numbers of house church Christians and it was wrong to try to drag them kicking and screaming into the Three Self. "Is it not an abuse of political power," he asked, "and an inflexible refusal to see the difficulty caused to a segment of patriotic Christians in terms of their faith, to compel them to join the Three Self?"[14] At a session of the National People's Congress in Beijing in 1988, Ding, the most prominent Protestant Christian representative at the conference, openly attacked the leftists who still seemed to be calling the shots in the Religious Affairs Bureau. "All civilized nations stress separation of church and state," he said. "China should be like this. We shouldn't need the government to control every aspect of religion."[15]

It was a bold and striking declaration, especially given Ding's previous record of routine support for the Communist Party's control on religion. By December 1988, Ding's apparent change of heart went even farther. At a Shanghai meeting of the Three Self he asked the unthinkable question, "Do we need the Three Self? Go home and think about it."[16]

Ding himself certainly did some more thinking. On a visit to the U.S. in February 1989, he went farther than ever by suggesting it was time for the Three Self to close shop. In an interview with a Christian news organization, News Network International, he said, "Today the Three Self is probably not good because the church is the Body of Christ. Christ is the head of the church." It could have been someone from the Fangcheng Fellowship speaking, or Wang Mingdao himself, not the man who in the 1950s had denounced fellow Christians who refused to join the Three Self as "counterrevolutionary." In the same interview he even hinted that the Three Self might be phased out altogether, perhaps by 1991.[17]

But Ding had spoken out of turn. Not long after his return to China, he denied saying these things. He now said that what he meant was that the Three Self had taken on too much administrative authority for China's churches as a whole. Still, further elaboration of Ding's thinking in *Tian Feng* suggested that Ding and the top *lianghui* leadership would have liked at that moment to set up the CCC as the sole determinant of church life, not under the direction of the RAB.

Ding *did* for a time appear to be a changed man. Nothing suggested this more clearly than his response to the student demonstrations that burst out in Beijing, and later in other cities across China, after the death on April 15, 1989, of former Communist Party secretary-general Hu Yaobang. The world was mesmerized as the student protest against corruption in government stretched into weeks. The Soviet Union's Gorbachev came and went, the Asian Development Bank had its annual meeting in the city, and the government still didn't seem to know what it should do.

Students demonstrated on the campus of Nanjing Seminary with a banner that read, "Let righteousness flow down like a river." In

Beijing, seminary students joined the daily throngs of demonstrators from all walks of life who protested for a better and more honest government. On May 18 and 19, 1989, they carried a banner reading, "God so loved the world" (Gospel of John, 3:16) and carried a cross. Ding, again with considerable courage and boldness, issued a statement in late May praising what the students were doing. He said, "I am glad that Christians are making their presence felt in these demonstrations. I am very glad that the students in Nanjing Seminary are taking an active part."[18]

THE TANKS ROLL IN

Any hope that the government in Beijing might compromise with the students vanished in late May 1989, when Premier Li Peng announced martial law in the city. By the time the shooting began in Beijing late in the evening of June 3, Deng Xiaoping had already secured the support of the regional commanders of the People's Liberation Army for a total suppression of the student movement. Hundreds, perhaps thousands of Beijing citizens, including many students, were killed as soldiers in trucks and tanks fought their way toward Tiananmen Square.

The vice president of the CCC, Zhao Fusan, took advantage of his sojourn in Paris to defect to the West. Ding was in no position to defect, and almost certainly wouldn't have in any case. A tide of greater repression of Christian activity swept in with the post-Tiananmen era.

Party officials spoke about the dangers of "Christianity fever" in China. In January 1991, the new Communist Party secretary-general, Jiang Zemin, selected in the aftermath of Tiananmen to bring the nation back to "normalcy," called for tighter controls on China's five major religions (strangely listed as Roman Catholicism, Protestantism, Buddhism, Islam, and Daoism). Otherwise, he warned, "illegal elements" might try "using religion or religious activities to stir up disorder."[19]

But across China, urban-based house churches and legal "open" churches began to notice a new development: hundreds of students, previously uninterested in religion, were coming to church or wanting to discuss the Christian faith. In Fuzhou, capital of Fujian Province, more than eight hundred students came to one meeting to learn more about Christianity. In Peking University itself, several reports spoke of entire dorm rooms (six to eight beds) becoming Christian. Hitherto, the "Christianity fever" that was changing China's countryside seemed to have bypassed China's emerging new intelligentsia. Now this important component of China's life and future was beginning to pay attention to the Christian faith. What was the attraction of Christianity to intellectuals in the post-Tiananmen era? One suggestion was that China's traditional Confucian view of man as inherently good was shattered under the tanks that rolled into the center of Beijing in early June 1989.

China's authorities, for their part, worried about "democracy" and other subversive ideas creeping back into Chinese life through a process they called "peaceful evolution"—meaning by stealth—and about the effect that the spread of Christianity might have on Communist Party control. In 1991, Document Number 6 was issued by China's state council. It reinforced the restrictions spelled out in Document Number 19 of 1982 and reiterated the demand that any religious activity in China be registered at the local level with the Religious Affairs Bureau or the Three Self. In 1994 this registration requirement was spelled out once again in Document Number 145, while a decree announced simultaneously, Document Number 144, spelled out yet again that no foreigner could conduct any religious activity in China without first getting permission from the relevant national-level organization of that religion. This decree was aimed at cracking down on the growing number of foreign Protestant Christian pastors and teachers involved with the rapidly expanding house church networks in China.

Throughout the 1990s, China's Communist Party sought to ensure that the social and cultural forces unleashed by the "open door" policy would not eventually undermine Communist control. By 1993, the threat of mass popular discontent with party control seemed to be diluted by the astonishing surge in the growth of China's economy. Anyone visiting China would have found many signs that China was physically changing: more cars, smarter stores, better-dressed young people, a sense of an emergent middle class. Some analysts reasoned that the regime had sealed a Faustian bargain with the Chinese people: if living standards continued to rise rapidly for almost everyone, then ordinary Chinese wouldn't protest against continuing Communist control.

Still, China's leadership was worried. Reports of uninterrupted growth in China's Protestant communities suggested that the party in some areas of national life simply didn't have control of the population. In November 1993, President Jiang Zemin announced a new framework for religion: "to make religion adapt to socialist society."[20] Cadres in the UFWD, the RAB, and the Three Self were ordered to think of ways to execute this policy.

One way was simply tighter control at the grass roots. Throughout the mid-1990s there were repeated waves of assault on house church networks—arrests, imprisonments, and beatings. Again and again, unregistered groups were told to register or face arrest. Many of them preferred to disband or go into hiding than to submit to what they considered the liberal and heterodox theology championed by the Three Self.

DING REVERTS AGAIN

Bishop Ding, having courted foreign evangelicals in the 1980s and having rather bravely supported protesting students at the end of the decade, might have ended his official career on a conciliatory note vis-à-vis the majority of China's Christians. But in a bizarre twist, Ding in the last years of his life reverted to the Modernist, authoritarian, ardently pro-Communist instincts of his earlier career in the 1950s. On his official retirement as chairman of the Three Self and President of the CCC in 1996, he retained his office as "president" of Nanjing Theological Seminary and became anything but "retired." At age eighty-four, he became the principal cheerleader for a nationwide campaign to promote what he called the "Theological Construction" of Chinese Christianity.

Ostensibly, the goal was to rejuvenate theological inquiry in China and move Chinese Christianity beyond what most of the *lianghui* leadership regarded as unreconstructed theological conservatism. But, as one American who spent a year at Nanjing watching the process firsthand observed, "the campaign was a transparent counterattack against theologically conservative evangelicals within the *lianghui* who had grown increasingly assertive in their challenges to senior church officials."[21] During 1998–2000, the Three Self and the CCC tried to impose upon the entire structure of China's "open" churches this new theology. It was widely regarded by local Three Self pastors as yet another effort to ram Modernist dogma down the throats of China's Protestants, much as the Three Self had done in the 1950s.

Major repercussions erupted at Nanjing Seminary itself, where the student body was predominantly evangelical and mistrusted Ding's Modernist nostrums. When Bishop Ding preached a sermon on Easter Day in 2001, he barely touched on the Resurrection itself before launching into a heavily politicized message. The students in the chapel started tittering and snickering. Later, three graduate students, convinced that Ding wasn't even a Christian believer in any real sense, called him up at his home and tried to evangelize him. He was furious, and at a faculty meeting at the seminary, referred to the students as "running dogs of Taiwan," a throwback to the Maoist terminology of the Cultural Revolution. The same three students had already provoked Ding's anger by refusing to sing Communist patriotic songs at the eightieth anniversary of China's May Fourth Movement, a major student protest movement of that date in 1919 that has often been regarded as the starting point of China's political radicalism. The students argued that the May Fourth Movement was a national, secular event and that, since Nanjing Seminary was a place for studying the things of God, any celebration at the seminary ought to reflect Christian submission to the Lord.

Jason Kindopp, then a Ph.D. candidate at the George Washington University in Washington, D.C., spent 2000–2001 at Nanjing studying how the Three Self worked. He became convinced that the resistance to Ding's "Theological Construction" was so widespread in the Three Self churches that the viability of that organization was itself at risk. He said, "In contrast with Mao-era campaigns, when Protestants' only recourse was to exit the official church or remain silent, opposition to the TCC [Theological Construction Campaign] has been concerted, sustained, and vocal, raising questions of the *lianghui*'s viability as a tool for controlling China's Protestants.[22] According to Kindopp, Bishop Ding was unable to persuade anyone at the Chinese Academy of Social Sciences, some of whom Kindopp knew described themselves as Christians, to support the campaign.

It is unlikely that any of the other top leaders of the Three Self and the CCC will redirect the organization's course while Ding is still alive. The current president of the CCC is Cao Shengjie, a *lianghui* careerist without any formal theological training who is known to have cultivated political connections all of her adult life and is assumed by most observers to have been a longtime party member. She has been given the mischievous monicker by many Three Self pastors opposed to her of "Old Mrs. Marx and Lenin" (*malie lao taitai* in Chinese). A senior Chinese theology professor at a Three Self seminary said that even the theologically liberal officials of the World Council of Churches in Geneva dislike her visits. "She sounds like an old Maoist propagandist," they told him.

The Three Self projects a fantasy picture of Chinese Christianity to the outside world, denying most of the time that Christian house churches even exist. At a conference in Los Angeles in February 2003, Three Self official Matthew Deng said that on each of his eleven trips to the U.S. he had been asked about "underground" churches in China. "I always say," he began, "that there is no underground church in China. The impression we have is that the church in China is not underground. If a church meets with one hundred people, do you think it could be secret?" Well, it could be, if the price to pay for coming into the open is to have "Theological Construction" jammed down your gullet.

It is disturbing that Bishop Ding, after seeming to toy in 1989 with the idea of scrapping the Three Self, has in his golden years returned to a rigid, authoritarian perspective of how to control Protestant Christianity in China. In an interview at his home in Nanjing in November 2002, Bishop Ding said that he didn't think his faith had changed much over the years, although he thought his "theology" had. As to the Bible, Ding admitted, "In many ways my interpretation of Bible passages would be considered liberal and un-Christian, perhaps." I asked if Ding had any regrets in his long career in China's church. Did he, for example, regret any of his accusations against Wang Mingdao in the 1950s? No, he said firmly, he didn't regret the attacks on Wang Mingdao. But he did say that when he had joined in the anti-rightist campaign in 1958 he had accepted as truth accusations by the Communist Party that, after Mao's death, the party itself admitted had been false. He explained, "That was partly due to my acceptance of the indoctrination of the time concerning the infallibility of the party." Ding was admitting that five decades earlier he had accepted Communist propaganda that contradicted biblical assumptions as truth.

During his career, Ding has at times undoubtedly demonstrated in both word and deed a commitment to key aspects of a Christian view of reality. Yet he has also contradicted his own ideas with conviction much closer to classic Marxist theory than to anything traditionally Christian. "I know that socialism is the best social system to have appeared in human history," he said in 1999.

REVIVAL OF THE THREE SELF

The Three Self continues to live at the beck and call of the Religious Affairs Bureau, or to give it its most recent official name, the State Administration of Religious Affairs (SARA). This is the political agency that reports to the United Front Work Department of the Communist Party on how China's religious life is being administered and controlled. Privately, Three Self officials often complain about the interference and restrictions imposed even on China's "open" churches by SARA officials. They decide how many pastors the Three Self can ordain in any six-month period, how many meetings Three Self pastors can hold in any one-month period, and who is permitted to teach and graduate from China's seventeen official Protestant seminaries.

All SARA officials are Communist Party members, and thus are not permitted to adhere to any religion. The director general of SARA appointed in 1995, Ye Xiaowen, fifty-one, is a Communist and a militant atheist who is vigorously opposed to the expansion of Christianity. Yet he regards himself as qualified to comment on matters of Christian theology. At a Three Self meeting in the year 2000, Ye opined, "From a deep level of analysis, theology in Chinese Christianity...still has conservative, even mistaken views in its ranks."[23]

I met Ye for the first time in Los Angeles in February 2002. At least three aides sat around taking copious notes while he answered my questions with the ebullience of a recently crowned regional tire salesman. Under the bluff cheerfulness lay an unmistakable toughness. Perhaps a precinct lieutenant in *The Sopranos* would be a more accurate description.

Why on earth did China need an organization like his, I asked? Was he not aware that even some Chinese scholars were questioning the usefulness of his organization? Ye reacted smoothly to these provocative questions. His organization was needed, he said, to ensure religious freedom in China. Well, I pointed out, many countries had discovered that religions could operate freely, peaceably, and fruitfully with no government supervision and control. The U.S. had enjoyed such a system for two centuries, I said. "The U.S. is a very young country," Ye replied. "What works in the U.S. might not work anywhere else." I asked him if he thought Christianity had been expanding too quickly in China, an assertion I had heard attributed to Ye, but which I had not seen attributed to him in any written document. He hesitated, then said, "Christianity that is patriotic is good. Christianity that is foreign-controlled is harmful."

An American official who has been to China and is familiar with the work of SARA was surprisingly blunt about Ye Xiaowen. "Ye Xiaowen is the biggest thug of all," he said flatly. "I am not surprised that his star is rising." Ye has consistently been a hard-liner and some Chinese officials claim he had a close relationship with Hu Jintao,

China's latest general secretary of the Communist Party. Yet he faces opposition from China's legal establishment and from some scholars in the Chinese Academy of Social Sciences. These critics, though careful not to say it in public, believe that SARA should be dismantled. They regard SARA's and Ye's thuggish attacks on religious groups, especially Christian groups that steer clear of political opposition, as harmful to China's ongoing modernization, not to mention to China's world image.

At a conference outside Los Angeles in February 2003, Ye Xiaowen made a major address that was designed to flatter his Protestant Christian audience and show that SARA was a boon to religion in China. "I can tell you with pleasure," he said in his tire-salesman mode, "that Chinese Christians are running their church independently and have thus removed the 'cap' [he probably meant "garb"] of 'foreignness.' It has become a religion that eulogizes love and traditional culture." Some might question how Ye acquires such deep theological insight.

Ye's task in Los Angeles was not theological at all; it was propagandistic. Well aware of the poor publicity that has followed the brutal arrests of house church Christian leaders and Roman Catholic priests and bishops, not to mention Falungong demonstrators, Ye Xiaowen was eager to show that such reports from China were "groundless abuses and attacks" and reflected old-fashioned bias. "As a result of the constant reports by some American media," he complained, "people in the United States [have] reached a wrong conclusion that there was religious persecution in China and the Communists showed no respect for the freedom of religious beliefs." He added, "As director general of the State Administration of Religious Affairs, I told them that our respect for the freedom of religious belief is sincere and consistent." He concluded, "A fond dream of Chinese Christians is to integrate Christianity with the traditional Chinese culture and do their part in the rejuvenation of the nation, the unification of humankind, and promotion of world peace."[24]

None of China's house church leaders, of course, would dissent from this final sentiment. What they would object to is Ye Xiaowen credibility and his organization's ability to help implement these goals. Though persecution of Christians is sporadic rather than uniform, it still exists in vicious forms across the country. It is a grim and cruel reality, but an important aspect in the growth of China's Christianity.

Chapter Nine

CHINA'S "JERUSALEM"

THE CONFERENCE ON ISLAM IN ITALY was very interesting. But outside the city was even more so: the wonderful sights of Florence. I wandered out to the Piazza della Signorina and the area in front of the Palazzo Vecchio. Then it began to dawn on me rather vividly that, amid the splendors of Italian High Renaissance were Chinese Christians from Wenzhou, working very hard—and apparently succeeding—at making a living in the retail business. Standing at a small table in front of the Palazzo Vecchio and flanked by Nigerians selling woodcarvings and Albanians selling lighters was a rather attractive Chinese woman in her thirties selling silk scarves. "Where are you from in China?" I asked.

"From Wenzhou."

"Are you a Christian?"

"Yes."

"How many of you are there here?"

She told me that she was part of a group of some twenty-five Wenzhou Christians who were living in Florence and conducting a retail business. She was in a hurry to go elsewhere and I couldn't pursue the conversation.

WANDERS FROM WENZHOU

Two years later I was sitting at a table in an outdoor restaurant on Barcelona's Gran Via Corts Catalanes Avenue enjoying a glass of wine at the end of another conference, this one on journalism. The talk got around to the many foreign immigrants you could see all over Spain, especially in Barcelona.

"You don't have to take this as an actual wager for cash," I said, stabbing in the dark, "but I can almost guarantee you that within fifty feet of any European cathedral you will find a Wenzhou Chinese Christian selling something."

"Okay," everyone said benevolently, mildly amused by my eccentricity. "Why don't you go and find out tomorrow?"

The next day, around 10:00 A.M., I approached the fine Gothic West doors of Barcelona's fourteenth-century Cathedral of La Seu. Two Chinese were there, brothers it turned out, playing on two classical guitars. Hovering around the edge of the Sunday morning tourist audience was a tall Chinese woman selling their CDs. Was she from Wenzhou, I asked, and was she a Christian?

She was. The two guitarists, both friends of hers, were music graduate students from Beijing studying classical guitar at the University of Barcelona. They too had become Christian since arriving in Spain for their studies.

I spent the day and the evening with them, visiting the Chinese church they attended, and learning about the Wenzhou presence in Barcelona. There were three Chinese churches in the city, they said, and the largest of them consisted of merchants who hailed from Wenzhou.

Later, in Hong Kong, Dennis Balcombe told me about preaching several times at a Wenzhou Chinese church in Paris that had several hundred members. Another Hong Kong Chinese friend told me about large communities of Wenzhou Chinese in Khabarovsk, Russia, Bucharest, Romania, and Budapest, Hungary. For generations, Chinese business families have been dubbed "the Jews of Asia" for their commercial success throughout East and Southeast Asia. Wenzhou business families were often called "the Jews of China," for wherever they went they usually succeeded in undercutting and even driving out the non-Wenzhou Chinese. Early in 2003 a popular book at airport book kiosks in China was about "China's Jews"—not the real Jewish community that had settled in the city of Kaifeng, Henan, from the tenth century onward—the remarkably energetic, sharp-witted, and hardworking traders of Wenzhou.

Everywhere the Wenzhou retail merchants went, it seemed, at least from the 1980s, they also started churches. This was certainly true in China itself. In Beijing, Wenzhou Christian merchants started not just churches, but also schools teaching the Chinese how to reach out to their neighbors with the Gospel. Wenzhou communities settled in many other large cities in China. Overseas, the pattern was repeated. In Italy alone, according to Dennis Balcombe, by 2003, there were no fewer than eleven Wenzhou Chinese churches, springing up from Florence to Rome. What was it about Wenzhou that caused this religious fervor? Why is this city known among China's Christians as "China's Jerusalem"?

The first time I visited Wenzhou, in March 1993, I already knew that it had one of the highest percentages of Christians of any Chinese city: at least 10 percent and probably more (in the year 2002, several experienced observers said the total for the entire municipal area of some 7 million may have reached about 14 percent). I had heard that there were literally hundreds of churches in the city. The night of my arrival in late March, around 11:00 P.M. I wandered out of the Ou Jiang Hotel and down the street to talk to the peddlers who had set up makeshift stores in the center of town. Even driving into the city from the airport, it was obvious that the city had gone through a retail business explosion since Deng Xiaoping's economic reforms in the 1979. Shoe stores, luggage stores, clothing stores, furniture stores, toy stores, kitchen-utensil stores, button stores—Wenzhou liked to boast that it was the "button capital" of the world—outlets for just about everything, line every street in the city.

As I wondered along in front of the diverse storefronts, I had a hunch that the Fu Yin Printing Company was more than just any old printing company. The Chinese syllables *fu yin* were also Chinese for "Gospel," though, of course, in the case of the print store, the character used for *fu* was "wealth" and that for *yin* was "print." It was a rather clever Chinese pun. It was late, so I started asking questions directly about Christianity in Wenzhou; I was scheduled to be in the city for just two days. The two young men at the store warmed to me at this point and invited me back to the small business office behind the counter. There I was introduced to another young man and the wives of the first two I had met. All were in their mid-twenties, all were second- and third-generation Christians, and they were pleased to meet a foreigner who had come to Wenzhou because of its reputation as a strong center of Christianity in China.

I asked how many Christians they thought there might be in this city of 6 million (in 1993). "Several tens of thousands," they said. Why had the church grown so fast? "It is just God's blessing," they said matter-of-factly.

God might indeed have blessed Wenzhou, for all I knew, but as a reporter I wanted more than a theological or metaphysical explanation for the city's religiosity. On the drive to the airport thirty-six hours later I noticed something that had escaped my attention driving into town. Clearly visible paper crosses were pasted on the doors of several apartments in the housing blocks along the main road. I asked one of the guides what he thought these meant. "They are probably unofficial Christian churches," he said, as though it was rather obvious.

I returned for a more extended visit in 1998, on the same China journey when I met Zhang Rongliang and other "uncles" in Zhengzhou who helped to produce the "United Appeal." Through conversations on that trip, and then yet another visit in 2002, I gradually pieced together the Wenzhou story.

A ONE-LEGGED SCOTSMAN

Unlike the city of Xian or Beijing, home to the Jesuits from 1601 for more than a century, or even Guangzhou, where Robert Morrison had arrived in 1807 to begin his Bible translating, Wenzhou had no Christian presence at all until the second half of the nineteenth century. In fact, isolated as it was by mountains on three sides and the ocean on the fourth—there was no railroad or airline connection until the 1990s—the city was firmly locked into Buddhism and Chinese folk religion until the 1870s. It had managed to resist efforts by the Taiping rebels to capture it in the 1850s and 1860s, and boasted about its supposed divine luck with self-designations like "City of Great Good Luck" and "City of Golden Glory." Not until an eccentric one-legged Scotsman called George Stott, of the China Inland Mission, first showed up in 1867, did Christianity have any presence in Wenzhou.

The locals didn't exactly welcome Stott. Just because he was a foreigner the local Chinese for the first few years threw pebbles at him or mocked him as he limped by. But precisely because he was an invalid, his sheer courage impressed a few of the Wenzhou citizenry. Some of them stopped to hear his initially stumbling preaching in their rare dialect. (Wenzhou dialect Chinese is so different from all other Chinese dialects that it is incomprehensible to people who have not studied it. During the 1979 Sino-Vietnamese war, the Chinese army employed Wenzhou "code-talkers," much as the U.S. Army used Navajo Indians during World War II.)

A handful of Wenzhou youths became Christians. Stott persisted in his missionary work, and in 1878 built the city's first Christian church, on Chengxi Street. But local resistance was considerable. Antiforeignism was endemic to this part of China and was easily stoked up every time the French or the British made a move to impose the notorious "unequal treaties" of the nineteenth century. The church on Zhengzhou's Chengxi Street was burned down in 1884 during antiforeign riots, but then rebuilt in 1898 on the same site. Two years later, the Boxers rampaged through Wenzhou, killing several missionaries and local Chinese Christians. "The blood of the martyrs was the seed of the Wenzhou church," commented Wu Baixin, a thoughtful Henan intellectual. The Chengxi church building itself survived, and in 1998 celebrated its hundredth anniversary. It was by now a Wenzhou historic landmark, and the Three Self, which ran it, had opened up a Christian bookstore alongside the main building.

When Communism rolled over China in 1949, Wenzhou was ravaged by the same anti-Western campaigns as the rest of the country. The Protestant churches were forced to unite under the umbrella of the Three Self. The only alternative was imprisonment. In 1958, hard on the heels of the "anti-rightist campaign" that had begun in 1957 and resulted in the jailing throughout China of hundreds of thousands of intellectuals, Wenzhou was declared to be a "religion-free" zone, China's first officially atheist city. Churches and temples were closed and teachers hectored their students on the need to resist "superstition." Only when Mao's Great Leap Forward campaign was finally abandoned in 1962 and China returned to a degree of normalcy were the churches permitted to reopen once more.

Even this reprieve, however, was short-lived. In 1966 the Cultural Revolution broke out. Churches all over Wenzhou were closed once more and pastors or prominent laypeople were humiliated by being marched through the city wearing dunce's hats. But in contrast with Beijing and Shanghai, where the severity of the Cultural Revolution briefly brought even clandestine house church gatherings to a halt, in Wenzhou the Christians kept meeting, often on the hillsides outside the city. "Taiwan Christians were flying Gospel tracts and Bibles over the South China Sea by balloon," said Wu Baixin, who spent some time investigating the phenomenon of the Wenzhou Christian revival. "The evangelists never stopped evangelizing." Tanghe "uncle" Feng Jianguo, who has maintained good relations with the Wenzhou house churches, noted that "Wenzhou had the earliest revival church in China. From the earliest missionary times it just kept growing."

MIAO ZHITONG

One man who is familiar with what happened during the Cultural Revolution is Wenzhou's most prominent house church "uncle," Miao Zhitong, the greatly loved leader of the main Wenzhou house church network. Born in 1942, Miao lost both his parents before he was twelve and was brought up by Christian relatives. He had a powerful Christian experience at the age of eight in a local Pentecostal church, in the first year of Communist rule in Wenzhou. But by Miao's own account he was a "prodigal" until twenty-three, when he repented his wayward teenage years, got serious with his faith, and started along a pathway of evangelism. The timing wasn't great: he sensed a call to be a full-time preacher in 1967, at the very height of the Cultural Revolution. It wasn't long before he began to receive what became annual arrests, beatings, and sessions of torture. At one point he was hung by the arms before being pushed into a pool of sewage where it was hoped he would drown. He managed to wrestle himself away and plunged into a clean creek before the police grabbed him, took him to a Buddhist temple, tied him to a pillar, and then beat him with bamboo rods. Only the presence of a large group of Christians who showed up at the temple and bravely clamored for his release prevented Miao from being beaten to death on the spot.

Released after a time, Miao was picked up again in the early 1970s at the tail end of the Cultural Revolution. He was handcuffed behind his back, made to wear a dunce's cap, and pushed through the streets wearing a big placard that read "counterrevolutionary head of superstition." As the parade crossed a bridge, Miao was ordered to stand on the parapet. He thought they planned to push him off the bridge and kill him, so he prayed fervently. A sudden storm blew up, the parade was called off, and he was taken back to prison. The next day there was another "struggle meeting," this time in the prison itself. Ordered to stand up and confess his political "sins," Miao quite simply began preaching to the officials and fellow prisoners. "I preached about judgment and said that if they didn't repent they would go to hell," he recalls. "They were dumbfounded, but they listened to what I said."

Just when the cadres realized Miao had fooled them by turning his "confession" into a sermon, another storm blew up and the meeting adjourned once again. After futile efforts to force Miao into admitting various political crimes, the authorities eventually gave up and ordered him to go home. But Miao did nothing of the sort. He started mobilizing Christian churches in the eastern counties of Zhejiang Province, including the surroundings of Wenzhou, in 1972. Largely because of organizing by Miao and others, the Zhejiang house churches were probably more active than those in any other part of China by the time the Cultural Revolution came to a decisive end with the arrest of the Gang of Four in 1976. Miao says he remembers being arrested at least once every single year in the 1970s. Between 1968 and 1988, he said, he had been arrested at least twenty times, the most recent occasion being a 143-day detention in 1995. "During the first few years of arrests, they accused us of counterrevolutionary superstition," he said, "but after 1980, when the Three Self reemerged, the charges against us were because we wouldn't register with the Three Self."

ZHEN DATONG

Another of the house church leaders in Wenzhou whose Christian work became intense during the Cultural Revolution was Zhen Datong, the son of Christian parents in Wenzhou. However, Zhen absorbed the school-taught atheism of the regime until his own coming of faith in 1969. "The church in Wenzhou was very good during the Cultural Revolution," he said over a lunch of noodles in his fourth-floor apartment. "We never stopped meeting. The China Inland Mission had laid a good foundation here. The old Christians knew how to pray."

And pray, presumably, they did. Hong Kong Chinese Christians visiting relatives in the Wenzhou area in the year 1974 returned with stories that 50,000 active Christians were in the Wenzhou area, an unheard of figure for a large city (then around 5 million) during the Cultural Revolution. Zhen, like Miao, paid a heavy price for his evangelistic activism. He was arrested in 1974 and jailed for nearly three years, then again in 1994 for fifty-three days for holding an unauthorized Christian training class, then again for ten days in 1997 in a new, nationwide upsurge of repression of unauthorized Christian meetings. "I was arrested in 1997 for being a 'key leader' in the church," Zhen observed. "They are the criminals, not I."

A UNIQUE COMPROMISE

Somehow, the unusually isolated location of Wenzhou and the amazing economic takeoff of the city after 1980 led to a compromise between Wenzhou's house church Christians and the authorities that set a unique pattern for the city. In the year 2001, Zhejiang Province had the highest per capita GDP of all of the provinces of China, surpassed only by the major cities Beijing, Shanghai, and Tianjin. Wenzhou itself since the early 1980s has periodically been held up as a model of entrepreneurship. In the city of Wenzhou, a phenomenal 95 percent of the GDP was generated by private enterprise.[1] By 1990, a mere decade after Deng Xiaoping's "open door" policies, Wenzhou's GDP was $1.5 billion, six times the figure for 1980.[2]

Partly because there was no easily reachable rural hinterland, Wenzhou's traders traveled to the farthest parts of China, and then overseas, in pursuit of entrepreneurial opportunities. Wenzhou people estimate that there are some 1.5 million Wenzhou traders in other parts of China, and perhaps as many as half a million overseas (including in the U.S.). There was also an expansion of "townships" within the larger Wenzhou municipal area, from eighteen in 1978 to 110 in 1990. This helped diffuse the power of the city's central authorities. In addition, because the children of long-established Christian families were beginning to move into administrative positions of authority in the city, the efforts of the provincial Religious Affairs Bureau to enforce registration of all house churches began, in the late 1980s, to be diluted by unusual kinds of local exceptions.

The most striking of these has been the profusion of highly visible "house church" buildings throughout Wenzhou. These are often gigantic, ornate structures evocative of large European or North American churches, topped by huge red crosses that are landmarks as you make your way out of the center of town, along the expressway leading across the Ou Jiang River to the west. The churches have indeed registered, but with the local municipal authorities as "places of religious worship," not with the Three Self. The buildings are often as large as a mid sized European cathedral, five stories high with huge sanctuaries, large basement-level meeting areas, and assorted additional rooms for Sunday school, intercession, and Bible teaching meetings.

Clearly visible on the main expressway from Wenzhou Airport to the city center, for example, is Bethel Church, on Five Good Religions Street. The impressive structure, whose original name was "Twin Village Church," was completed in just five months in 1998. The main funding came from Wenzhou's prosperous business community, but Seventh-Day Adventist churches overseas also pitched in. The total cost was about $100,000. When the church was first completed, it seemed to soar straight up out of suburban rice fields. Urban sprawl has since caught up. Today, though it still towers over the moderately built-up neighborhood that has grown up around it on the original rice fields, it seems more hemmed in than before, like a European Romanesque cathedral trapped by arteries of downtown traffic.

The second-floor sanctuary of the church is ornate and expensive-looking. Behind the raised platform is a large, red Chinese character *ai*, Chinese for "love." To the right on the same rear wall, is the Chinese translation of the Apostles' Creed,[3] and to the left is the Lord's Prayer in Chinese. The total seating capacity of the church is 800. It has been used several times for house church conferences.

There is no full-time pastor. Authorized laymen take turns leading the service and keeping the civic registration current. There are no doctrinal controls over the content of Sunday school teaching or the sermons preached. Bethel Church, as far as anyone could tell, was largely left alone by the authorities, as were almost all of the other churches of Wenzhou.

Across the Ou Jiang River, in a much smaller, privately built house church in the Yueqing District, a student of philosophy at a university in Wenzhou, who wished to be identified only by the name "Ali" (pronounced *ah-lee*), said that he thought that 12 to 15 percent of the local population was Christian. He said, "The elders of the church in this area went through severe persecution during the Cultural Revolution.

The government expected that the Christian population would decline, but it increased. A lot of businessmen and government officials are Christian, as their parents are. We can guess that the government compromised a lot."

Five years earlier, this wasn't the case. In 1997, the Religious Affairs Bureau worked strenuously to cut down Christianity in Wenzhou. During a period of some six weeks during November and December, hundreds of unauthorized Buddhist temples and Christian churches were bulldozed to the ground. In 1998, I visited the site of one of the church demolitions. All that remained of what had once been a four-story building was a small, ground-floor walled area with sealed-up windows. It was in the Yong Fu San District in the eastern part of the city. A teenage girl bicycling by stopped to watch two foreigners taking photographs of the destruction. "There is a lot of Jesus in this city," she said breezily, before resuming her ride home.

The church and temple destructions took place, according to Zhen Datong, because China's president and party leader of the day, Jiang Zemin, had visited Wenzhou earlier in the year and been amazed at the visible evidence not just of Christian symbols, like the cross atop city churches, but also mirrors used in some Buddhist ceremonies to deflect forces of evil. Jiang himself gave no orders to remove Wenzhou's religious symbols, but zealous provincial and city underlings interpreted his dismay as equivalent to an order. In the "destroy-the-mirrors-and-remove-the-crosses" movement that followed, several hundred churches and temples were destroyed. Yuan Zhiming, the Chinese documentary filmmaker exiled to the U.S. in 1989 who has spent hundreds of hours interviewing key Chinese Christian house church leaders, returned from one trip to Wenzhou with dramatic footage from one of these demolitions.

Attempts by Wenzhou's Communist Party leadership to trim the sails of the city's flourishing Christian community were not limited to the destruction of church buildings. John Pomfret, the Beijing correspondent of the *Washington Post*, came back from a reporting trip to Wenzhou late in 2002 with a story about near civil disobedience from Wenzhou pastors resisting an edict that had come down earlier in the summer to halt all Sunday-school teaching. Instead of meekly backing down, as the city's Religious Affairs Bureau anticipated, several of the pastors banged on bureaucratic doors all the way up to Beijing. No law anywhere prohibited the teaching of religion to children under the age of eighteen, the pastors insisted, even though the Public Security Bureau had often acted as though there were in various parts of China. Bishop Ding Guanxun, president of the Nanjing Theological Seminary and one of the founding leaders of the Three Self and the China Christian Council, agreed. He weighed in with a letter to the Chinese People's Political Consultative Conference, an official advisory body with no legal powers but occasionally some influence, in Beijing.

The CPPCC did not respond to Ding's letter, but as Pomfret's story indicated, Wenzhou's pastors, as well as the influential Wenzhou business community, lobbied hard and successfully with the government in Beijing and the All-China Federation of Industry and Commerce to put an end to this arbitrary persecution. Unable to get any backing from Beijing, and threatened with legal action all the way up the ladder of judicial process, Wenzhou's RAB backed off from trying to implement the Sunday-school ban. But it did not give up the struggle against religion altogether. Well aware that the majority of Wenzhou churches, both Three Self and house church, were going about their religious business their own way, the RAB tried hard to require the churches to get official approval for all of their activities for the following year, 2003.

CHINA'S "ANTIOCH"

Wenzhou's Christians are somewhat self-conscious about their city's reputation as "China's Jerusalem," and a few would prefer a different analogy, "China's Antioch." During the expansion of the Christian faith beyond the boundaries of Jerusalem in the first half of the first century, Antioch, according to the New Testament (Acts, chapter 11, verse 26), was the first city in Roman-ruled Palestine where followers of Jesus were known as "Christian." Miao explained,

"There was a prophecy a long time ago [during the Cultural Revolution] that Wenzhou would be like Antioch."

Wenzhou had a good foundation for growth from the Cultural Revolution onward because the biblical and theological teaching by the city's mostly evangelical pastors had been very thorough before 1949 and continued to be so even when the Cultural Revolution forced all Christian teaching to go underground. In the past decade, however, problems of theological differences have arisen in the city. "Uncle" Miao, with his Pentecostal background, cooperated closely with Henan's "uncle" Zhang during the 1980s, especially after Balcombe's Charismatic teachings became influential in both Henan and Wenzhou. But in the 1990s a powerful overseas Chinese teacher, Reverend Stephen Tong, of Indonesian Chinese background, began to make trips into the Zhejiang area with a strong Presbyterian message of conservative evangelicalism. To the Charismatically orientated pastors, the new message read as "once-saved-always-saved," a theological magic wand that could ensure Christian salvation once repentance and baptism had taken place, no matter what heinous things the believer did subsequently. This new teaching was quite unsympathetic to the Charismatic zeal to which Miao had become accustomed. In Miao's telling of the story, the strong, Calvinist-based reformed theology introduced by Stephen Tong all but "destroyed" the leadership structure of the largest Wenzhou house church network.

Nevertheless, Miao and the house church leaders in Henan and Wenzhou have a daring new vision for China's still young and rapidly growing Christian church. Miao Zhitong explained how the vision first started in the summer of 2002. "A long time ago," he recalled, "we had this vision in Wenzhou and Henan. We had this idea of going back along the Silk Road. When I was writing *Lilies Among the Thorns* [a collection, in Chinese and in English translation, of house church stories published in Hong Kong in the early 1990s][4] in 1989, I was standing in front of a map of the world. God gave me a great vision. There were two armies. One was from Henan. This army would go along the Silk Road to Afghanistan. The second army was in Wenzhou and would take the ocean route to the

Persian Gulf. I was not the only one to have this vision. A lot of Henan coworkers had it too."

Referred to simply as "Back to Jerusalem," this vision has become familiar to the Christians of China's house church Christian networks, and to the many foreigners who have met with them. Wenzhou may be China's "Antioch" or it may really be "China's Jerusalem," but the city's Christians have a longing that they share with an overwhelming majority of China's Protestant Christian population: to move out on a missionary road that will take the Gospel back to the Middle East, from which it originally came to Europe, North America, and finally China.

Chapter Ten

BACK TO JERUSALEM

EARLY IN FEBRUARY 2002, a group of Koreans and Americans gathered to meet with several dozen Chinese at a four-star hotel just outside of Beijing. The American group included Dr. Luis Bush, a prominent Protestant evangelist and the chairman of the AD 2000 movement, an international effort launched in the 1990s to coordinate world missionary efforts in as many continents as possible, and striving to accomplish great things by the beginning of the third millennium. Also present were Americans of Korean background, increasingly active in helping to train China's emerging generation of evangelists.

The most striking feature of the large gathering was the Chinese participants. Several were leaders of China's major house church networks who did not usually meet with one another in any public setting, much less in the heart of the heavily policed Chinese capital. More surprisingly, a dozen of the group were junior clergy from churches connected to the Three Self, an organization whose leadership for much of the past three decades has either continued to deny that house churches exist or has actively cooperated with government crackdowns on China's unregistered Protestant Christian groups. An American participant in the meeting observed, "Never in history had these leaders been able to come together. Xu Yongze had tried in 1997 but was jailed for three years. This time, they not only came together but wanted it known in the outside world that they had done so."

This was one reason the participation of Luis Bush was so significant. Bush was a leader in international evangelical Protestant circles. He counted people like Billy Graham among his friends and confidants. It was Luis Bush who coined the term "the 10/40 window" at a major conference on Protestant global evangelism in Manila, the Philippines, in July 1989. The numerals 10/40 refer to the latitudinal band of the globe covering 10 degrees above the equator and 40 degrees below it. This geographical swath of the earth contains the overwhelming majority of major ethnic and religious communities and nations that have thus far strongly resisted conversion to Christianity. Since that day, evangelical Protestant churches around the world have prayed daily for "the 10/40 window," and missionary strategy has been dominated by the challenge of penetrating the window.

By privately meeting with China's major house church network leaders, Luis Bush was in a sense conferring upon them the seal of recognition from global Protestantism. Of course, American evangelist Billy Graham had met privately in 1988 with China's preeminent twentieth-century Christian evangelist, Wang Mingdao. But Wang at age eighty-eight was no longer active in China's Christian growth. Bush was taking a certain risk in meeting with the house church leaders. If Beijing's public security bureau had known about the gathering, they probably would have interrupted it and arrested some of the Chinese leaders. Bush and the other Americans might have been detained and summarily expelled from China. It would have been more than a simple personal embarrassment. Evangelical Christian groups in the U.S. associated with him might have been denied further access to China's official Protestant Christian leaders of the Three Self.

THE BEIJING FORUM

The meeting, later called simply "The Beijing Forum," greatly encouraged the Chinese house church leaders. It was the first time they had ever gathered for any conference in Beijing, the very heart of the regime that so often had tried to crush their networks. It was also significant that a top American evangelical, well known in international missionary circles, would be willing to confer with them about not only the continued evangelization of China, but also about Christian missionary outreach to the entire world. One of the matters that surfaced most vividly at the Beijing Forum in February 2002 was how to help China's Christians implement their dream of going "Back to Jerusalem."

The forum discussed both China and global missions. One of the house church leaders present articulated an idea that had been in circulation throughout the house churches for at least five years: China would like to raise 100,000 Christian missionaries to send out to the world, and would like to do so in honor of the Morrison bicentennial in 2007.

A few of the Americans present were familiar with this notion: 100,000 Chinese missionaries on a global evangelization expedition. Bush was dumbfounded. For a comparison, the total estimate for American Protestant and Catholic missionaries working overseas in any given year is around 40,000 to 50,000. The U.S. annually sends more missionaries overseas than any other single country by far; the current effort is built on two centuries of experience and the considerable wealth of ordinary Americans. Could 100,000 Chinese be prepared for missionary work and sent out by the year 2007? Almost certainly not. But the process could begin. In fact, even before the Beijing Forum of February 2002, it had already begun.

There has always been an overall global missions concept among several house church networks. "Even in 1994," said Xing Liaoyuan of the Tanghe fellowship, "when we sent out the first seventy evangelists, we had a vision to take the Gospel to the whole world. We have a mission today to send out missionaries to all countries. We have the same vision as the others to take the revival back to Jerusalem." According to some of leaders the Tanghe and Fancheng fellowships, by 2000 the two networks will have sent a total of about sixty missionaries across China's southern border for work in Burma.

(One of the "uncles" who went to help them out had a run-in with Burmese authorities and was jailed for several months in a filthy Burmese prison.) The Born Again had also sent a handful of missionaries into Pakistan by 2002.

"Back to Jerusalem." It was impossible not to hear this term from Chinese house church Christians of all ages in all parts of the country. The origins of the movement are as complex as they are dramatic.

The first time the notion that China's Christians had a role to play in evangelizing the world, and in connection with Jerusalem, seems to have been in the 1920s in Shandong Province. In 1921, Jing Dianying founded a small, independent Christian group. It was called the Jesus Family, and was not dissimilar in format to the Little Flock, founded by China's most famous twentieth-century Christian, Watchman Nee. The Jesus Family was so radical in its interpretation of how Christians should behave that it believed members should sell all their possessions and distribute the proceeds among other family members. The five-word slogan of the Jesus Family was "sacrifice, abandonment, poverty, suffering, death." This turned out to be the fate of the group's members who set off on foot spreading the Gospel in nearby towns and villages. They were frequently scorned and beaten. The group's vision of taking Christianity on foot to the whole of China and to the nations beyond China's northwestern borders was not called "Back to Jerusalem," but the "Northwest Spiritual Movement." Members believed that Jesus would return any day and that the best way they could spend their time was evangelizing. By the late 1940s an estimated 20,000 Chinese believers were scattered in more than one hundred Jesus Family groups throughout the country, all of them believing they were called to bring the Christian message from China into the heartland of Central Asia.

GOING NORTHWEST

But the best-known Chinese forerunners of today's "Back to Jerusalem" vision among China's Protestant Christians were members of what in English was called the "Back to Jerusalem Evangelistic

Band" (in the sense of group). The Chinese name, translated literally, was "Preach the Gospel Everywhere Band." It had a very specific origin during World War II, when many Chinese Christian seminaries and missionaries—those who had not been interned by the Japanese—relocated to China's western and southwestern provinces. One of these Christian training centers was the newly formed Northwest Bible Institute, in Fengxiang, Shaanxi Province. The principal of the college was Hudson Taylor's grandson, James Hudson Taylor III. The vice principal was Mark Ma, a Henan-born Christian who had been a government schoolteacher until coming to the Christian faith in 1937.

MARK MA

While Ma was in prayer one evening in November 1942, he had the distinct impression that God was calling him to go to China's farthest, northwestern province of Xinjiang to preach the Christian Gospel. Ma had no interest in this part of China and no desire to go. On Easter morning five months later, while praying with Christian coworkers from the Northwest Bible Institute on the banks of the Wei River, he spoke for the first time about the conviction he had received back in November. Immediately, one of the women in the prayer group said she had received the same "call" several years earlier.

Greatly encouraged, Ma returned to the campus, only to learn that eight of the students at a sunrise service that day had expressed a similar sense of divine calling in that geographical direction. According to Ma's testimony, on asking God in prayer what all of this meant, he felt that God was saying to him, "Since the beginning at Pentecost [the event in the Book of Acts, chapter 2, when the Holy Spirit is described as coming upon the followers of Jesus after the Resurrection and Ascension], the pathway of the Gospel has spread, for the greater part, in a westward direction: from Jerusalem to Antioch, to all of Europe; from Europe to America and then to the East; from the southeast of China to the northwest; until today from Gansu on westward it can be said there is no firmly established church. You may go westward from Gansu, preaching the Gospel all the way back to

Jerusalem, causing the light of the Gospel to complete the circle around this dark world."[1]

Ma says that he then got into an argument with the Almighty. "That section of territory is under the power of Islam and the Mohammedans are the hardest of all peoples to reach with the Gospel," Ma complained. The Almighty replied, "Even you Chinese, yourself included, are hard enough, but you have been conquered by the Gospel." Ma then asked why Western missionaries hadn't seemed to have had any success in preaching Christianity to the Muslims. God replied, according to Ma, "It is not that their hearts are especially hard, but that I have kept for the Chinese Church a portion of the inheritance; otherwise, when I return, will you not be too poor?"[2]

This retort ended the argument for Ma, who added in his account of the prayer experience, "Therefore my hope is that our Chinese church will with determination and courage hold fast to this great responsibility and, depending upon our all-victorious Savior, complete this mighty task, and taking possession of our glorious inheritance, take the Gospel back to Jerusalem. There we shall stand on top of Mount Zion and welcome our Lord Jesus Christ descending in the clouds with great glory!"[3]

MECCA CHAO

At the May 1942 meeting at which Ma decided the group was to be called the Back to Jerusalem Evangelistic Band, he told his small group of fellow enthusiasts that God was calling Chinese evangelists and missionaries not just to the outlying provinces of China, including Xinjiang and Tibet, but to Afghanistan, Iran, Saudi Arabia, Iraq, Syria, Turkey, and Palestine (which at the time was still a British mandate territory). It probably didn't seem too unusual a challenge to some of the group. One of them, a young man whose last name was Chao, had experienced a strange vision shortly after his own conversion to Christianity as a teenager. He saw a piece of paper being held in front of him with the name "Mecca" on it. Neither he nor any of his Christian friends or pastors had any idea what it meant. But he felt that he was supposed to make "Mecca" his Chinese given name.

Chao's spiritual pilgrimage wasn't exactly orthodox. He drifted away from church, was drafted into the Chinese Nationalist army, and only recovered his faith while a prisoner of war of the Japanese. In prison he had another vision—a map of Ningxia, the Chinese province that held a large number of Muslims in it. In 1947 he was freed from prison and found his way to the Northwest Bible Institute. It was here that Pastor Mark Ma explained the significance of the word "Mecca" to him.

By 1949 Ma, Chao, and others had made several daring and risky expeditions into China's far west, but their efforts were brought to a halt by the Communist conquest of China in 1949. Several members of the Back to Jerusalem Band spent many years in prison where they were subjected to the usual gamut of mistreatment: beatings, torture, humiliation at the hands of other criminal inmates. Some of them remained in China's far west, somehow surviving the Great Leap Forward of 1958–1961 and the Cultural Revolution of 1966–1976. Ma eventually made his way back to Chongqing, where as late as 2001 he was still receiving Christian visitors from Hong Kong and the west. Chao was still alive and conducting evangelistic efforts as late as 1987, according to James Hudson Taylor III, who in Kashgar met an elderly woman who had herself gone out to Xinjiang in 1947.

It is hard to determine exactly how many Han Chinese Christians made the trek out to China's west. A handful of them are still active in small house churches scattered in Xinjiang cities. A British woman missionary in Chongqing in 1949 wrote in one of her missionary reports that she knew at least five different Chinese Christian groups that wished to take the Gospel out of China in a westerly direction. "The thing that has impressed me most," she reported, "has been the strange, unaccountable urge of a number of different Chinese groups, quite unconnected with each other, who have left their homes in east China and gone forth, leaving practically everything behind them, to the west." All separately felt it was urgent to take Christianity to the westernmost areas of China as a prelude to carrying it even farther west.

SIMON ZHAO

The leader of one of those groups, the Northwest Spiritual Movement, survived an astonishing forty-five years in prison in Xinjiang in order to keep alive the original "Back to Jerusalem" vision and impart it to the current leadership of China's house church networks. His original Chinese name was Zhang Haizhen and he came from Shenyang in Liaoning Province. Zhang, who took the Christian name Simon and a new Chinese surname, Zhao, arrived in Kashgar with twenty or so teammates toward the end of 1948. The Communists, however, were already asserting their control over this part of China, and they sealed the borders with Soviet Central Asia. Zhao and his team, who had tried to sneak across illegally, were arrested and charged as traitors. All were imprisoned, and several of them died in prison. Zhao was sentenced to an astonishing forty-five years in prison, where for at least three decades he was routinely beaten and tortured, mainly because he refused to renounce his faith. In 1988, five years before the end of his term, he was released. He walked out of jail a bent, wizened man in his seventies with a long white beard and the wire of an antique hearing aid hanging down from his right ear to a plastic, battery-powered receiver in his shirt pocket. "Simon Zhao's physical appearance was unique and added to his ministry," a house church leader commented later. "He looked like an ancient sage, with a long white beard and white hair."[4]

By chance, some of Xu's Born Again network were in Kashgar, heard about Simon Zhao, and sought him out. They were astonished by his story and by the fact that he had maintained his faith nearly half a century in a labor camp. The Henan Christians of all networks had known about the Back to Jerusalem movement of the 1940s, but none had actually met anyone from the original groups. Finally, in the 1990s, Xu Yongze's sister, Xu Yongling, traveled by bus from Henan to Kashgar to persuade Zhao to return with her and share his stories in Henan. Reluctantly, Zhao did as requested, spending the last few years of his life sharing the Back to Jerusalem vision and his own decades-long prison experiences with many house church groups in Henan. He died in Pingdingshan, Henan Province, on December 7, 2001.

It isn't clear what rekindled the Back to Jerusalem fervor among China's house church Christians from the mid-1990s onward. It could have been the influence of Zhao's story or simply the spontaneous reemergence of the same vision that animated the Northwest Bible Institute students and others back in the 1940s. Certainly, the enormous confidence that the house church networks had acquired during the phenomenal expansion of the 1980s was part of the explanation. The enthusiasm for the project wasn't limited to any one network, but common all over China. "My parents' church in Xian was meeting for a time with Uighur [a Turkic minority that is the largest non-Han group in Xinjiang] students from the university," said Mary Li, the pretty Beijing website professional we met in chapter 5. "They have this big picture of using the Silk Road to take the Gospel to Jerusalem." Xing Liaoyuan, one of the top Tanghe leaders, said, "We have the same vision as the Back to Jerusalem Evangelistic Band and the Northwest Spiritual Movement of taking the revival back to Jerusalem. The reason we had the Chinese mission [when the seventy youthful evangelists were sent out during March–October 1994] was that we wanted to send missionaries all over the world."

A handful of China's Christian house church leaders have actually been to Jerusalem, to Christian prayer gatherings organized there. Zhang Rongliang and Sister Ding visited Jerusalem for a Christian prayer conference in 2001, and Miao Zhitong of Wenzhou traveled to Israel in September 2002.

"Through my visit to Jerusalem," Zhang said, "I was greatly encouraged to love Jerusalem, and since then I have had even more of a burden for the city." Zhang was touched by the presence of some ten thousand Chinese workers in Israel, and would like to organize Chinese Christians to pastor them. But he seems to have been moved principally by the Jewishness of Israel. He said, "I went three times to the Western Wall, then to the Mount of Olives and to the Garden Tomb [an alternative site, according to some Protestants, for the actual Crucifixion and entombment of Christ]. That gave me more love for Christ. I feel the Wall shows the presence of God. The tomb of King David is also a very sacred place." Ding was also deeply moved by the prayer conference in Jerusalem. It was on her return to China that she began to speak to different house church groups on the importance of twenty-four-hour prayer chains.

The Christians of China's house churches almost overwhelmingly accept the premillennialist vision of the biblical end times. That is, they believe that Christ will return and inaugurate a reign on earth of a thousand years, based in Jerusalem. Before that happens, however, premillennialists believe there will be climactic developments in the Middle East, of which the present troubles are only a foretaste. "What is happening in Israel makes me believe even more in Biblical prophecy. I think Israelis themselves will come closer to the [Old Testament] Bible," said Zhang Rongliang.

A PRO-ISRAELI CHINA?

Early on in the reporting for this book, in 2002, I learned that there was an overwhelmingly pro-Israeli feeling among China's Christians, which contrasted sharply with China's official government position of supporting the Arabs in general and the Palestinians in particular. In addition, many house church Christians said that they prayed strongly for a U.S. victory in the war against Iraq. The future strategic significance of an important component of China's population being pro-Israeli is well worth considering.

Paradoxically, the fact that China's government is seen by the Arab world as supportive of their side in the Arab-Israeli dispute heartens the house churches in their hopes of evangelizing the world's Muslims. "The Chinese church is getting ready to go to the 10/40 window," Zhang Rongliang told some Americans in the summer of 2001. "Chinese people are more suitable than Americans to go to the Muslim world. Muslims prefer Chinese to Americans. They don't like Americans very much. The Chinese government supports [Middle Eastern] terrorism, so the Muslim nations support China. Besides, we have a lot of experience of persecution."

Zhang has a broad, but not yet detailed, theology of missions to the Muslim world. For him, as well as for other Chinese Christians seeking ways to implement the Back to Jerusalem vision, there is no thought of evangelizing the Jews living in Jerusalem. The city itself is merely symbolic of the Gospel having traveled around the earth and now returned to its place of origin. Zhang elaborates, "It was the Apostle Paul who took the Gospel to Europe and now, after 2,000 years, it has come to China. When the disciples left Jerusalem to go toward East Asia and Europe, they were only a few people. They went barefoot. Now the Gospel has reached China and we have several Christian networks. We believe that now that the Gospel has reached China it will follow the old Silk Road back to Jerusalem. Once the Gospel comes back to Jerusalem, it will mean that the Gospel has been preached to the whole world. We have the view that Chinese missionaries will be part of the mainstream on the highway back to Jerusalem. The Muslim religion is the biggest obstacle on the road back to Jerusalem."

To this end, there are several small missionary-training seminaries in different parts of China that are training Chinese Christians as missionaries to the Muslim world. Some Chinese have enrolled in Arabic-language programs at major Chinese universities. Some of the smaller, underground missionary seminaries have brought in Arabic-speaking Christians to train a new generation of Chinese missionaries to work in the Islamic world. Some Americans who encourage the Back to Jerusalem effort in China estimate that there may already be several hundred Chinese house church Christians operating as missionaries—perhaps filling professional positions like engineers, interpreters, or ordinary laborers—throughout the Middle East.

Zhang Rongliang says that Chinese communities in both Saudi Arabia and Kuwait have requested that China's house churches send pastors and evangelists to help Christian communities in those countries reach out—at considerable risk—to the Chinese workers living there and to the Muslims among whom they live. "In China, the hearts of ordinary workers are often very closed," he says. "Overseas they are more open."

Several American groups have lent support to China's Back to Jerusalem enterprise. A recently initiated U.S. website, *www.backtojerusalem.org*, provides both a history of China's Back to Jerusalem movement and a focus for efforts to assist it. Eric Watt, president of a mission organization called Reaching Unreached Peoples, is prominent in a loose network of Americans, Europeans, and Koreans who are doing what they can to assist China's Christians in the Back to Jerusalem venture. Watt (son of Reagan-era Secretary of the Interior James Watt) doesn't like the idea of dumping Western missionary experts on China. He prefers to find a few foreigners who can train Chinese house church leaders on how to instruct their own people in missions.

Surprisingly, despite their experience of persecution and their heart for spreading the Gospel globally, Chinese, Watt says, can sometimes be even more culturally crass than Americans. He cites the case of a Chinese evangelist in a Muslim region of China who invited his Muslim neighbors to a banquet, featuring pork, to celebrate the establishment of a new Christian community. "Back to Jerusalem," he says, "is more of an icon than a specific missionary strategy. Christian believers in the Pacific Rim are the future of global Christianity and global missionary efforts."

There is no doubt that China's engagement in the Middle East and the Islamic world in general will continue to grow as China's energy needs become increasingly dependent on petroleum imports. China's Communist government, moreover, has had no qualms about selling advanced military equipment to any nation in the region prepared to pay for it, from Saudi Arabia to Iraq, from Iran to Afghanistan (at least until the ouster of the Taliban regime in 2002). Along with Chinese arms sales and petroleum import agreements will go hundreds and eventually thousands of Chinese technicians and workers. Some of these, without question, will be as eager to spread the Gospel as many Americans have been when given similar opportunities to work in the Islamic world. There will, no doubt, be strong resistance by the governments and by the Islamic authorities of the Arab world to the presence of Chinese Christian missionaries presumed to have been merely technical experts or actual workers. But in its efforts to isolate its people from hearing anything about Christianity, the Islamic world, especially in the Middle East, will no longer be able to resort to the usual complaints about the "decadent West" or the perils of globalization. Globalization is indeed here to stay, and the Christian component of it, more and more, will have a Chinese accent.

Chapter Eleven

CATHOLICS

AT AROUND 9:00 A.M. on a Sunday morning, Beijing's Southern Cathedral is showing signs of a very active Catholic church. The sanctuary is packed with worshipers attending one of the several Sunday services, groups of children are being led off to English-language-for-Catholics lessons, and a handful of foreigners are beginning to show up for the 10:00 A.M. English-language service.

In the courtyard before the main entrance to the church a glass case houses a Chinese description of the cathedral. Below it is an English translation of sorts:

> Cathedral. The Cathedral of Immaculate Conception of Blessed Virgin Mary. Situation in 141 Qianmen Xidajie Avenue Beijing. Today here is also the Bishop's resident.

> The Italian Jesuit Father Matteo Ricci arrived in Beijing in 1601. The Emperor of China bestowed him the land and funds to build a chapel here. He lived here and worked [hard] for the propagation of the Gospel and cultural exchanges.

> A church was built here by German Jesuit Father Adam Schall in 1650. The Ching Dynasty Government granted

him a lot of silver coins for it and the Emperor Shun Zhi twenty-four times came here and have had heart to heart [talks] with Father Adam Schall. But the church was burnt away in 1775 and in the year 1900 it was set on fire. So the present cathedral was rebuilt in 1904. Xuan Wu Men. Nan Tang.[1]

That inscription tells a large part of the story of Catholicism in China. But it omits some important details. For example, in 1900 the rampaging Boxers set the cathedral on fire and murdered thousands of Chinese Catholics in Beijing alone. It doesn't mention that from 1966 the cathedral was closed for a decade and a half by the Red Guards and used as a storage facility. Its cross was torn down in case the citizens of Beijing were tempted to recall that there was a God more important than Mao Zedong.

CHINESE CATHOLICS UNDER COMMUNISM

The story of Catholicism in China under Communism is tragic and heroic, pragmatic and sophisticated. When Mao's victorious legions rolled into Beijing in 1949, Roman Catholics—as they were still called in China then—were already set on a collision course with the new regime. Unlike the Protestants, whose leading institutions had been carefully infiltrated for years by Communist Party members or by people openly sympathetic to Communist rule, China's Catholics braced themselves for a struggle that their leaders had for years indicated might be a life-and-death combat for the very existence of the Catholic faith in China.

Morning Catholic mass at the Southern Cathedral in Beijing

The great strength of the Church of Rome throughout the world has always been its impressive and visible hierarchical structure, the disciplined chain of command—occasionally challenged by dissident bishops and priests, though seldom for long—from the pope down through the bishops to each local parish priest. But this source of unity and strength in places of religious freedom can become a clear and vulnerable target in times of major political upheaval. In some ways, it is a miracle that Catholicism survived the onslaught from China's Communist rulers in the 1950s.

ANTONIO RIBERI

In some ways, the Catholic Church in the twentieth century was slower than the Protestants in turning over leadership of the church to native-born Chinese. It wasn't until 1946 that the Vatican removed China from the jurisdiction of the Propaganda Fidei ("propagation of the faith")—i.e., supervision of all foreign missionaries—to a national church in its own right. By 1949, four-fifths of all China's Catholic bishops were still foreigners, and at the grass roots, two-fifth of all Chinese Catholic priests were foreign-born.

From 1946 on, China's Catholics were quite visibly under orders from a Catholic superior who was deeply involved in trying to prevent the Communists from coming to power in China. His name was Archbishop Antonio Riberi (1897–1967), an Italian who had been assigned to China as an internuncio—that is, someone who both represents the Vatican as an ambassador in the diplomatic sense and, on the Vatican's orders, ensures the implementation of Vatican policy within the country.

Archbishop Riberi clearly saw himself as an ecclesiastical general in the global Cold War. In 1947, he forbade all Roman Catholics from joining any Communist organization. In 1948, he organized the Legion of Mary—in China's case, a Catholic organization dedicated to resisting and turning back Communist influence in China. As the Nationalist and Communist armies wrestled for control of China, Riberi also declared that it would be a sin for any Catholic to fight on the Communist side. Since Communist armies were composed largely of ordinary peasants drafted into its ranks because they happened to reside within areas controlled by the Communists, rural Catholics faced a difficult choice: to obey would almost certainly mean death at the hands of the Communists, to disobey might mean excommunication from the church.

In 1950, while China's Protestants were pushed into the "Three Self Reform Movement" (later renamed the Three Self Patriotic movement), a parallel effort was being organized in the countryside to mobilize China's Catholics to support the new regime. "Catholic Reform Committees" were established in North China by 1949 to propagate the Catholic version of Three Self, sometimes known as the "three autonomies": self-propagation, self-support, and self-governance. Riberi's response was outright opposition. He ordered all foreign-born Catholic priests to stay in their stations, whatever was happening around them. When the Catholic Reform Committees were later subsumed by the United Front Work Department into the Chinese Catholic Patriotic Association in 1951, Riberi flatly refused to have anything to do with it or to permit any Catholic bishop or priest to cooperate with the organization.

He was not in a strong position. The Vatican had not withdrawn its recognition of the Nationalist government, the Republic of China, after Mao's victory and the departure of Chiang Kai-shek to Taiwan. The Korean War in 1950 had exacerbated tensions between China and the West in general. In May 1951, Riberi was first put under house arrest, then unceremoniously bundled into a third-class compartment of a train from Beijing to Hong Kong. At the border he was ordered to cross the bridge into the British colony.

Although no official expulsion order was ever issued to either Protestant or Catholic missionaries in the country, by the end of 1951 a full-scale exodus was in progress. Sixteen Catholic priests, missionaries, brothers, and sisters were effectively ordered out of China by the end of 1952, leaving only 787. By 1951, nineteen Catholic priests, including two archbishops and two bishops, had been killed or had died in prison. More than three hundred Chinese Catholic priests were rotting in prison by the end of 1953.[2] In 1958, China's government finally cracked down on the last American Catholic prelate in China, Bishop James E. Walsh. (He was arrested, convicted in 1960 of "organizing spies, counterrevolutionaries, and criminal activities," and not released until 1970, at the outset of the thaw culminating in the U.S.-Chinese "ping-pong diplomacy.")

Thus began the long dark night for China's Catholics.

CHINESE CATHOLIC PATRIOTIC ASSOCIATION

The nation's Chinese priests were immediately pressured to become associated with various "reform committees" or to sign manifestos denouncing their superiors. If they didn't, as had been the case with Protestants refusing to join the Three Self, they were likely to be condemned as "counterrevolutionaries" and arrested. Many simply dropped out of sight and, at the risk of their lives, carried on their priestly duties underground. Some displayed astonishing bravery when faced with demands to publicly affirm the regime's policies. In early June 1951, Father John Tung (Tong Shizhi) was asked by the authorities to speak at a mass meeting in Chongqing Cathedral in denunciation of Archbishop Riberi and on behalf of the Patriotic Association. He agreed to speak, but his address enraged the watchful officials. An attack on Riberi, he told his astonished audience, would be followed by an attack on the pope and then an attack on Christ himself. Instead, he said, he would offer himself. In his own words,

> It is best, it seems, to offer my whole soul to God and to the Holy Church; and my body to my country. If she is pleased with it, I do not refuse it to her. Good materialists, who deny the existence of the soul, cannot but be satisfied with the offering of my body.[3]

A month later he was arrested, and in 1965 was reported to be working in a labor camp in a remote area of China, but in good spirits.

Across China the choice of Chinese Catholic priests was stark: either cooperate with the government—and hence risk perpetual separation from the mother church in Rome—or refuse and be subject to arrest, imprisonment, beating and torture, and quite possibly death. In August 1951, Father Beda Chang, director of the Bureau of Chinese Studies in Shanghai, was arrested with two other priests, charged with opposing student control of Catholic schools, supporting the Chinese Nationalists on Taiwan, and engaging in "counterrevolutionary activities." Father Chang died in prison within three months, with strong evidence that he had been either beaten to death or had collapsed into a coma after repeated interrogation and probably sleep deprivation.[4]

The regime's assault on the Catholic Church in China went on. By the end of 1955, some 1,500 Catholics in Shanghai alone were in custody, including the outstanding figure of resistance to Communist rule, Gong Pinmei, or Bishop Ignatius Kung, as he was known at the time (using the old Wade-Giles romanization). Gong was accused of being a spy and a saboteur, but despite the usual recipe of mistreatment while in prison, he never broke. He was not released until 1988, thirty-three years later.

The frontal attack on the Catholic establishment in China produced brutal results. By the end of 1955, resistance to joining the government-organized "Anti-Imperialist Movement for the Love of Country and Church," the latest effort to control Catholics, was down to about 30 percent among the priests and bishops. The departure of the foreign-born priests and bishops, the arrest and imprisonment of hundreds of others, and the disappearance into the underground of yet more left the Catholic Church in China with a desperate shortage of the people—"patriotic" or not—to actually run it. Where were the candidates for ordination? Where were the bishops to ordain them if they could be found? The Catholic Patriotic Association had just come into formal operation as a national organization in 1957, but by 1958 there was a severe need for senior clergy.

CPA vs. Rome

In 1957, the government organized in Beijing a National Conference of Catholics, attended by 241 archbishops, bishops, priests, and laity from one hundred dioceses. In February 1958 the CPA announced that it would call for the election of new bishops in dioceses throughout China. Elections were duly held and names of qualified and approved candidates emerged. Naturally, no candidate with any record of opposing China's Communist government was elected.

As required by Catholic canon law, Beijing then sent the list of names to the Vatican for formal approval by the pope. Rome adamantly rejected the proposed list, primarily because the Catholic Patriotic Association had formally declared that Rome itself had no right of ecclesiastical jurisdiction over Catholicism in China. Catholicism in China was now "patriotic," beholden for approval by the CPA, above that the Religious Affairs Bureau, above that the United Front Work Department, and above that the Central Committee and Politburo of the Chinese Communist Party itself. The Vatican responded that if any Chinese priest permitted himself to be consecrated by a bishop in defiance of approval from Rome, he would risk excommunication.

Despite the Vatican's objections, China's "patriotic" consecrations went ahead. By mid-1958 as many as forty new priests had been consecrated on instructions of the CPA, and by 1962 no fewer than forty-two new bishops had been consecrated as well. By the late 1990s more than one hundred bishops had been consecrated in China under the auspices of the Catholic Patriotic Association.

For a number of reasons, Rome didn't permit the sword of ultimate separation to fall upon China. Instead, it responded with surprising subtlety and flexibility. It declared that the consecrations had been "illicit" but that the ceremonial form had nevertheless been correct. The consecrations were therefore "valid." This was to be the posture of Rome toward the CPA from the 1960s on. In other words, the Vatican never accepted the right of the CPA to decide the religious order of Catholicism in China, yet it never formally cast into outer darkness those priests and bishops who had been taken over by the CPA. Several U.S.-based organizations criticized the Vatican severely for this posture. Chief among them is the Cardinal Kung Foundation, dedicated to the heroic life of Cardinal Kung and countless bishops and priests like him who resisted Communist control to the point of martyrdom. The foundation's website today blasts the CPA as "Communist-created, Communist-controlled, blatantly schismatic, [a] pro-abortion organization founded by the devil himself."[5]

The long-run advantages to be reaped by the Vatican's patience and subtlety were at the other side of a grim valley of persecution and suffering. After the first clash of the early and mid-1950s, Catholics again came under fire, along with Protestants and intellectuals in general as China lurched into the anti-rightist campaign of 1957–1958, followed by the Great Leap Forward of 1958–1961. More Chinese Catholic priests were rounded up, interrogated, and cast away into labor camps, along with many Chinese intellectuals who were Catholics or who had enjoyed any sort of relationship with Catholic institutions in China or the West before 1949. Conditions in labor camp were especially grim during the Great Leap because of the man-made famine that swept through China during 1960–1962. Estimates of the number of Chinese who died as a result of the Great Leap policies reach as high as 47 million.[6] An ecumenical brotherhood of Christian suffering grew up in many labor camps as Catholic priests and Protestant pastors, previously often at loggerheads over doctrinal issues, joined together to fight the bullying of state atheism under the guise of "reeducation."

In 1962, things let up a little in China. Liu Shaoqi and Deng Xiaoping, in many ways the arch-opponents of Mao's economic and social radicalism, assumed day-to-day leadership authority within the Communist Party: Mao, for the time being, was assigned to a secondary level of authority. Though the "people's communes," into which the entirety of China's peasantry had been herded during the Great Leap, were not yet abolished, peasants were permitted once more to farm private plots. In the cities, small-scale consumer commercial activity resumed. The stranglehold on China's social, cultural, and religious life was momentarily loosened. Catholic churches in China were permitted to resume services and a measure of normalcy appeared at hand.

But it was over in the blink of an eye. By late 1965, Mao was already plotting his comeback to power with a literary campaign and what became the tornado of China's Cultural Revolution. If the anti-rightist campaign had been intimidating and the Great Leap disruptive, the Cultural Revolution was devastating on all of China's civic life, including religion. Churches, mosques, and temples were vandalized and closed. The Three Self, CPA, and other authorized organs responsible for religions in China (Buddhism, Islam, and Daoism) were themselves subjected to humiliations by Red Guard groups. Personnel of the CPA, along with those of the Three Self, were assigned to reeducation camps and left to molder there for years.

Toward the end of the Cultural Revolution, many observers feared that religion had been entirely removed from the landscape of Chinese life. Mao's radical leftist wife Jiang Qing declared in the 1970s that Christianity in China had now been consigned to the museum. Many foreign observers were ready to believe what the government officials were telling them: "religion no longer exists in China."

SURVIVAL AND REVIVAL

Catholicism in China survived and eventually revived, for reasons interestingly different from those that explain the emergence in the 1970s of a vibrant, evangelistic new Chinese Protestantism.

A CATHOLIC IDENTITY IN THE NORTH

According to Richard Madsen, a scholar from the University of California at San Diego who has specialized in China's Catholicism, most of China's Catholics were located in rural villages in the provinces of Hebei and Shanxi. In some of these villages, Catholics had constituted the overwhelming majority for more than one hundred years. Chinese Catholic officials told me that of the 12 million Catholics (about 4 million in the Patriotic churches and up to 8 million in the underground churches) one-quarter lived in Hebei Province, the northern province in the center of which Beijing is located.

Madsen found that a powerful, clannish sense of identity had grown up over the decades in the predominantly Catholic villages of north China. China's Catholic villagers saw themselves as belonging to a pre-Vatican II world in which what mattered was to adhere to the

"God teachings"—the basics of Roman Catholic belief—in a manner that symbolically connected Chinese Catholics not just to their nation's past, going all the way back to Matteo Ricci, but to a grand scheme of church history whose origin, ultimately, was Adam and Eve. Even not very devout Catholics, Madsen found, believed that it was important to organize and attend Catholic funeral ceremonies at the death of anyone in their family or village community. The Catholic Church, Madsen discovered, had come to be regarded as the social and cultural entity that lent legitimacy to social activities of the village. Catholic ceremonies in these communities became a way of expressing social identity. Madsen observed that villagers in the rural communities of Hebei province dedicated themselves to making their village "a miniature Christendom, a self-enclosed world of God."[7] In effect, Catholicism for the villagers of rural Hebei came to constitute, according to Madsen, "a kind of ethnicity."[8]

For much of the 1960s and 1970s there were no priests at all in these village communities. Yet it became clear, once Catholicism reemerged from the catacombs in the 1980s that there had been no disruption in the continuity of Catholic tradition. According to Madsen, mothers would "baptize" their children even without a priest, by pouring water over them as infants and saying, simply, "I baptize you in the name of the Father, the Son, and the Holy Spirit."[9]

Many of their regular priests were imprisoned, but even so, a strong "underground" resistance emerged in much of rural Hebei to the Patriotic clergy. In the 1950s a handful of clandestine consecrations of priests had taken place in China, the officiating clergy consisting of foreign prelates visiting China. In 1978 many of China's underground bishops requested permission from the Vatican to select and consecrate successor bishops without direct approval from Rome as a way of ensuring the continuity of Apostolic consecrations in China. The Vatican consented.

PARALLEL ROADS TO ROME

When the Cultural Revolution was at an end, normal patterns of worship and spiritual life needed to be resumed. The CPA climbed out of its Cultural Revolution tomb in December 1979 by arranging for the consecration of Michael Fu (Fu Tieshan) as bishop of Beijing. But with the reinforcement of China's underground Catholic clergy as a result of the 1978 Vatican-approved consecrations of underground bishops and priests, a situation emerged that was unique in global Catholicism: parallel, and sometimes competing, hierarchies of Catholic priests and bishops, one licit and one not. The clergies of the various communities did not officially recognize one another, often competed for the loyalty of the Catholic laity, and frequently over-lapped in their jurisdictions. The mutual antagonism was occasion-ally aggravated by the emergence of a new and in some ways characteristically Chinese phenomenon: Patriotic priests and bishops whose allegiance was supposedly only to China's home-grown Catholic hierarchy, one by one committed themselves to Rome through contacts with visiting Roman Catholic prelates.

In effect, Roman Catholic Christianity was infiltrating Chinese Communism.

By 2002, according to Patriotic bishops and clergy I interviewed in China and representatives in Hong Kong of the Roman hierarchy, at least two-thirds and perhaps as many as three-quarters of China's seventy-two Patriotic bishops had formally—albeit privately—sworn allegiance to Rome. Even more strangely, both establishments, the CPA and the Vatican, seemed entirely comfortable with this unusual cohabitation, though rivalries and displays of one-upmanship were also quite apparent. Also, in surprising contrast to Protestant Three Self leaders, who often deny the existence of "house churches" in China, ordinary priests and top clergy in the CPA discuss their rela-tions with the underground church as though this were the most nor-mal thing in the world.

In Beijing, Father Francis-Xavier Zhang (Zhang Tianlu), a CPA priest attached to the Southern Cathedral, had a fascinating tale to tell of moving from the underground to the Patriotic side of Catholic life in China. Born in 1970 to a devout Catholic family in Hebei, he encountered for years only the underground side of Catholicism. In fact, he spent a decade of his Catholic life "underground." His father, however, who had helped protect underground priests, grew disenchanted in the late 1980s over what he considered their "arrogance." In any event, in 1988, Zhang's father made the momentous decision to travel by himself to Beijing and interview Bishop Fu.

Did Fu believe in the pope, Zhang's father asked?

"Yes, of course."

Did he believe in the four elements (the Catholic formula of "one, sacred, catholic, and apostolic" church)?

"Yes."

What was the main purpose of the CPA? The older Zhang and Fu spoke for two hours and the visitor was won over. In 1988, the younger Zhang, who had been baptized "Francis-Xavier" by an underground priest at the age of four outside a Chinese prison, entered seminary in Beijing and began his journey to priesthood.

He showed obvious promise. After his graduation in 1993, Fu sent him for further training in Cambridge, England. This was followed by visits to the U.S., where, Zhang said, Bishop Joseph Lewis Bernardin of Chicago (made a cardinal in 1982) was his "best friend." Zhang seems to have received huge favor from the Catholic establishment in the West ("I was deacon for so many cardinals," he said). He also met with Pope John Paul II, who spoke to him about the Catholic Church in China for four hours. "Go back to China," the pope told Zhang.

Zhang obeyed, and in 1997 was ordained in Beijing. He now presides over a hum of activities in the South Cathedral, ranging from "Couples for Christ" (in English) to Sunday school for forty-eight Chinese Catholic children every Sunday, practice sessions for five choirs, and English training for 468 Chinese students every week. Zhang is an obvious supporter and admirer of Bishop Fu, who, after all, gave him a considerable push during his priestly career. But he also seems to maintain a healthy contact with China's underground priests and bishops. "Relations with the underground are quite good," he said in August 2002, noting with some satisfaction that two bishops from Tianjin who were previously underground had now joined the Catholic Bishops Conference, which is not formally recognized by Rome.

Tianjin, according to Madsen, had an unusually complicated ecclesiastical situation in the early 1990s. When the office of bishop of Tianjin became vacant in 1992, the CPA's choice was Li Hongchen, an underground bishop. But there was already an ordained bishop, also of the underground, Li Side. At the time of the CPA's installation of Li Hongchen, Li Side was kept under arrest lest he would provoke demonstrations against the new appointment. A bitter war of mimeographed broadsheets ensued, with Li Side's supporters arguing angrily that he was already the Rome-approved bishop of Tianjin and should thus take priority. Li Hongchen, however, was more acceptable to the CPA because he agreed to work within the structure and not challenge it directly. Madsen recounts a High Mass that he attended at the Tianjin Cathedral in 1992, officiated over by the CPA bishop, Li Hongchen, while outside, a hundred "underground" Catholics kneeled to recite the rosary in protest as noisily as possible.[10]

In Shijiazhuang, the capital of Catholic-heavy Hebei Province, Father John-Baptist Zhang (Zhang Shijiang) operates a social service center at the CPA seminary that takes care of the aged and provides help to victims of flood, earthquake, and other natural disasters. The social service, named *beifang jinde,* has thirty full-time workers, a few of whom are Catholics from outside China. "Mother Teresa was our patron," John-Baptist explains. "Every year we received from her [organization, the Missionaries of Charity] a million yuan [about $125,000]." Father Zhang of Shijiazhuang is rather proud of the relative independence of his organization, and compares it favorably with the Amity Foundation of Nanjing. "We are decision-makers," he insists. "The government never tells us what to do. No one can change our policy."

Father John-Baptist Zhang says, "People don't care very much any more about the divorce between the official and the unofficial church. The Vatican is very clear that it will not get into conflict with the government. I hope normalization takes place. It will be good for China and for Catholics."

Several hundred miles away in Xian, Shenxi Province, Bishop Li Du'an has excellent relations with the CPA hierarchy: he is, after all, the CPA bishop of that diocese. Yet he is clearly in close contact with many underground clergy in the Xian diocese. Fortunately, he does not have to deal with a rival underground bishop. Bishop Li believes that normalization between the CPA and the Vatican could occur as early as in two or three years. According to him, the Chinese government requires that the Vatican cut off its diplomatic ties to Taiwan and agree "not to interfere" in the internal affairs of the Patriotic church. Bishop Li acknowledges that Rome cannot forswear its tradition in perpetuity of having the final say in the appointment of bishops throughout the global Catholic hierarchy, but he insists with seriousness that "the Chinese government really has the wish for normalization." "Normalization is good for China and for the world, so that the world can know that there is religious freedom in China." As to the underground priests within his diocese, Bishop Li says, "Our relations are okay. They now think our way of doing things and organizing the church is acceptable. Our relationship is still not to the point of cooperation, but we are not opposed to each other."

POINTS OF CONTENTION

Despite the good wishes for normalization expressed by Father John-Baptist Zhang in Shijiazhuang and Bishop Li in Xian, many difficult obstacles must be overcome. There are complex diplomatic, organizational, historical, and personnel issues to resolve. In addition, Madsen in his seminal book, *China's Catholics*, worries that a climate of anti-modernity among many Chinese Catholics, especially in the rural areas, renders them ill-equipped to display the "moral qualities of civility" that could contribute to China's gradual evolution to a society where civic culture eventually took precedence over politics. He is also concerned that China's rural Catholics have "the potential of becoming a nucleus of rural rebellion," further aggravating church and state relations in China.[11] In many instances, Madsen says, China's Catholics, both underground and Patriotic, avoid harassment from officials in China by the simple expedient of bribery. As a Hong

Kong scholar explained to Madsen, "Religious Affairs officials love money more than they hate religion."[12]

Taiwan. The matter of the Vatican's recognition of Taiwan is an obvious diplomatic challenge and at the top of the list of issues preventing normalization of Beijing-Vatican relations. The Vatican is the last sovereignty in Europe to recognize Taipei and not Beijing as the seat of China's government, and Taiwan's Catholic hierarchy has understandably been devotedly pro-Rome on every issue. Many in the Roman hierarchy would be very reluctant to "dump" Taiwan after so many years of diligent loyalty to the Holy See.

Chinese Catholics, as well as Protestant Christians, would be intensely opposed to any initiative by the regime in Beijing to resolve the Taiwan situation through force. Aside from the obvious loss of life this would lead to on both sides of the Taiwan Straits, a violent political action by China against one of its own provinces in the East China Sea would destabilize the whole security system in Asia. It would possibly provoke massive rearmament by Japan (including the development by Japan of its own nuclear weaponry) and almost certainly frighten many of the nations of Southeast Asia into a new, East Asian version of NATO predicated on the assumption that China, once it had tasted blood in Taiwan, might want to sate its hunting ambitions farther south and east.

Of course, not many of China's Catholics and Protestants are educationally equipped to make this strong strategic argument against a Chinese military assault upon Taiwan. But all of China's Christians understand that the internal social tensions arising from military action by China may lead to a crackdown on China's Christians precisely because this community, historically, has had strong ties with the outside world. In effect, most of China's Christians believe that hostilities across the Taiwan Straits would lead to renewed persecution of Christianity in China.

As many Protestant house church leaders made clear to me, they support the contention of the central government that Taiwan is part of China and not eligible for sovereign independence. But they believe that, with their own occasional contacts with Taiwanese Christian leaders over the years, they could play a role in dissolving tensions across the Straits.

Continued Harassment. In November 1989, just months after the massacre in Tiananmen, China's underground bishops convened clandestinely in Shanxi Province to organize their own bishops' conference, a rival to that of the CPA. The meeting had, of course, been observed by the PSB, who have always gone to extraordinary lengths to penetrate China's underground Catholic circles. Several arrests followed. What worried the authorities most was the timing of the underground bishops' conference. They assumed that these Catholics were not only taking up the student challenges, but were drawing inspiration from the considerable role that religion played in the civic opposition to the rule of Communism in Eastern Europe. The Berlin Wall collapsed (figuratively) in November. By the end of December, every single Communist regime in Eastern Europe (save quirky Albania and Yugoslavia) had thrown out their Communist leaders. Mark Zhou, a Chinese now studying in the U.S., recalls how in 1991 his political instructors at a Changchun university stressed how dangerous Christianity had been to Communism in Eastern Europe in 1989.

Joseph Zen, Hong Kong's current co-adjutor bishop, said that there was "continual harassment" of Catholic clergy in China. Brett M. Decker, an editorial page writer for the *Asian Wall Street Journal* and a keen observer of Catholic life in China, put it more bluntly. "At Christmas and Easter," he said over lunch in Hong Kong, "like clockwork they beat up priests and throw them in jail." In one notorious instance in April 1992, Bishop Fan Xueyan, eighty-five, of Baoding, Hebei, died in police custody the day before the end of a ten-year prison sentence. His body showed signs of torture when it was returned to his family.[13]

How much of this sort of thing was known either before it happened or shortly afterward by CPA officials like Bishop Fu Tieshan, or by Liu Bainian, secretary of the CPA and head of the Catholic Bishops' Conference in China? Liu is widely known as a Communist Party member and, according to Catholic observers in Hong Kong, "is manipulating everything." Technically, Bishop Fu is above him, but

Liu Bainian reflects Communist Party thinking and is in the chain of command leading directly back to the Communist Politburo itself.

Governance. There are also profound questions of Roman Catholic governance. Even in Communist-controlled Eastern Europe, the Communists did not totally defy the Vatican in the selection of Catholic bishops. One of the ironies of the twentieth century is that the appointment of Karol Wojtyla as archbishop of Krakow in 1962, a big step toward the papacy, was due to the Polish Communist Party vetoing other names for the job put forward by Poland's then Cardinal Wyszynski. Wyszynski, for various reasons, thought Wojtyla unsuited to the Krakow job. The Polish Communists, by contrast, assumed with historically classic misjudgment that Wojtyla would be more politically malleable than any of Wyszynski's candidates.[14]

The "Polish" solution for Catholicism in China is dear to Vatican diplomats but not to any Chinese officials. In theory it seems reasonable: the CPA, for example, would propose three candidates for a bishop's position, and the Vatican would indicate its preference. The CPA in the past has listened to practical-sounding requests from the Vatican. For example, because the CPA did not acknowledge any fealty to Rome, one great twentieth-century event passed by China completely: Vatican II. Throughout the sixties until the Cultural Revolution, and then from 1979 on, masses in China were always said in Latin. But in the 1990s, with relations between the Vatican and the CPA softening, the CPA agreed to adopt vernacular Chinese as the language of the mass.

Also in the 1990s, increasing numbers of CPA Chinese priests went to Europe and the U.S. for further studies and training, and overseas Chinese Roman Catholics were permitted to teach in China's twelve CPA-run seminaries. One of many who did so frequently was Bishop Joseph Zen from Hong Kong. Before being appointed bishop in Hong Kong, Zen taught in several CPA seminaries. He was not prepared for what he discovered. "I was really surprised when teaching to find such deep faith after so many years and to find these young priests so courageous and to learn that the government was not so worried about them." The instructional materials now used in China's

CPA seminaries, Zen said, were identical to those used in Catholic seminaries outside China.

By the beginning of 2000, a number of observers thought that the normalization of Vatican-China relations was within sight. But in January, the CPA consecrated five new bishops in Beijing without a papal mandate. CPA seminarians in the city were so upset that most of them boycotted the consecration service. The slight to Rome, however, was reciprocated—whether deliberately or not it is hard to tell—when Pope John Paul II announced the canonization of 120 Chinese Catholic martyrs, more than sixty of whom had died during the Boxer Rebellion in 1900. The date for formal announcement of the canonizations was October 1, the national day for the People's Republic of China, and thus, to the CPA, a deliberate insult. Even China's foreign ministry chimed in, saying that the canonization was "extremely hurtful to the feelings of the Chinese people and to the dignity of the Chinese nation."[15]

"The Religious Affairs Bureau is frightened that, if China gets too close to Rome, its influence will be reduced," Hong Kong-based Catholic scholar Kim-kwong Chan told me.

Squabbles in some Chinese provinces also hamper the organization of the church. For example, it is difficult to determine who should take precedence: a CPA bishop who has pledged loyalty to Rome or an underground bishop who asserts his authority based on long loyalty to the Church despite long years of persecution.

A GROWING FAITH

Despite these obstacles, there is good evidence to show that China's Catholics are not doing a bad job of reaching out in the cities to a secularized society deeply impacted by consumerism and the scramble for economic advantage. Shanghai, once the stronghold of urban Catholicism in China, still contains the best seminaries and the largest number of Catholic churches. There, I met a twenty-something Catholic Chinese woman who had entered the Church in an unusual way: through the phone book.

Elizabeth (not her real name), while attending college in Shanghai in the late 1990s, had been influenced by the Charlotte Brontë novel *Jane Eyre* as well by the life of Mother Teresa. She became interested in Christianity generally, and in the summer of 1998 began calling all of the churches she could find in the Shanghai phone book. She left messages, but not a single Protestant church replied. The only church that responded was Catholic. The friendly voice at the other end of the line invited her to attend a Catholic newcomers' class.

She began to attend regularly, despite the heat, liked what she heard, and in December 1998 was baptized in Shanghai into the Patriotic Catholic Church along with twenty others. She shared her newfound faith with her family, who didn't go along with it, but didn't object either. "I tried to share my faith with my colleagues, but they pushed me away," she explained. "So now I try to live out my faith and give a good impression of the Christian life."

According to Elizabeth, Catholic Christianity is thriving at the grass roots in Shanghai. At the baptismal service in 2001, in the same church where Elizabeth was baptized, she said, there were two hundred baptismal candidates, ten times the number at her own baptism in 1998. Elizabeth is also quite familiar with rural Catholicism in Shanxi Province, where, she says, some villages are 98 percent Catholic. "The Catholics there are allowed to open orphanages and old people's homes without getting permission," she said. "If it were Shanghai, they would have to use government names and terms."

In Hong Kong, Bishop Joseph Zen, who has not been permitted back into China since writing an article in the 1990s critical of the situation of Catholics inside China, complained to me that China's Protestants were "winning" the war for the souls of Chinese because the Protestant system of evangelizing was much less formal than Catholicism. "The Protestants are more active," he explained. "So they are conquering a good part of the world to their side. Our system is rather rigid. You have to go through a catechuminate for a year before being baptized."

Father John-Baptist has the most positive spin on things. "People trust us [the Church]," he said, "because they realize we are doing a lot of good for society. We do no harm to the Communist Party or to Chinese society. The Church is more mature than before. Secularism is a big challenge for the Church. I think in China faith is getting stronger."

Although obstacles are still major, he is surely right.

Chapter Twelve

PERSECUTION

CHINA'S LONG RECORD OF INTOLERANCE to all religious groups is part of the original Marxist-Leninist worldview that insists on dictating not just all politics, but all of society. Since the Deng Xiaoping reforms of 1978, private activities and initiatives in Chinese society are much more broadly condoned than during the time of Mao Zedong's imperial dictatorship of 1949–1976. Ordinary Chinese can travel abroad (though for some it is not so easy), start businesses, wear whatever clothes they choose, listen to a broad variety of music, and get married or divorced or have lovers without any interference by the state—most of the time. Compared with 1949–1976, China is a paradise of personal freedom.

Compared with most other major nations of the world, however, China still lags miles behind in terms of freedom of religion and freedom of expression. According to China's latest constitution, that of 1982,[1] "Citizens of the PRC enjoy freedom of religious belief. No state organ, public organization or individual may compel citizens to believe in, or not to believe in, any religion; nor may anyone discriminate against citizens who believe in, or do not believe in, any religion." The constitution goes on:

The policy of freedom of religious belief adopted by the Chinese government has the following basic contents: *Respecting and protecting freedom of religious belief.* [emphasis mine] In China, every citizen enjoys the freedom to believe in, or not to believe in, any religion. Within a religion, every Chinese citizen has the freedom to believe in any denomination or division. Each citizen has the freedom to adopt or reject a religious belief.

This means that believing in or not believing in religion is a citizen's personal affair, and no state organ, public organization or individual may put pressure on any citizen in this regard. All citizens are completely equal, are entitled to equal rights, and at the same time must perform the duties prescribed by law, whether or not they are religious believers. [2]

All very impressive. But then comes the figurative small print:

Protecting normal religious activities. [emphasis mine] All normal religious activities held at special sites for religious activities or in believers' homes according to religious custom shall be managed by religious organizations and believers, and shall be protected by the law.

No one shall interfere with them. The Regulations on the Management of Sites for Religious Activities promulgated by the Chinese government specify: The site for religious activities shall be managed by the administration organization of the site autonomously.[3]

The problem lies both in defining what "normal religious activities" are and in the content of the "Regulations on the Management of Sites for Religious Activities." "Normal religious activities" does not include Christian evangelism in the ordinary sense that religious freedom is defined in most modern societies. As for those "site" regulations, they were designed to prevent Christians, or adherents of any other faith, from moving across jurisdictional boundaries to share their faith with other Chinese.

Those Christians who are arrested and imprisoned often still face severe torture at the hands of the authorities. Until 2003, the only photographs of the Chinese prison system available in the West had been smuggled out by investigators like Harry Wu, who had simply driven up to buildings in China's *laogai* labor camp system, taken out a camera, and clicked away. But in the spring of 2003 some astonishing photographs appeared on the Internet depicting Chinese police officers torturing Chinese Christians, all with names attached.[4]

For example, one photo shows Li Jingwei, a policeman in his twenties, sitting idly in a chair, one knee crossed over the other, and smoking a cigarette, while Shi Suhuan, a Chinese Christian woman in her forties is forced to kneel painfully on bricks with her arms stretched high in the air. One of the more hideous photographs shows Cai Xiangdong, a Christian in his forties, being pinned down on the floor in a detention center in Xiayi County, Henan Province, as an older policeman called Xie pours water into his stomach through his mouth. This torture is sometimes called the "Chinese water torture." If it is carried through to the end, the victim's stomach becomes so bloated that the stomach skin becomes agonizingly sensitive to any kind of touch or blow.

I asked several Chinese now living in the U.S. how they could be sure such photographs were authentic. Why, after all, would a policeman want to be identifiable in a photograph showing him torturing a prisoner? I received from different people two answers that tend to support each other. First, "in China you can do absolutely anything for money." In other words, the policemen could be bribed into having their photos taken while "working." Second, the policemen in this case were apparently told that the photographs would show them diligently performing their duties and might lead to promotion.

PERSECUTION OF CHRISTIAN DISSIDENTS

Late in 1998, the website Hong Kong Voice of Democracy listed fifty-eight Chinese who had been arrested, usually on charges of having "organized illegal organizations," in the previous few months. Though thirty-eight of these had been released at the time of the website's last update, December 26, 1998, those still held included people like Wang Ce, chairman of the Alliance for Democratic China–Liberal Democratic Party. Wang Ce, fifty-three, is an evangelical Protestant Christian who earned a Ph.D. in politics at the University of Hawaii, then moved to Spain, which he used as a base to develop a Chinese version of Christian democracy. He entered China through Macau in 1998. In 1999 he was arrested and sentenced to three years, and was referred to in the Chinese press as "a convicted spy." Wang Ce was eventually released in January 2002 for good behavior in prison. He returned to Spain and involved himself primarily in business activities.

Wang Xizhe is another heroic political dissident, whose political protest goes back to 1974 (before dissidents like Wei Jingsheng had even been heard of). Wang, sixty-one, was the author of a startling "big character poster" that appeared suddenly in the city of Guangzhou in 1974, criticizing Mao and his leftist acolytes in the Communist Party for having betrayed the ideals of the Cultural Revolution. In effect, Wang attacked the Maoists from the left. During the Democracy Wall movement in Beijing in 1978–1979 he continued to be active, this time supporting criticism of Communist Party rule that came from critics on the right. He spent a total of seventeen years in Chinese prisons. He managed to escape to Hong Kong late in 1996, barely half a year before the British territory reverted to Chinese sovereignty, and eventually acquired political asylum in the U.S. Wang, now cochair of the U.S.-based China Democracy Party, vigorously protests the arrest of other political dissidents in China.

In August 2000 Wang Xizhe was baptized a Christian while attending an Oakland, California, seminar on Christianity and politics in China. The baptizing clergyman was Dr. Jonathan Chao, founder of the China Graduate School of Theology in Taiwan, and for many years one of the most respected and best-informed observers of China's Christian scene.

China arrested and sentenced many of these prominent political dissidents because of their political activism, not their Christian faith. Many of them did not acquire their Christian faith until after their incarceration or exile. Since becoming Christians, these Chinese political dissidents have continued to carry on their activism to democratize China and to improve the conditions of its people.

WANG BINGZHANG

I had first met him in the early 1980s, soon after he arrived from China, where he had been trained as a medical doctor. He moved to New York City via Canada in 1980, and became very active in China's fledgling democratic movement. It was pre-Tiananmen, and most Americans seemed pleased that China was beginning to open up and somehow concluded that real democracy might not be far away.

Wang Bingzhang (now fifty-six), quietly, with an earnest dignity, begged to differ. In New York in 1982 he started a quarterly pro-democratic magazine called *China Spring* along with a new movement of Chinese living outside China, the Free China Movement. He relentlessly criticized the human rights violations and undemocratic actions by the Chinese government. I liked him and admired his courage in pursuing a one-man challenge against a totalitarian system in the world's most populous nation.

I next met him at a conference of Chinese Christian intellectuals on the eastern shore of Maryland at the beginning 2002. Bob Fu, a doctoral candidate at Westminster Theological Seminary who had been a house church leader in China, had gathered a group of Chinese and a handful of Americans to hear about his launch of a new non-profit organization God Bless China Inc., dedicated to promoting democratic values and religious freedom in China. Wang was his usual modest self, and seemed to remember me. He was still active in democratic work outside China, he told me, but he approached it now from a slightly different perspective; he had become a committed Christian.

I was traveling extensively in China during the summer of 2002 and so missed a sinister event that was widely reported in the U.S. and Taiwan. Wang Bingzhang had been visiting Hanoi, Vietnam, with two other dissidents in late June 2002. It isn't clear what he was doing there. It is quite possible he was meeting Chinese dissidents from the People's Republic who had slipped across into Vietnam, perhaps to discuss a political party he had tried to form inside China, the China Democratic Party. More than six months later, Wang's travel companions to Vietnam, Yue Wu and Zhang Qi, were able to reveal what happened on June 26, 2002, barely a week before his scheduled return to the U.S. According to them, the three were having lunch in their hotel (not far from Vietnam's border with China) when ten Chinese-speaking men dressed in Vietnamese police uniforms showed up and ordered them into a car for a drive to a waterfront location on the Sino-Vietnamese border. Wang resisted and was beaten before being shoved into a waiting car. The three were then transferred to a boat and transported to China. The men who had kidnapped them demanded a ransom of $10 million and stole their passports and money. They were then left tied up at a Buddhist temple in Fangchenggan, a city in Guangxi Province in China's southwest. There the Chinese police, conveniently, found them.

For a while, the three were held in detention and under investigation in Guangdong Province. Late in 2002, Yue Wu and Zhang Qi were released. Yue Wu left China, went to Paris, and raised the alarm about Wang. Wang was charged in the city of Shenzhen with the very serious crime of pro-Taiwan espionage and advocating terrorism. He was sentenced in December to life in prison. Two months later, his appeal was denied. Wang had been in trouble in China before. In 1998 he had been deported for attempting to make contacts for his democratic movement inside China. Wang had also once, perhaps imprudently, indicated that he thought that the Communists might someday be driven from power by force.

The Chinese authority's version of events reads like poorly composed fiction. A spokesman for China's national counterespionage agency, the Ministry of State Security, gave the following account of

Wang's arrest and kidnap in *China Daily*, often the conduit for government-originated stories: Wang and his friends had been kidnapped in Vietnam by a gang that transported them to China, then left them tied up in the Bohu Temple in Yunnan when they failed to provide the ransom money. The heroic local police had rescued them, but it turned out (rather conveniently) that Wang was wanted by the police of neighboring Guangdong province.

Like the charges against Wang, the kidnapping story is very questionable: If the purported kidnappers were so clever that they could acquire Vietnamese police uniforms, why would they pick an almost penniless Chinese dissident to hand over $10 million? Wang ran a huge risk in entering China and making contact with sympathizers from opposition groups so close to China's border. But the notion that he was engaged in "terrorist" activities is simply not believable. As he was being led away after his "trial" in Shenzhen in early March 2003, Wang, who had not been permitted to say anything during the proceedings, shouted at a handful of sympathizers in the court, "I've been kidnapped. This is political sabotage."

HAN DONGFANG

One of the most impressive of all Chinese political dissidents to have attempted to reenter China and been thrown out is Han Dongfang, forty, the only Beijing worker at the time of the 1989 Tiananmen democracy protests to have become well known to foreigners covering the event. Filled with patriotic idealism, Han at seventeen had joined the People's Armed Police, a law-enforcement division of the People's Liberation Army. Though his leadership talents quickly drew the attention of his superiors, he became revolted by the opulent lifestyle of the officers—meat and alcohol at dinnertime in contrast with the coarse *watou* dumplings served to the enlisted men. An argument with his superior officer led to the tearing up of his Communist Party application. Han left the PAP and for three years worked first as a librarian in Beijing Teacher's University, then as a refrigerator car worker for the railroad. He traveled all over China, learning much about how ordinary people lived across the country.

When students started demonstrating in Beijing in 1989, Han found himself swept up in the movement. He was not especially interested in the somewhat pampered students, but he wanted to improve the lives of workers. Han became spokesman for the short-lived Beijing Workers' Autonomous Federation, a makeshift umbrella group that had attracted twenty thousand workers in a matter of days. He was so tired in the last few days of the protests that when soldiers began moving onto Tiananmen Square early on June 4, he had to be practically pulled out of a tent for his own safety. "Han Dongfang, you are not the same as other people," some of his coworkers in the square said to him. "In the future our country will need such a leader as you, we need a Chinese [Lech] Walesa. Other people can die, we can all die, but you must not die."

Han didn't come close to dying in the square, but after he voluntarily surrendered himself two weeks later, he was, after interrogation, deliberately placed in a cell containing twenty inmates infected with either tuberculosis or hepatitis. He became infected with TB. His health deteriorated so severely that the authorities finally decided in 1992 to release him so he could die at home and not on their watch. International human rights physicians intervened and Han was flown to the U.S. where he eventually had to have one of his damaged lungs surgically removed.

While recuperating in New Jersey in 1993, Han became a Christian, was baptized, and almost immediately tried to get back into China. He hadn't broken any law, he insisted; he was Chinese, he told everyone, so he had a right to live in his native country. But the authorities didn't see it this way, arrested him in a hotel in Guangzhou, drove him to the Hong Kong–China border (Hong Kong was then still British), and literally pushed him out of China. Since 1997 Han has been making regular broadcasts into China about labor conditions in the mainland via Radio Free Asia. He often asks anonymous callers from China if he can tape their calls and play them back in his broadcasts.

He is not an admirer of the Communist regime in China, but he doesn't hate it or call for its overthrow. "Now I see that to make people more angry, to make them hate more is not a way to solve problems," he says. "This is Mao's idea. We should change ideas." He adds, "I believe that the power of God comes from forgiveness and love. I feel a real release from hatred. In religion, God works a miracle in each person. I have found the reason for my life from my faith." Perhaps because he tells everyone that he is trying to improve conditions of workers in China, not overthrow the regime, Han has received informal word back from the authorities in China that he will be permitted to reenter the country in the event of a family bereavement or other personal emergency.

PERSECUTION OF "CULTS"

China's suppression of Protestant and Catholic Christian activity was so egregious throughout the 1990s that despite an overall improvement in U.S.–China relations and China's declared intent to join the World Trade Organization, the U.S. Congress in 1998 passed the International Religious Freedom Act in part to help cope with problems of religious freedom in China and other countries. The act required the State Department to monitor religious freedom worldwide through the office of an appointed ambassador for International Religious Freedom (currently John V. Hanford III) and to issue an annual report. Despite a lot of grumbling from some parts of the State Department, embassy staff around the world generally complied, equipping the U.S. government with what is probably the most comprehensive annual survey of religious freedom throughout the world.

FALUNGONG

The year after the signing of the International Religious Freedom Act by President Clinton, the State Department found itself monitoring one of the most vicious crackdowns on a religious group in China since the 1970s. The group was not technically a religion, since it had no places of worship and no formal creed. Falungong, also known as Falundafa, did demonstrate some attributes of a religion, or at least a sect or cult, from the moment it burst upon the awareness of the world in April 1999. Some ten thousand Falungong followers, or "practitioners," staged an unannounced demonstration outside the Chinese Communist Party headquarters in Zhongnanhai, Beijing.

Falungong is a meditation system that combines breathing and mental visualization exercises to enhance personal health and power. Its original appeal was to intellectuals and to ordinary, often middle-aged Chinese who saw it as a means of acquiring better health. Falungong belongs closer to China's traditional *qigong* (pronounced "chee-goong") exercises than any form of religion. *Qigong* is an ancient and culturally indigenous meditation system rooted in the philosophy and religion of Daoism. It was savagely repressed in China during the 1950s and 1960s as "superstition." In the more relaxed cultural setting of China in the 1980s, *qigong* went through something of a revival in China, particularly among China's aging Communist elite, who, it was rumored, were kept alive longer than expected by *qigong* masters. China's military was also interested in *qigong* because of its connection with the martial arts.

Falungong, which suddenly became very popular in China in the early 1990s, is different from traditional Chinese *qigong,* not only in its peculiar blending of Buddhist and Daoist doctrines, but also in the divine role accorded its founder, Li Hongzhi. Li Hongzhi was born in Jilin Province in north China in either 1951 or 1952, became interested in *qigong* in 1988, and founded Falungong in 1992. As the leader of the Falungong, Li claims that no one knows who he really is, that he has borne the sins committed by mankind over hundreds of thousands of years, that he can see through buildings, make himself invisible, and levitate, and is a few cuts above both Mohammed and Jesus. Because of pressure from the authorities, he emigrated to the U.S. in the 1990s.

Chinese history has been pockmarked by violent political changes. These were often provoked and sometimes led by leaders of heterodox religious movements. Well before the Communists, the Chinese coined a special term for these religious groups: *xie jiao* (literally, "evil religion"), which embraces both the pejorative word "cult" and an approximation to "anti-government" or "mutinous."

When Falungong practitioners courageously, but perhaps rashly, confronted the Chinese government head-on with demonstrations in Tiananmen Square and other public places, China's Public Security Bureau cracked down on them with a harshness not seen since the suppression of democracy activists in June 1989. Falungong followers were jailed, beaten, brainwashed, tortured, and on many occasions killed in detention. The 2002 State Department religious freedom report asserted that "several hundred" Falungong practitioners had died while in detention since 1999.

The vast majority of Chinese do agree that Falungong is indeed a *xie jiao*. This view was reinforced by the alleged self-immolation of a Falungong follower on Tiananmen Square in 2000 and by a story widely reported in the Chinese press that Falungong activists had at times murdered people to ensure that, after death, everyone would go to the right place. Falungong representatives in the U.S. have strongly denied that Falungong practitioners deliberately kill themselves or others.

OTHER "CULTS"

Christians, who have no sympathy for Falungong as a doctrine or a movement, were nonetheless aghast at the violence meted out upon its peaceful practitioners. Christians have long suffered persecution by the Chinese government. As Beijing became determined to stamp out cults such as the Falungong, several Christian groups found themselves labeled as an "evil religion" by the government.

In the 1990s, the "Shouters" group, also known as the Local Church, was harshly and vigorously suppressed. The Local Church (or Little Flock) emerged from the teaching and ministry of Watchman Nee (1903–19720), Ni Tuosheng in Chinese, certainly the most influential Chinese Christian teacher of the twentieth century. Watchman Nee's books sold in the millions in the West, particularly in the U.S., from the 1970s on, and they continue to be widely read, mostly by evangelical Protestants. Nee, greatly influenced by the British Protestant group the Brethren, wanted to form a church that was completely independent, and in his view, completely biblical in its worship and practices. As a result, the Little Flock from the outset tended to keep apart from other Christian groups.

Witness Lee (1905–1997), Li Changshou in Chinese, unrelated to Watchman Nee, became closely associated with the Little Flock's work and leadership in the 1930s. In 1955, Watchman Nee was arrested in China, and remained in prison until his death in 1972. Witness Lee departed for Taiwan in 1949 and skillfully nurtured the Little Flock there until it became a large and prosperous Christian group. In 1962 he moved to California, and continued to develop the Little Flock until it was a worldwide movement with members estimated today at 250,000.

China's authorities also threw the epithet of "cult" at Xu Yongze's Born-Again Movement (also known as the Full Scope Church or "Weepers") when he was arrested in 1997. Officials of the Three Self often repeated this charge to justify the widely criticized crackdown on the Born-Again Movement.

In 1999, the standing committee of the National People's Congress, prompted by the Falungong challenge, enacted a harsh new law giving security authorities almost unlimited powers to suppress cults. In May 2000, a secret document distributed in Beijing by the General Office of the Ministry of Public Security to all public security offices at the provincial level officially listed seven groups as "cults." In 2001, the Public Security Bureau issued a detailed listing of Christian and other groups in China that were to be treated as "cults" and suppressed. Some of them might be listed in any standard American "cult" list: for example, the Immortal Real Buddha Sect and the Children of God, originally founded by Moses Berg in the U.S. in 1968. But the list also included the Local Church and the Born-Again Movement. These government documents were smuggled out of China and published in both Chinese and English in 2002 with a foreword signed by leaders of four evangelical Christian groups and by the probable source of the documents, Li Shixiong; Li has political asylum in the U.S. and is president of the New York-based Committee for Investigation on Persecution of Religion in China, Inc.[5]

One Christian group that was treated very harshly in 2001 and received extensive reporting and commentary in the 2002 State Department report on International Religious Freedom was the Church of South China, an offshoot of the Born-Again Movement that had spread very rapidly in Hubei Province in central China. Police raids during May through August of 2001, led to the arrest, beating, and torture of several members. In a raid in August 2001 the leader of the Church of South China, Gong Shengliang, was captured, beaten, tortured, and eventually put on trial and sentenced to death, along with two other members. One woman, Gu Xuegui, was tortured to death in prison in September 2001. Several other women were tortured in prison with an infamous Chinese invention called *dian bang*, ("electric stick"). *Dian bang* has been used extensively against every conceivable variety of political and religious dissenter in China, including Tibetan monks. Looking like a rather short nightstick, the *dian bang* can deliver an electric shock of very high voltage, enough to cause extreme pain and skin blistering. After meeting clandestinely in central China with members of the Church of South China who had been arrested, beaten, and tortured, *New York Times* reporter Nicholas Kristof narrated how "interrogators stomped on the fingers of male prisoners and stripped young women naked and abused them." The abuse, according to the women who survived to tell their story, included applying the *dian bang* to their breasts and lower sexual organs.

Originally, five of the church leaders were sentenced to death, but the world outcry was so great that the three death sentences handed down to Gong Shengliang and others were commuted to life in prison. Gong's life, however, is hardly safe. A report from Hubei Province in May 2003 indicated that he continues to be repeatedly beaten, has lost hearing in one ear, has blood in his stool and urine, and suffered from frequent fainting spells.

A Genuine Cult

Since the mid-1990s, more and more Protestant evangelical house churches have been targeted by one of the strangest quasi-Christian cults—in China or anywhere—since Hong Xiuquan decided in the mid-nineteenth century that he was the younger brother of Jesus and started the Taiping Rebellion. The cult is called "Lightning from the East" or, more plainly, "Eastern Lightning" and appears to have started in 1989 or 1990 in Henan Province, where probably the fastest Christian growth in China had occurred. The name "Eastern Lightning" comes from a well-known Bible verse (Matthew 24:27) referring to the Second Coming of Christ: "For as lightning that comes from the east is visible even in the west, so will be the coming of the Son of Man."

Adherents of Eastern Lightning believe that God has revealed himself in three separate dispensations: the Era of the Law (Jehovah in the Old Testament), the Era of Grace (Jesus in the New Testament), and the Era of the Kingdom (the female Messiah). The basic belief is that neither God nor Jesus quite finished the job they were trying to do. God's management of things, according to EL, is developing all the time. The latest development is the incarnation of Jesus, as a woman named Deng, now believed to be in her thirties, in Henan Province, China.

The Asian edition of *Time* magazine ran an informative story on Eastern Lightning in November 2001 with the witty headline: "Jesus is Back, and She's Chinese."[6] There are no known photographs of Deng, and EL followers are ambiguous about whether she is still alive. Jesus, the EL cult declares, managed to bear people's sins, but now the new incarnation will sweep away all human corruption. Furthermore, in an apocalyptic twist, EL argues that China (a.k.a. the "dragon" in the Bible's Book of Revelation) is collapsing from within, part of an overall judgment by the female Christ on the world.

Under ordinary circumstances, the EL and its lunatic theology might be discarded with Elvis sightings or headlines for a supermarket tabloid. But far from being an eccentric but harmless offshoot of Christianity, EL has ravaged China's house churches and attempted to ravage underground Catholic churches, Patriotic Catholic churches, and even Three Self churches through a brutal campaign of kidnapping, beatings, blackmail, and, according to some Protestant house church leaders, even murder. Every single Christian group I met with in China, whether official or underground, had horror stories of what EL has been doing. I debriefed several victims of the kidnappings, including thirty-four leaders of the Tanghe who had been kidnapped in one swoop in April 2002 and held for up to two months in six different EL safe houses.

Xing Liaoyuan, right hand to Feng Jianguo of the Tanghe network, described in detail what happened to him and the thirty-three other leaders when they were abducted. The whole operation had been cleverly planned for more than a year. EL had sent to the Tanghe leadership a man posing as a Singapore Chinese from the well-known, internationally respected evangelical training group called the Haggai Institute, based in Singapore. (Haggai has emphatically denied any connection with Eastern Lightning.) This Edward Yu said that Haggai would like to conduct special Gospel training sessions for all of Tanghe's top leadership, starting April 23, 2002. For security reasons, Yu said, the thirty-four leaders would have to split up into six groups and meet with the trainers in six different locations in China, from Heilongjiang in the north to Henan in central China.

Xing was taken with five others to a small township called Renqiu, in Hebei Province. Cell phones were removed ("for security reasons," the EL kidnappers said) and on their arrival in a third-floor apartment, their shoes were also locked in a closet. Then some sort of drug was put in their drinking water. "At night I didn't sleep," said Xing. "It made me confused. Then I had terrible stomach pains."

The six Tanghe leaders in Xing's group were told that they would have a chance to share their own (orthodox) Christian teachings with some others in the same apartment area. But in Xing's case, after the drugged water didn't produce sympathy for the teachings of EL, they assigned an attractive woman to seduce him. "They sent a girl to my room to tell me how bad her marriage was," he said. Xing said he might have fought his way out, but two women in his group were being held, and there were four EL men guarding the apartment.

Ni Faxing, a Shandong evangelist who came to Beijing, told me a similar story involving water-drugging and attempted seduction. Ni was kidnapped early in 2002. Some newcomers to his Beijing house church group told him that a group of Christians in Hebei Province wanted him to come and teach. He took them at their word, caught a train to Baoding, in Hebei, and soon found himself held prisoner in a second-story apartment.

For five days nothing happened, so Ni agreed to go with the group to a house on the outskirts of Baoding. He was even allowed to call his wife twice. After a few days, Ni also got the seduction treatment. "If you were single," a woman cooed to him, "you would be an ideal husband for me. Divorce your wife. I want to marry you." Though neither Xing nor Ni succumbed to the seduction treatment, I heard tales of some men who were so weakened by sleep deprivation that they were unable to push the women away from their beds. The EL kidnappers would then take photographs of the church leaders in compromising positions and threaten to show them to their congregations.

In Ni's case, the deception was complex and seemed to involve the participation of the local police, presumably after bribery. Men who were dressed as police came to the house, said the city was on the lookout for Falungong followers, and demanded a fine in lieu of arresting Ni. Ni eventually made his escape by claiming that his next-door neighbor back in Beijing was a high party official who would treat the group with extreme severity if he were not allowed to leave immediately. He had been kidnapped for fifty-nine days. Ni was lucky not to be beaten up, probably because he was physically powerful and told his captors that he was excellent in the martial arts. I heard stories of several women beaten so badly by EL kidnappers that they were crippled for life. Ni told me that the young son of a Christian leader who had denounced EL had been murdered a few days later.

In the case of Xing and the other Tanghe leaders, two of the kidnapped women managed to escape after three days and raised the alarm with the remaining leadership back in Henan. At this point a very intelligent woman leader of Tanghe took a bold initiative. Luo Ying, in her thirties, who had, like most of the Tanghe and Fangcheng leadership, been arrested several times and served time in the *laogai*, took a train to Beijing and went straight to the headquarters of the Public Security Bureau in Beijing. She said that she knew she couldn't trust the provincial PSB in Henan because they had been harsh on Christians and might well be bribed by EL.

On April 26, 2002, Luo Ying introduced herself to an officer in the PSB headquarters in Beijing. But he already knew who she was, producing a thick dossier with details of her arrest in Henan in 1996. The PSB told Luo Ying, interestingly, that they knew that the Tanghe fellowship was not a "cult," though the PSB nationally had once labeled it as such, and that EL had now become a serious national menace. They said they would be more than happy to cooperate with house church leaders in suppressing EL, and would agree not to investigate or try to stop Tanghe's own evangelistic efforts in the process. The PSB even praised Luo Ying for doing something that no other house church leader had done, approaching them at a national level in order to cooperate in suppressing a real crime. Within a few days the PSB had secured the release of all the kidnapped Tanghe leaders and had made a few arrests. But it seems that the EL's ultra-secrecy and destruction of evidence was so thorough that it was extremely difficult to prove any particular EL member's involvement in the kidnapping.

Eastern Lightning has thrived in China at least in part because of the beneficence of the U.S. government. Some time in the 1990s the man regarded as the founder of Eastern Lightning came to the U.S. with a false passport and applied for political asylum. He claimed that his religious faith was "Christian" and that he had been persecuted for his faith while living in China. Several Christians in China say that EL's founder, and presumed leader today, Zhao Weishan, originally belonged to the Shouters but left to form his own group, which later became Eastern Lightning. I have not been able to determine whether there was a direct connection between Witness Li's followers in China and the emergence of EL. Zhao Weishan is a man in his fifties who appears to be residing in the New York area. It would be surprising if he was unaware of the kidnappings being conducted in China by EL members. Some Chinese Christians in the U.S. have tried to initiate legal proceedings to investigate Zhao, so that he could be deported if he is found to be complicit in the kidnappings. EL has even attempted to infiltrate Chinese evangelical Christian churches in the U.S. Members of Chinese Protestant churches in the San Francisco Bay Area have found EL leaflets on the windows of their cars in church parking lots.

A handbook for EL activists that was obtained in China has a chapter on "spying," presumably, on target Christian churches. "Don't put other people off," the handbook says. "Be a normal person and leave a good impression. Be well mannered, dress neatly and normally." Interestingly, the handbook instructs EL followers not to spy on the Three Self, Catholics, Eastern Orthodox, Daoists, Muslims, or Buddhists, but on "those who believe in Jesus, pray to Jesus, and thirst after God's revelation."[7]

These instructions notwithstanding, EL has in fact targeted both Three Self churches and Patriotic Catholic churches. Catholic bishop Li Du'an of Xian complained to me that EL had been trying to lure away from the Catholic Church Catholic laity and priests in his own diocese. One report from overseas Christians keeping in touch with Protestants in China said that 80 percent of a group of house churches in Inner Mongolia had been taken over by EL. Several house church leaders have "fallen"—sexually compromised, bribed, or frightened by EL threats—into joining the group. All of the house church networks I am familiar with agreed to work closely together to educate their congregations about both the falseness of EL doctrines and the dangers of its practices.

Perhaps the most promising sign of change at the official level in China is the slow-dawning understanding by the Public Security Bureau in Beijing that there is a big difference between a religious group, Christian or otherwise, that believes in strange, even "superstitious" things but is otherwise law-abiding and patriotic, and a band of thugs seeking to enlarge their national and international influence through lying, kidnapping, blackmail, torture, and possibly murder.

Unfortunately, as in so many facets of change involving the Chinese regime, no one should hold his breath while waiting for this to take place.

Chapter Thirteen

ARTISTS, WRITERS, AND ACADEMICS

PUSHING THE CULTURAL AND LEGAL ENVELOPE was strong in China during the late 1980s in much of journalism, especially on TV. In the spring of 1988 Beijing's Central Television aired a daring, six-part documentary, *River Elegy*, produced by Yuan Zhiming, a prominent documentary producer. The theme of the series was that popular symbols of China's historic greatness, such as the Great Wall and the Yangtse River, should be regarded as emblems of captivity and restriction. *River Elegy* argued that they had hindered China from access to the great progress and discoveries taking place in other parts of the world, especially in the West. The final episode of the series, "Ocean Blue," shows the Yellow River emptying itself into the Pacific as an emblem of China engaging with the outside world openly and confidently. "The dream of *River Elegy*," Yuan wrote later, "was born out of concern and hope for China."[1]

That sentiment wasn't shared by many of the old reactionaries still powerful in the Communist Party and the People's Liberation Army. While students, intellectuals, and many others hailed *River Elegy* for pointing to the new, more open, pro-Western direction China should be taking, old-guard revolutionaries were outraged, accusing Yuan of "vilifying the Chinese people and the symbols of the Yellow River and the Great Wall."[2] When the authorities after the Tiananmen massacre began looking around for people to blame, Yuan Zhiming was an obvious target. But he succeed in eluding a national search, escaping finally to the U.S. At Princeton University, to which many reform-minded Chinese intellectuals flocked, he encountered a group of committed Chinese Christians who were pro-democratic, but who did not believe that democracy, in and of itself, would solve all of China's problems.

Neither Yuan nor his collaborators on *River Elegy* had ever been to the West before fleeing China. On his arrival in 1989, Yuan was shocked and disillusioned; he heard about crime, suicide, homelessness, declining moral standards, and family breakdown. Yuan began to read the Bible, became friends with many Chinese Christians, and was baptized in August 1990. He then decided to deepen his knowledge of his new faith by attending the Reformed Theological Seminary in Jackson, Mississippi, where he studied Christianity in greater detail during the 1990s.

Yuan never doubted that China, for its own basic health, must sooner or later become democratic. But, based partly on what he saw in the U.S., Yuan also came to believe that a successful democracy in any country had to be constructed on more than tried and true institutions. "If a person lacks a firm and overcoming faith," he wrote later, "he or she is easily tossed around on the sea of life. No democracy can be built on this." He admitted, however, that many of his fellow dissidents, including those who had worked with him on *River Elegy*, didn't share this perspective. He wrote,

> Democracy is not merely an institution nor simply a concept, but a profound structure of faith. At times I have called this to the attention of my friends in the democracy movement who have been in America for quite some time, but continue to lack a deep understanding of democracy. I told them that just because they have read Montesquieu and Locke and have seen an American presidential election,

it does not mean that they have found the fountain of democracy. The root of democracy is the spirit of Christ.[3]

In retrospect, as Yuan told British journalist Ian Buruma, he thought that *River Elegy* was superficial because it left out "the most important thing, the core of Western civilization, which is Christianity. Without that, you cannot have democracy or human rights."[4]

While many Chinese dissidents would disagree, the idea became more and more powerful in Yuan Zhiming's mind. He set out to produce a new TV documentary, in many ways even more ambitious than *River Elegy*. This was a multi-part series that aired for the first time in Taiwan in 2000 and was spread throughout China and Southeast Asia as a VCD. The English title, *China's Confession,* doesn't do justice to the Chinese name *shen zhou*, which is an ancient name for China, approximately "Land of God." Yuan—whose seminary research focused on connections between the *dao* of Chinese philosopher Lao Zi's book, the *dao de jing,* and the biblical sense of God, the Holy Spirit, or Christ—interprets the whole of Chinese history as a tragic letdown from a previous era when, he says, the Chinese worshipped God (*shangdi* in Chinese) and sought to live moral lives. The narrative of *China's Confession* tells us:

> This was the ancient land of God where people believed in God, feared heaven, obeyed the Tao (i.e., the *dao* of Daoism), and worshipped God.... Our ancestors held firm their belief, which is: the justice of God will prevail, nothing could escape the sight of God, and sinners will receive their punishment. This belief is the moral power of promoting the good and discarding the wrong. It is the moral cornerstone of an ideal universal society. It is the dream of Confucius.[5]

According to Yuan's view of Chinese history, the real downturn in the behavior of Chinese toward one another occurred about 2,500 years ago, when China was plunged into a turbulent era of internal regional warfare called the "Spring and Autumn" period (770–476 B.C.).

Leaving aside the historical validity of Yuan's argument that the Chinese worshiped God at the origins of their civilization and lived in an upright moral universe, *China's Confession* attempts to account for the fact that despite China's cultural early greatness, God's revelation of Himself as recorded in the Bible took place in the Middle East, not in China. Like many Chinese intellectuals, Yuan sought a moral historiography of China that suggested God hadn't simply bypassed Chinese civilization. According to Yuan, God did actually set the moral foundation in China for what could have been a righteous and benevolent civilization.

Well financed by overseas Chinese Christian backers, Yuan used dramatic excerpts from several Chinese historical dramas about ancient China to illustrate his point. He flew in one of Beijing's top TV documentary narrators for several days to help out. Toward the end of the documentary, there is news footage of Mao at different stages of the revolution, including the fanatical Red Guard idolatry of him in 1966. Aired on TV across Southeast Asia as well as Taiwan, *China's Confession* is unlikely to be released legally in China in the near future. But *China's Confession* has been shown secretly to Christian groups all over China. Those Chinese Christians I spoke to were full of praise for what Yuan was trying to do. They said they knew a number of people who had become Christian after watching the documentary. Yuan is also an accomplished preacher; tapes of his sermons are in wide circulation across China and are listened to enthusiastically.

Yuan's objective is very ambitious. "Our goal," he explained in his modest home in Petaluma, California, "is to change the perception of China by the Chinese. If you go to any city and ask the average person, 99 percent of the people don't understand Christianity. They don't even know what the question is. Some people in China don't even know that there are Christians in China."

To counter this lacuna in basic knowledge, Yuan in 2001 embarked on an even more ambitious documentary, a multi-part series on Christianity in China. Making many trips in and out of China that year, Yuan took his film crew to Christian communities the length and breadth of China. At one point, early in 2002, they filmed a Christian rock concert in the city of Daqing, close to the Russian border. Having a total of some four hundred hours of interview and narrative film, Yuan is calling his latest project *The Cross*. It seeks to explain to ordinary Chinese what major contributions Christians have made to Chinese life in the past century and more. He says, "We want to let government leaders see the movie. The most important thing is to make people realize that Christianity is related to Chinese culture. It is not a Western religion. The main purpose is to tell the Chinese people that the God of the Bible is the God of the Chinese people."[6] Yuan would like to have the English-language version of *The Cross* shown on American TV.

CULTURAL CHRISTIANS

A significant group of Chinese scholars have taken up a different, though perhaps parallel, approach to "reintroduce" Christianity into China. Many often refer to them as "cultural Christians."

The term was coined a few years ago, and some say that Bishop Ding himself laid claim to having invented it. But the man with whom the term most fits is a linguistically gifted scholar with formidable knowledge called Liu Xiaofeng. Born in Sichuan in 1955, Liu belongs to the Cultural Revolution generation. On finishing middle school at eighteen, Liu, like everyone else, was assigned to labor in the countryside. After the Gang of Four was overthrown, Liu was admitted to Sichuan College of Foreign Languages in 1978. There he learned French and German, which formed the basis of his remarkable career as a scholar, writer, and champion translator.

After completing his B.A. in Sichuan, Liu was admitted to the *sanctum sanctorum* of China's humanities institutions, Peking University, in 1982. He acquired an M.A. in aesthetics in 1984, taught at the newly formed Shenzhen University on the Hong Kong border for a few years, and was then given a fellowship to study theology in Basel, Switzerland. There he developed a profound interest in twentieth-century Christian theology and came to his own, personal Christian faith.

Liu transferred to Hong Kong in 1993 to head up the Institute for Sino-Christian Studies at Tao Fong Shan in Hong Kong. There he began what may turn out to be the most ambitious translation project attempted in China since the scholar Yen Fu rendered Social Darwinists, Nietzsche, and others into Chinese nine decades ago. Yuan's goal is to expose Chinese intellectuals to the broadest range possible of historical and contemporary Christian theology.

Starting with his initial interest in aesthetics in the 1980s, Liu wrote several books that became widely and enthusiastically read all over China by young people asking ultimate questions about themselves, about China, and about such weighty topics as God and history. Works such as *Romanticism, Philosophy and Poetry, Salvation and Freedom,* and *Toward the Truth of the Cross: Introduction to Twentieth-Century Christian Theology* explored recent Western Christian thought, taking into account China's historical and contemporary cultural history. As a Singapore Chinese scholar put it, "The starting point for the entire thought structure of Liu Xiaofeng is the question of modernity for China," a question first puzzled over by the New Culture scholars eighty years earlier. He added,

> Liu Xiaofeng has a gigantic ambition with his theory: To promote the expansion of Christian scholarship in China's university system; and at the same time, present his intellectual views through book series and periodicals in order to build a foundation for Christian scholarship in the midst of tension and competition in Chinese intellectual cultural space, so that the values system of the "sacred" may have its own cultural capital.[7]

Some Christian scholars outside of China object to the term "cultural Christian," because it does not make clear whether such a person was a Christian believer. Professor Edwin Hui, of Regent College in British Columbia, Canada, preferred the more accurate, but somewhat cumbersome term, "mainland Chinese studying Christianity" (MCSC). Liu himself seems satisfied with "cultural Christian," whom he described as someone who had "faith in Jesus Christ" but was not baptized or a member of any identifiable church.[8] The need not to be identified with any church or denomination is characteristic of Liu, who dislikes being categorized as "mainstream Protestant," "evangelical," or any other heavily freighted name.

Liu's writings have had a major impact in China not only on those Chinese who think of themselves as Christian, but on those who are interested in broad analysis of China in the context of the world's current cultural and philosophical era. "His books affected me deeply," said Mark Zhou, a Chinese who became a Christian believer in China but who has for many years studied in the U.S. "When I read *Toward the Truth of the Cross,* I found myself crying. It is very moving."

In Beijing, a young writer called Yu Jie, who received his M.A. in literature from Peking University in 2000, calls himself a "cultural Christian" because he is not yet a believer though he does attend some church activities. "I have some friends around me who are writers, artists, musicians, professionals," says Yu Jie. "Some are baptized as Christians, and some are not. Christians are fewer among writers than nonbelievers, but the trend is toward Christianity." Yu Jie, who has written about the Russian writers Solzhenitsyn and Dostoevsky, shares Liu Xiaofeng's view that Chinese culture is lacking the spiritual dimension of literature evident among the Russians. He explained, "I think the Russian intellectuals contributed more to the world and their own country than Chinese intellectuals did to theirs. The contribution of Russian intellectuals is a treasure to the world. They are appreciated by Western countries. But there are no such people in China."

Liu Xiaofeng's larger point is that throughout history the Chinese have lacked any kind of transcendent religious character at their root. Foreign scholars of Chinese culture who note an absence of the philosophical or metaphysical speculation central to European history have also voiced this view. Liu wrote, "The historical rationalist core of Chinese culture has lacked the religious temperament of love and fear." China, he believes, has lacked the moral sense of the tragic that helped give birth to the richness of Russian literature, especially in the nineteenth century. If the May Fourth generation had absorbed that deeper, moral component of Russian wisdom alongside the mechanistic revolutionary science of Lenin, Liu believes, China might have steered away from the most devastating of Mao's experimentation of the 1950s and 1960s.

ACADEMICS

Liu, of course, doesn't speak of politics. He played no role in the student democratic protests at Peking University and thus escaped the crackdown that followed Tiananmen. But his pioneering writing and thinking appear to have provided a politically acceptable umbrella for the study of Christianity across the whole of China. From modest beginnings at Peking University in the early 1980s, institutes for the study of Christianity, or similarly named academic entities, have appeared in more than twenty Chinese campuses. None of these is permitted to "teach" Christianity—in that sense it is not unlike a contemporary U.S. college campus—but scholars who openly profess their Christian faith staff many of these institutions.

At Peking University, the departments of philosophy and religious studies have a director, Zhao Dunhua, who is sympathetic to Christianity, though not a Christian himself. Zhao has invited overseas Chinese scholars, mainly evangelicals, to speak on Christian theology. One Chinese graduate student estimated that there were at least two hundred Christian students at Peking University. Some of them, he said, attended the local Three Self church in Haidian District, where the university is located. Others were involved in various urban house churches close to the campus.

Robert, we'll call him, had spent a few months studying Christian theology in an American university. When he returned to Beijing, he said, he was astonished to bump into Christians in so many different parts of society. "China is full of hope," he said over coffee in a university cafeteria. "After I came back to China I found Christian believers in every field, among professionals in Beijing, managers, businessmen. It's fantastic."

A Peking University graduate student of religious studies spent a summer on a sociological project trying to find out how many religious study groups or house churches there were in the Chaoyang District of Beijing, a locality heavily populated by students, scholars, and professionals. She concluded that there were at least 20,000 small groups (sometimes as small as three to four people) in this area of Beijing alone, and that large numbers of these were Christian groups.

Reports after 1989 showed that as many as 10 percent of students on many Chinese college campuses were Christian, but there is no way of verifying this figure independently. Jane at Peking University says she thought at least 20 percent of students on the campus were religious believers of one kind or other. One university that actually polled its students anonymously was People's University, also in the north of Beijing. Familiarly known as Renda, as Peking University is known as Beida, the university is known to have several teachers who are professing Christians. One Renda professor who says he is "not yet" a Christian, but is exceptionally well informed, is Yang Huilin, director of the Institute of Christian Culture at People's University.

In 2001, Yang conducted a study of four hundred students at Renda, randomly selected, and asked a number of direct questions (the answers were returned anonymously). A total of 3.6 percent of those questioned said they were Christian, and some 60 percent of the polled group said they were interested in Christianity. Of those who expressed interest in Christianity, only 5 percent attributed this to contact with a church. More than half, according to Yang's survey, had acquired that interest through reading, lectures, and optional courses. Overall, Yang said, he was encouraged that most students thought it no longer a problem to be known as a Christian on campus.

I asked Yang if he thought Christianity was growing significantly in China. "Of course, greatly," was his response. But he added an interesting comment. "China doesn't need a new religion," he said. "It needs a new value system and a new way of thinking. Christianity has been developing in China rapidly for the past ten years. But it may not be good for Christianity." Why not? Yang didn't spell this out, but he implied that Christianity might become too enmeshed with politics and grubby economic life. He went on, "With globalization and post-modernity, we cannot find a clear value system and clear definitions and judgment. In this case, Christianity would find a very wide space. It is one of the strong points of Christianity to set up an absolute value system."

Yang said at least ten Chinese contemporary novelists had a strong religious identification and some were actually Christians. Those with a strong Christian coloration to their writing, he said, were Lao She, Xu Dishan, Bing Xing, and Mu Dan. Yu Jie, the Beijing writer who admires Liu Xiaofeng, agreed with this view. So did another Beijing intellectual, Xiao Dongfang, who is well acquainted with many of the reform-minded intellectuals who came to the fore under former Premier Zhao Ziyang in the second half of the 1980s. "In Beijing," Xiao said, "we see more and more people in writers' circles who are Christians. There is a new literary style called *sheng jing ti* ("biblical" in Chinese). It means objective, truthful, terse."

ARTISTS

That description could well be applied to the works of the man who is probably China's best-known Christian artist, both inside and outside China, Yu Jiade. Yu paints in a number of styles, most recently in oil, but some of his most remarkable paintings are traditional Chinese watercolor renditions of well-known Bible scenes in the New Testament. Many of his paintings hang in Nanjing Theological Seminary, and for a while Yu's work was used in Christian calendars and other items sold by the Amity Foundation in Nanjing.

Yu's story has the epic, tragic tone that is virtually the hallmark of China's best creative minds of the past fifty years. Born in 1939 into a Christian family, Yu studied in a high school specializing in art in Harbin in 1952–1956. Then, still a teenager, he entered Nanjing University Technical College. Then his family suffered in the anti-rightist movement of 1958, mainly because his father had been a Protestant Christian minister. His family was sent off to China's underdeveloped northwest, to Xinjiang Province, to develop this part of China along with thousands of other exiled youth. About a tenth of all the students shipped out to Xinjiang belonged to "rightist" families.

Once in Xinjiang, Yu was subjected to intense "struggle" sessions to change his political and, indeed, his religious thinking. In his artist's studio in a modest apartment in Qingpu, about an hour's drive out of Shanghai, Yu began to weep as he described what had happened to him. "I had to say that I would not accept God," he sobbed. "In my heart I said to God, 'How could I abandon my faith? How could I abandon you?' I told God that all the others were saying that they were no longer Christian. I told Him that in my heart I would still believe in Him."

"I still had my faith in God," Yu went on, "but I felt that I was like the second son in the story of the Prodigal Son. I acted just like the others who said they were no longer Christians. At the time there were no Christians that I knew about. I once went into a building in Xinjiang that said 'Christian Church' on the outside. When I entered it they said that Christianity had already been eliminated. I felt that we Christians were a place, like a church, but without God."

Yu's turbulent time in Xinjiang took him through both the Cultural Revolution and the "Down to the Countryside" movement in which all the young people were involved, willingly or not, in 1969–1974. Yu was a laborer and a carpenter until the end of this period, when he was summoned back to a town in northern Xinjiang. Gradually, his economic situation improved. He started by working in a bank, then found himself commissioned by various govern-

Chinese Christian artists

ment agencies to paint heroic pictures of Mao Zedong being greeted by rapturous peasants from minority groups, or, after the fall of the Gang of Four, of the newly emerging leaders like Hua Guofeng and Deng Xiaoping. Yu says the he painted one of the thousands of paintings seen all over China of Mao Zedong, sitting next to Hua Guofeng with his hand on Hua's thigh, saying, "With you in charge, I am at ease."

By the early 1980s Yu had been promoted to a middle-level cadre, though he refused to join the Communist Party because of his Christian faith. "In 1985," he said, "I had a strong desire to paint secretly, to depict the stories in the Bible. At that time the Three Self encouraged me to paint, using the traditional Chinese style. Chinese Christians wanted the Jesus of history, but some foreigners wanted me to paint a Jesus that looks Chinese."

Yu Jiade, Christian painter

Yu stays at home most of the time; painting passionately the themes he loves. He prefers the intense, detailed style of oil, but his watercolors are extremely popular. He is frequently commissioned to depict biblical scenes in the fluid, swirling, highly evocative style in which many Chinese artists excel. "I think that now I am liberated," Yu says. "Society doesn't care about me now. I am still rather conservative. I feel the only role Christian artists have to play is to spread the Gospel. I think I can still do a great deal." Yu's dream is to go to America and have an exhibition there and to send one or both of his daughters to the U.S. for studies. The younger daughter is a gifted painter in her own right, but currently does illustrations for advertising clients.

In Beijing, an entirely new generation of Chinese Christian painters is emerging, some of them living in a community setting in a village called Song Zhuang, about nineteen miles due east of Tiananmen Square. The houses are probably less than twenty years old, but they have been comfortably "gentrified" by artists who moved out of Beijing in the 1990s. My escort on this visit was an intense young artist called Wang Zengmi. Wang had been something of a rabble-rouser during the turmoil in Beijing just before June 4, 1989. In fact,

Wang, not Christian at the time, was known as a *huai ren* ("bad man"), a mocking allusion not only to his dissident politics but to his reputation as a man of low personal integrity. Wang hadn't been detained after the Tiananmen massacre, but had difficulty selling his unconventional, modern paintings.

Through a mutual acquaintance, Wang met a traveling house church evangelist from Shandong, Ni Faxing (whose story of an encounter with one of China's most dangerous quasi-Christian cults comes in the last chapter). In 1996, Wang heard Ni preach at a youth meeting in Beijing and became a Christian. His wife was converted too. He soon decided that his calling was to evangelize China's community of young, and often deeply unhappy artists.

In 2001, he traveled to the village of Song Zhuang and shared his faith with several of the artists there. One of them was an exceptionally gifted oil painter originally from Xinjiang, a woman called Chen Yiwei, who became a Christian while Wang was in the village. Chen Yiwei's radiant oil landscapes, with actual wheat stalks in the foreground, have a sort of golden tone that seems somewhat mystical. She does not paint biblical or "Christian" scenes as does Yu Jiade, but her landscapes evoke an unusual blending of peace and spiritual triumph. Her husband, Wei, at thirty-six, two years younger than his wife, soon followed her into the new faith. They then decided to turn their yard into the place for Christian baptisms. They had a pond in the shape of China built in the center of the yard for water baptisms. The baptizing is usually done by Wang Zengmi.

In Chen Yiwei's simply decorated home an indefinable atmosphere of calm and quietness prevails. Chen Yiwei herself is one of the most sweet and tranquil personalities I met during my three months of reporting in China. "Everything has changed," said husband Wei of his life after his conversion. "Before we became Christians we used to fight all the time. After that we found a real new love for each other."

But Wei has no pat solutions for China. "We need patience," he says. "It is difficult to preach the Gospel in China." Wang, the artist-evangelist who led Chen Yi and her husband into their new faith, is more outspoken. He said, "As painters and artists we naturally have a feeling for history. We feel we are the conscience of society. But in my opinion, this conscience must be based on the Lord, otherwise it is just a personal attitude." Wang also believes that his own sense of calling has to do with China's destiny as well as with the Christian call to evangelize. He says,

> From the first, I had a burden from the Lord to share the Gospel with artists, because I myself am an artist. But in addition I have a vision that God will bless China. How will he do this? He will bless the culture. It is not that China will be Westernized. Many things like socialism, nationalism, capitalism, cannot save China. The democratic party or dictatorship cannot save China. Only Jesus can. So we can say that only Jesus and the conscience of intellectuals and artists can save China.

Wang has become a zealous evangelist. One of his more recent converts is a young man who did not tell his first name, but his last name is Qi. He is, in fact, the grandson of one of the most talented Chinese artists of the twentieth century, Qi Baishi. As we drove out to the Song Zhuang village, Qi, in the car with us, seemed almost enraptured by the changes that he said had come into his own life. It struck me as remarkable that an artist should regard himself as called to evangelize the artistic community, traditionally a notoriously quirky and unpredictable set of people.

MUSICIANS

The domain of music, too, has recieved that sense of "calling" early in the twenty-first century. In December 2001, the Forbidden City Concert Hall held the first performance of Handel's *Messiah*, in Chinese, since the Communist takeover of 1949. Nor was this a sneaky little event tucked away and unadvertised. A mostly Chinese audience, from Beijing's Christian community, packed the concert hall. The glossy program, in both Chinese and English, contained comments by Ludwig van Beethoven about Handel, with a pithy and eloquent note on the musical work itself by Ravi Zacharias, not a musician but an internationally known Christian speaker.[9]

The man responsible for this unusual cultural event was a talented young conductor from the Central Conservatory of Music, Su Wenxing. Su, of ethnic minority, heard about Christianity from his mother, who was a believer, but didn't become a Christian himself until a "tall American" who was teaching English at Su's first Beijing university, the Central University of Nationalities, began to tell him, quietly, about his own Christian faith. In 1996 Su became a Christian and began attending various house churches in Beijing. He met his wife in a Christian fellowship.

From the Nationalities University, Su went on to the Central Academy of Music, where he studied conducting, got an M.A., and soon afterward began to teach. He never concealed his Christian faith, though he was careful not to speak about it in the classroom. "The students know that I am different from other teachers," he said. "I am never rude. I don't insult them. Even when they are not very diligent, I don't punish them. I will say, 'I am disappointed.' They will be very ashamed. So they ask why I am different. I tell them, 'I am a Christian.' They are very curious about this. So I invite them to our home." Su goes on, "I can't tell them directly about the Bible, but we have discussions

Students at Christian Music Academy in Beijing

in the home that point to the Bible. They ask, 'Who is this man?' Meaning, who is Jesus? We often show them the *Jesus* film."[10]

He is remarkably open in public about his Christian faith, and has been written about in official publications such as the *China Daily*. Along the way, Su has been encouraged and educated by many older Chinese musicians who were Christian before the 1949 revolution and watched the Chinese government for decades suppress all public Christian musical performance. An elderly professor from the Tianjin

Conservatory of Music, who had graduated from the University of Michigan in 1932, gave Su private lessons on the history and substance of Christian music for three years before his death in 1999. Su has encouraged the development of musical education in China's house churches. He has also conducted a full orchestral version of Lu Xiaomin's Christian songs to be used as theme music for Yuan Zhiming's documentary, *The Cross*. When the professional musicians of the China Symphony Orchestra first heard Lu Xiaomin's compositions, they were surprised and touched. "She is a real composer," one of them told Su.

Su is not the only professional musician interested in training house church Christian leaders in professional musical schools. Just on the outskirts of Beijing is a music school called the Canaan School of Music where some fifty students are trained over a twelve-month period in the history of music, piano, guitar, sight-reading, vocals, and ensemble singing. The teachers, who work there at a fraction of the pay they could earn by teaching Beijing students privately, are all top-class musicians from major musical institutions in Beijing. The Canaan Music School is not registered. The Chinese government would almost certainly close it down immediately if it knew anything about it. But when I visited the school, I found the same intensity of purpose among the students that I had encountered in the rural and clandestine seminary described in chapter 6. The teachers, whom I cannot name, all say that the talent displayed by many of the students, all untrained in music, can at times be striking.

AIYAN

The cultural development in China's house church movement is well illustrated by the recent appearance of an attractive, slickly edited, clandestinely printed house church Christian magazine called *Aiyan* ("banquet"). The articles in *Aiyan* go well beyond the usual gamut of personal testimony stories typical of evangelical Protestant magazines around the world. The magazine also offers interesting articles about the history of Christianity, developments overseas, and even some touchy political problems. In one issue, an obviously well-read and intelligent reader asked the editors to explain how U.S. President George W. Bush could claim to be a Christian and yet lead his nation into war. (This issue came out after the war in Afghanistan.) The editor's reply is worth quoting at some length:

> I am not President Bush's advisor or secretary, therefore I can't speak for him. The following answer is just my personal understanding and assumption. As the king of a nation, Bush makes decisions based not only on his personal belief, but also on the consideration of national interests. When terrorist bin Laden and his followers attacked New York's WTC twin towers, it meant they had declared a war against the U.S. It's possible that from America's point of view, there was no other choice but to fight back.
>
> Meanwhile, we should know about our government's supportive position on fighting against terrorism. Bin Laden has also trained people and sent them to China's Xinjiang to commit acts of terrorism. So our government leaders have said, "China and the United States are both the victims of terrorism."

The editor goes on to detail al Qaeda's alleged connections with the "East Turkestan" separatist movement based in Xinjiang Province, which has—the Chinese authorities claim—committed terrorist acts against Han Chinese civilians in China's own capital of Beijing. Most interestingly of all, though, the editor makes it quite clear that, from a theological point of view, he supports the U.S. decision to go to war in Afghanistan. The editor writes:

> Some Chinese applauded the terrorist attacks on American civilians, but they have failed to realize their applause equals terrorists' murdering of Chinese civilians. Therefore, President Bush's decision to [declare] war against the terrorists is to maintain justice, [it] is also biblical.

The irenic tone of *Aiyan* is as striking as its pro-American view of international terrorism. The editorial response concludes that China's Christians pray not only for the people of Xinjiang (including, implicitly, the supporters of the East Turkestan movement), but for the Communist Party secretary of the province, Wang Lequn.

Aiyan is a striking contradiction to the Three Self depiction of China's house churches as made up of uneducated fundamentalists from China's sticks. To the contrary, it is a magazine that appeals to the many academics, writers, musicians, and other intellectuals who have joined the ranks of Christianity from all walks of the cultural life in China.

Chapter Fourteen

FOREIGNERS

IT IS JUST BEFORE 11:00 A.M. on a dismally rainy Beijing morning in June. One by one, a line of taxis is drawing up to a large, concrete auditorium in the same compound as the four-star Twenty-first Century Hotel, in the Chaoyang District. The passengers struggle out with their closed umbrellas and make for the entrance as quickly as they can in the rain. A growing throng of pedestrians heads for the same destination. They are all foreigners, at least half of them Asian-looking foreigners, and they are going to church at the Beijing International Christian Fellowship. There's just one hoop they have to dance through in order to be admitted: they have to show their non-Chinese passports. Blond hair and freckles, black skin and tight curly hair, gangly tall or fast-food obese, it makes no difference. You can look as un-Chinese as possible, but you still have to show that you're not Chinese. The passport inspectors are polite and attentive and request that everyone produce documentation. None of the arrivals seems to get antsy or object to this procedure, probably because it's been the custom for as long as foreigners have come to worship at this Japanese-built auditorium.

This is a place for foreigners only, and it's not the foreigners who want it that way, it's the Chinese authorities. They don't want their citizens beguiled or confused by these church-attending outsiders. But foreigners here are no more "controlled" than they have been ever since they began coming into China in large numbers in the middle of the nineteenth century. True, there are no foreign gunboats moored offshore, and that's certainly a good thing. But the government has failed to isolate its citizens from foreign missionary influences. Of the estimated 2,400 foreigners who flock to the BICF (Beijing's largest Sunday Christian place of worship) on any given Sunday, it's probable that 40 to 50 percent are in China for one purpose: to advance the cause of Christianity among the Chinese.

The theology at BICF is conservative and its relatively brief sermons would pass muster in any respectable U.S. Southern Baptist church. The worship team on this Sunday consists of a young French woman, an overseas Chinese woman, an African man, and a white American woman. The contemporary worship songs they are singing tend to be those preferred in Charismatic or Pentecostal settings. Visitors are greeted warmly before things get under way by the church ministers—all of them laypeople and not in China as clergy—and asked to introduce themselves publicly. On this rainy Sunday the newcomers are from eleven states in the U.S. and at least ten foreign countries, ranging from Belgium to Zambia. The outside reception area of this cavernous auditorium is covered with posters for different ministries: home groups, adult education, children's ministry, singles ministry, prayer ministry, men's ministry, special events, youth ministry. There are also posters that say "Willkommen," "Bienvenidos," or the equivalent in a dozen languages. If you are a foreign Christian in Beijing, this is probably the friendliest place to be on Sunday. It's also the place to pick up gossip on what is happening in other foreign Christian "ministries" in China.

The very notion of foreigners having anything to do with Christian activity in China would make Mao Zedong turn over in his Tiananmen mausoleum. After more than a century of foreign bullying—during which it wasn't always clear which foreigners were shipping in opium and which were handing out Christian tracts—many Chinese, Communist and otherwise, wanted to see foreign missionaries chased out of their country. In 1949, for most Chinese, Christianity was still a "foreign" religion. As noted, both European Jesuits and British and North American Protestants had labored diligently to introduce the Chinese to the Christian Gospel, the Jesuits in the seventeenth century, Protestants in the nineteenth. The Jesuits were brilliant and subtle, and had a strong patron in Emperor Kang Xi. The Protestants were sometimes brilliant—English missionary James Legge's translation of the Chinese classics remains one of the landmarks of Western Sinology—but not always subtle. In fact, Chinese in the nineteenth and twentieth centuries often deeply resented the attitude of many Protestant missionaries, especially those from North America, who seemed to want to change not just Chinese attitudes toward Christianity but the entire structure of Chinese behavior and culture.

The China Inland Mission and a handful of other missionary groups, to their great credit, did their best to honor Chinese culture by learning the language and dressing and eating like ordinary Chinese. But for reasons of safety—to protect themselves from theft and banditry—most missionaries lived in compounds. Another count against them was the fact that they belonged to foreign nations who always seem to be having their way with China. These anti-foreign and anti-Christian sentiments helped to fuel the May Fourth Movement of 1919.

But even after the Communist takeover in 1949, foreign Christians did not give up. Missionaries who had been expelled from China continued to pray for their fellow Christians in China, sometimes bumping into them joyfully in the late 1970s when it became possible to revisit the sites of their original Christian work. Other Christians from all over the world who sensed a God-directed "calling" to China organized prayer meetings, and in some daring cases tried to link up with overseas Chinese Christians who were able to visit relatives inside the People's Republic when practically no one else could enter the country.

But all in all, the great Christian revival in China that started when the Cultural Revolution was still under way in the 1970s and caught fire a decade later was entirely Chinese. Other than diplomats, very few foreigners of any kind were permitted to reside in China from the mid-1960s until the 1980s. Foreigners, of course, had planted the original seeds through their missionary work, but, ultimately they were not responsible for evangelizing China in the last half-century. China's Christian transformation was and is a native Chinese phenomenon.

Yet foreigners did play and continue to play a major supportive role at key periods. Foreigners in China today continue to share their faith, often in secret. Other foreigners have played a major role in changing the direction of Christianity in China through their visits, initiatives outside China, and close involvement with China's house churches.

DOUG SUTPHEN

One of the most remarkable of these individuals was an American ex-marine who had been converted to Christianity during a Billy Graham crusade in Anaheim, California, in 1966. Doug Sutphen, or to use his *nom de missionaire*, "Brother David," initially came to Asia in 1970 to help the Far East Broadcasting Corporation, an Evangelical Protestant radio network based, at first, in the Philippines. (It now

has transmitters in several other parts of Asia as well.) The FEBC played a major role in keeping Christianity alive in China during the Cultural Revolution. Its broadcast readings of the New Testament in Mandarin Chinese during these days, picked up on both medium and short-wave receivers, were often the only way a Chinese could learn anything at all about Christianity. Despite the enormous danger—

Doug Sutphen

many people were sent to labor camp if caught listening to foreign broadcasts—many Chinese became Christians while listening to FEBC's broadcasts.

Sutphen's work at FEBC was in the printing department. He quickly found himself drawn to FEBC's efforts to help the beleaguered Christians of China. In 1970 he met a remarkable Dutchman, Anne van der Bijl. Better known as Brother Andrew, he was badly wounded while serving in the Dutch army in Indonesia in the 1940s, converted to a strong Christian faith, and found himself in the 1950s driving a battered Volkswagen crammed with hidden copies of the Bible into Eastern Europe. Brother Andrew, who had also visited Protestant Christians in Cuba not long after Fidel Castro took over the country, was as concerned for China as Sutphen was. He encouraged Sutphen to develop as many contacts in China as possible.

Though unable to enter China because of his continuing work with FEBC, Sutphen worked energetically and imaginatively to build up teams of couriers who carried Bibles into China from all possible points in Asia. In Burma, where the border with China was relatively porous, foreigners or overseas Chinese would arrive with suitcases of Bibles and transport them to parts of the country where brave indigenous couriers would hazard the journey through jungle and over hills into the southern underbelly of China. Sutphen also recruited overseas Chinese visiting China from Hong Kong or Singapore to carry Bibles in their suitcases.

Then Brother David and Brother Andrew had an idea. Realizing that anything that remotely resembled a Bible might endanger any Chinese in possession of it, he arranged for the printing of small New Testaments, using China's post-1949 simplified-character script, in a format that was virtually identical (same size, same red color) as Mao's "little red book," or *Quotations from Chairman Mao Zedong*. This little Maoist red book had been toted around and waved by every teenage Red Guard ever since the Cultural Revolution began. An identical-looking book would arouse little suspicion. Within a few months, Sutphen, through his courier contacts, had arranged for the first printing of 25,000 of these New Testaments to be taken into China.

But travelers to China with normal loads of suitcases were often unable to carry more than fifty or so copies at time. So in the late 1970s Sutphen planned the first major shipment in large quantities: 30,000 to be taken in by businessmen and women attending the twice-yearly Guangzhou Trade Fair. It was called Operation Rainbow. Except for the discovery of two suitcases by Chinese customs officials, it went off flawlessly. Still, the contacts inside China wanted more: they wanted a million Chinese Bibles as soon as possible.

PROJECT PEARL

Thus began one of the most unusual and successful smuggling operations of the twentieth century, Project Pearl. One million Bibles, if assembled together, would weigh about 232 tons. Sutphen scoured Southeast Asia to find a tugboat large enough to accommodate a twenty-person delivery crew and a barge capable of transporting 232 one-ton blocks, each containing forty-eight boxes with ninety Bibles per box. All of the boxes were waterproofed. The tugboat was named *Michael*, after the archangel in the Book of Daniel. The barge was named *Gabriella*, the female version of the Angel Gabriel. It was cleverly designed so that, on arriving, the barge deck could be partially submerged and the blocks transported rapidly onshore by outboard motor-powered rubber boats. The delivery crew were carefully selected volunteers, all Westerners, most of them American. They had to commit themselves to total secrecy during the planning and training for the operation.

The crew sailed from Mindoro in the Philippines to a preselected beach near Swatow on the coast of China's Fujian Province, arriving around 9:00 P.M. on June 18, 1981. The phases of the moon and the movement of the tides had been carefully calculated. At one point, during the slow three-day journey up the China coast, tugboat and barge were passed by Chinese patrol boats. A heavily armed patrol boat appeared momentarily to be heading straight for the lumbering convoy and came within seventy-five feet. Strangely, the patrol boat veered off in another direction without noticing the Westerner staring stolidly ahead from behind the wheel of the tugboat. Before arriving off the Swatow beach, a 300-yard stretch of tree-flanked sand dubbed "Mike" for the operation, the Bible barge and its towing tug had to navigate between transport boats of China's navy. Below deck, a lot of praying went on.

The rendezvous went perfectly. Unloading the barge took two hours and multiple trips by the three rubber boats. From the beach,

2,000 Chinese Christians who had been assembled for the operation took the Bible blocks to shore. The blocks were broken up into watertight component boxes, and then passed onto assembly points. They were then quickly distributed aboard bicycles, cars, and trucks for journeys to locations in almost every province of China.

The *Michael* and the *Gabriella* successfully made their way out of Chinese waters. But not everything continued to go smoothly on the beach. Around 3:00 A.M., a Chinese army patrol showed up, alerted by fishermen that some "Russians" had been seen dropping off cargo a few hours earlier. (The Westerners all had beards and thus seemed "Russian" to rural Chinese.) Some of the local Christians were rounded up, but none was detained. Since most of the Bibles had already been taken away, the Chinese soldiers only confiscated a few boxes still on the sand. At first, they tried unsuccessfully to burn them, but finally dumped many of them into the ocean. One part of the shipment, intercepted inland, was dumped into a large outdoor latrine. Some fishermen scooped up the Bibles floating in the harbor, dried them out, and enterprisingly sold them back to local Christians. Some Christian villagers retrieved those dumped in the privies, washed them off, and put perfume on them. House church groups who received them often called those retrieved from the ocean "Wet Bibles." The privy-retrieved scriptures were sometimes called "Perfume Bibles." Project Pearl Bibles, which were small, black, soft-covered versions of the entire Bible, printed in the U.S., eventually showed up almost everywhere in China.

The CIA had kept the operation under surveillance from the moment that *Michael* and *Gabriella* left the Philippines and watched with growing astonishment by satellite as the tugboat and barge anchored, discharged cargo, and returned. Midway back to the Philippines across the South China Sea, a two-plane fighter patrol from a U.S. Seventh Fleet carrier did a 360-degree surveillance sweep of the smuggler expedition and dipped its wings in a salute before departing. On his return to Manila, Doug Sutphen was invited to the U.S. embassy to talk about his operation and was introduced to cheering marines in the embassy basement.

The Chinese reaction was less appreciative. Beijing was informed as soon as the Fujian Public Security Bureau grasped the dimensions of the operation: that Americans had landed right under their noses and unloaded 232 tons of prohibited literature. Word came down that Project Pearl should be considered a "counterrevolutionary" operation. Two Fujian Christians were arrested for questioning and imprisoned for three years.

Some Christian groups outside of China expressed dismay that Christians had "smuggled" Bibles and thus broken the law. Sutphen's response was that no Chinese law specifically prohibited the importation of Bibles, and that, in any case, if any such law existed, it would contradict God's own law that His Word should be freely available to everyone.

Operation Pearl had a major long-term impact on the overall availability of Bibles in China. Three Self officials were constantly being hectored on overseas trips by evangelical Protestants over the continuing scarcity of Bibles for China's Christians, whether Three Self or house church. Project Pearl was such an embarrassment that it became a major factor in prompting the establishment of the Amity Press in Nanjing in 1987. With major financial help from American Christian groups, Amity was permitted to print Chinese Bibles in very large numbers (mostly to be sold through Three Self churches). Up to 30 million copies were produced by the end of 2002.

The Chinese didn't take long to discover who "Brother David" was, but Sutphen did not seem to receive any harsh treatment from the authorities on subsequent visits to China. He was never prevented from returning there, and in fact he remained in close touch with house church Christians. He also developed friendships with several Three Self leaders, including Bishop Ding and other high officials with the Three Self. Like many American Christians, Sutphen loved China and the Chinese, Christian or not, and that admiration and respect communicated itself to every Chinese he ever met. In the late 1980s, Sutphen started East Gates International with Ned Graham, the youngest son of evangelist Billy Graham. In the 1990s he formed his own ministry, based in Washington State and called Love China International.

Like so many missionary pioneers of all ages, Sutphen is an original, well-focused man who could be astonishingly kindhearted and generous to people he hardly knew; it would be hard to think of many Americans or foreigners who loved China as unconditionally as he did.

DENNIS BALCOMBE

One of the most gifted Christians who has done much work in China is another southern Californian, Dennis Balcombe, from Los Angeles. Born in 1945 and converted to a zealous Christian faith at sixteen while still in high school, Balcombe's experience of starting in Christian work in China might be considered mystical by most people. He was attending an independent Pentecostal church in Almonte, outside Los Angeles, when the wife of the main American preacher suddenly started speaking fluent Hebrew. The pastor's wife had never heard Hebrew spoken in her life. She was "speaking in tongues," a Pentecostal or Charismatic phenomenon that was common in the early Christian church and which is extensively discussed in Paul's First Letter to the Corinthians (notably chapters 12 and 14). According to the Pentecostal understanding of tongues-speaking, a person receives from the Holy Spirit, in an intuitive way, the "interpretation" or translation of the message. Indeed, someone in the congregation received the "interpretation" in English and declaimed it aloud. An American Jew

Dennis Balcombe

who knew Hebrew happened to be in the church at the time and confirmed the accuracy of the translation. The gist of it was that Dennis Balcombe was going to be used by God as a missionary in China.

Balcombe, evidently, didn't argue with the message.

For a while, Balcombe attended bible college in California, but he was then drafted. He spent a year in Vietnam in 1969 with the First

Air Cavalry. During a one-week R-and-R in Hong Kong, he went into a Pentecostal church and heard another "prophecy" aimed at him, this time telling him that Hong Kong was the place he should go. Balcombe arrived there in the 1970s and began to study both Cantonese and Mandarin Chinese. Then he started to pioneer a new church. What was unusual about it was that, though he was a Westerner, indeed an American, the congregation was overwhelmingly Chinese and the main language was Cantonese, not English. Part of Balcombe's style was to call himself Chinese and, jokingly, an "egg" (white on the outside, yellow on the inside). Today, his Chinese Revival Church features the five-starred flag of the People's Republic of China in its sanctuary and weekly prayers for China's leaders.

Balcombe's fluency in the language and his passion for the country helped him to further his contacts in China when the country began to open up in the 1980s. Traveling to and from his English-teaching stints in Guangzhou, Balcombe was able to bring scores of thousands of Bibles. These would be stored in the home of a Chinese woman Christian in the city, then shipped by train to Henan. One of the earliest Fangcheng leaders he met on these trips was Ding Hei. As Ding Hei came to know Balcombe better, she became more interested in his Pentecostal background and teaching. In Guangzhou's Yexiu Park, Balcombe showed Ding Hei videos of Pentecostal meetings in Singapore. In 1986 he prayed for Ding Hei to receive the baptism in the Holy Spirit, a key moment in the spiritual lives of Pentecostals.

Ding Hei also learned about the new and exciting Pentecostal worship forms, including joyful praise tunes and dancing, that Balcombe had introduced into the Revival Christian Church in Hong Kong. This was introduced to other Fangcheng leaders, who were similarly impressed. They were so struck by what was happening in their own lives after being introduced to the Charismatic experience that they invited Balcombe to visit Fangcheng.

In 1988 he did so, but it was risky. Foreigners at that time were able to travel to Zhengzhou, capital of Henan Province, but were normally prohibited from traveling farther into the countryside. Ding Hei and others arranged for a motor-powered three-wheel taxi to pick

Balcombe up in Zhengzhou and drive him several hours through the night to Ma Cheng village in Shi Qi County, next to Fangcheng County. Balcombe had prepared for the journey with a twenty-day fast and prayed loudly in tongues during the bumpy hours on the tricycle. The driver was bewildered.

So were the leaders that Zhang Rongliang and others had invited to the first meeting with Balcombe. Zhang had used Balcombe's Chinese last name, so the hosts assumed that the visitor would be Hong Kong Chinese. "They were very surprised," said Wu Xinbai, a Henan intellectual who visited the village and later spoke with many of those who attended the meeting. "This was the first American missionary in Henan in forty-one years. It was historical," he said.

It was, but not just because of the rare appearance of a white-skinned *da bizi* ("long nose") in this rural corner of central China. Balcombe began to pray that the assembled Christians would receive the Pentecostal gift and that they, too, would begin to pray in tongues. That night, most of the Chinese gathered to hear Balcombe did just that. "After I prayed for these guys for half an hour or even two hours, the Holy Spirit would really come down," Balcombe recalled. "Sometimes the leaders would draw back and try to stop what was happening. But slowly but surely they began to open up to speaking in tongues. After about a year, the resistance was broken."

Broken, that is, in most of Henan Province. After the Fangcheng Christians acquired a new zeal in their evangelizing and saw more people being healed after prayer than ever before, Feng Jianguo of Tanghe, Zhong Rongliang's old cellmate, invited Balcombe to introduce the same message to the Tanghe fellowship. Balcombe didn't confine his message to just speaking in tongues. He also introduced the lively Pentecostal worship forms, including the "tambourine patterns," a form of percussion worship often adopted by women.

Though some of the house church networks would not accept Balcombe's Pentecostalism, notably the Born-Again Movement (though Xu Yongze has said he does not personally oppose Pentecostalism), the largest networks all did: Fangcheng, Tanghe, Wenzhou, and the two Anhui networks. Within a decade of Balcombe's first teaching, one-half to two-thirds of China's house church Christians belonged to the Charismatic fold. This was surely the most remarkable foreign missionary development in China in the twentieth century.

"We call Dennis Balcombe the second Hudson Taylor," said Fangcheng's Zhang Rongliang in 2002. "'Don't see me as a white guy,' he told us. 'I have a Chinese heart.'" Wu Xinbai put Balcombe's role historically, saying, "His influence was a turning point in the history of the Chinese church. Before Balcombe came, no one spoke in tongues. After he left, everyone spoke in tongues and people started to see healings. People saw the change when Balcombe laid hands on them. It was like a fire too big not to spread. After attending his meetings, people sometimes couldn't sleep for three to four days. One man who had been riding a bike got off every time he met someone and shared the Gospel. Before, the Fangcheng Christians had gathered in secret meetings. Now they shared in the street. Miracles just followed. I personally know many blind people who recovered their sight."

Balcombe spent much of 1988–1994 bringing other Pentecostal speakers into the churches where he had been welcomed: Canadians, Japanese, and English Christians with a "prophetic" gift. He also traveled widely in China to places where Zhang, Ding, and others had given him contacts. One of the churches where he prayed for the baptism in the Spirit was pastored by a woman preacher named Li Changxiu. This was the church where Lu Xiaomin, the prolific composer of Christian songs and hymns, had the breakthrough spiritual experience that led to her astonishing and continuing musical output.

Balcombe's travels were not without adventure. In the summer, he could not disguise himself with a thick padded cotton coat, face mask, and fur hat. Sometimes the only way he could go from village to village was in a coffin hauled by cart. There were some tense incidents. In 1992 in Henan, Balcombe had brought some eight Singaporean Chinese Christians to help with his ministry. Before he rose to speak, he had the strongest impression he should talk about persecution. The next day, at 11:00 A.M., the Public Security Bureau suddenly showed up and demanded admission to the meeting place. Balcombe was told to place himself immediately in the coffin. The police burst in, looked at the coffin, and started taunting the Christians. "Hey, you Christians can raise people from the dead, right? Why don't you do that with this cadaver?"

Without a second's hesitation a man in the group said, "Well, we could, but he has AIDS. Do you want us to do it?" The police backed off. In the confusion that followed, Balcombe was wheeled off to another village, with the PSB in hot pursuit. At the next meeting, the police arrested about 150 people, including some of the visitors with Singaporean or Malaysian passports. But Balcombe escaped once again by donning women's peasant clothes and sitting on the back of a bicycle that a Christian rode as furiously as he could back to Zhengzhou. He obtained duplicate passports for the Singaporean and Malaysian visitors who had been detained and arranged for them to leave China quickly.

Balcombe's luck didn't last forever. During the Spring Festival in early 1994, he and some visitors from Hong Kong were arrested in Henan and detained for five days in a government guest house in Zhengzhou. Though they were permitted eventually to return to Hong Kong, much of their video equipment was permanently confiscated by the police and a large amount of their money was simply stolen from them as they watched. Balcombe might have been able to reenter China if he had kept a low profile, but instead he traveled to Europe and the U.S. to speak out against the persecution of Christians in China. His appearance before a congressional hearing in 1995 may have been decisive in getting him banned from visiting China for the next eight years. He was finally permitted back in 2003.

JONATHAN CHAO

The third foreigner to have significant influence on Chinese Christianity is Dr. Jonathan Chao, founder and president of China Ministries International and director of Christianity and China Research Center, Taipei, Taiwan. Chao is Chinese through and through, but he happens to be an American citizen, having received his M.Div. from Westminster Seminary and his Ph.D. in Sinology from the University of Pennsylvania. Chao has long been known as one of the leading authorities on the church in China. From the late 1970s, working out of Hong Kong, Chao's Chinese Church Research Center incisively examined what was happening to China's house churches, both by insightful analysis of what was behind each new element in the Chinese government's efforts to control Christianity, and through interviews with Chinese who had visited Christian communities on trips to the mainland. Chao's often-brilliant analysis was indispensable to those trying to acquire hard data on what was going on in the grassroots Christianity movement in China.

Born in Liaoning Province in 1937, he narrowly escaped from China with his parents after the Communists took over in 1949, fleeing first to Hong Kong, then to Japan, then to Taiwan, and finally to the U.S. in the late 1950s. In 1978, he made his first trip to post-Mao China in the company of former Henan missionary David Adeney, who had been with the China Inland Mission in that province. During 1978–1982 Chao conducted six hundred interviews with Christian Chinese who had just come out of the country, compiling a broad informational database that proved to be invaluable to other scholars later on.

On the basis of his research and scholarship alone, Chao earned himself a prominent place among outside observers of China's Christianity. But Chao, at heart, was more than a scholar and observer: he was an evangelical activist. Chao continued to enter China in the 1980s, forming close links with many of the house church leaders. Unlike Balcombe, Chao was able to travel with relative safety to several different parts of China because he looked Chinese. He first met Xu Yongze in 1980 and helped Xu develop his own, at first thoroughly orthodox theology. From 1983 on, he gave daily thirty-minute radio teaching sessions on Christian theology for Trans World Radio, a Gospel network similar to FEBC but broadcasting from Guam and elsewhere in Asia.

As early as 1993, Chao tried to persuade Xu to tone down the sometimes seemingly hysterical spiritual retreat sessions of the Born-

Again Movement that led to the group's being called "the Weepers." "I affirmed their theology," Chao said, "praised their theological training, but criticized their emphasis on weeping." Chao also pointed out that some of the elements of Watchman Nee's theology that the Born-Again Movement had adopted were, in fact, not doctrinally orthodox.

Chao was by no means closed to the increasingly Charismatic networks of Henan. Chao, being of the Protestant Reformed position, didn't quite share the premillennialist Second Coming leanings of most of the house church groups, yet he made no effort to alter their viewpoint.

Starting in 1996, Chao may have become more closely involved than any other outsider in the sometimes confident, sometimes tentative attempts by all of the house church networks to come together in a unity movement. Chao's big concern was to provide convincing doctrinal evidence to the Chinese government and the outside world that China's house churches were not "cults." Starting in the spring, he began to work with house church leaders on the different aspects of the theology of each group to determine where it could fit together with other groups. The result of his theological counsel, nudging, and cajoling was the "Confession of Faith," signed by four house church leaders (including Xu Yongce's sister, Xu Rongling, under a pen name) in November 1998. Like the "United Appeal of the Various Branches of the Chinese House Church" of August 1998, the November document indicated that China's house churches were both orthodox and flexible in the way they accommodated the slightly different theological emphases of each group.

The house churches might possibly have been able to cobble together a statement of faith by themselves, but, undoubtedly, Chao's theological counsel was crucial in persuading them to realize that they had far more in common than in difference.

While not as flamboyant as Balcombe, Chao has not hidden from the media limelight. Early in 2001 he took American reporters, one from *U.S. News and World Report* and a TV crew from New York's

Channel One, into central China. The *U.S. News* story ran in April 2001 and was immediately criticized by many American Christians for revealing too much. The Channel One report that ran on ABC's *Nightline* probably triggered the decision by China's authorities to ban Chao from visiting China for an indefinite period.

Chao's role in China's Christianity was not limited to theological counseling of key network leaders. He also helped to establish and teach at several of the small, underground seminaries in different parts of China. This infuriated the Three Self as much as it did the PSB. "Jonathan Chao and his friends have carried into China a lot of books with the idea of not being patriotic because the government is atheist," complained Presbyter Ji Jianlong, general secretary of the Three Self. "Jonathan Chao's influence on the believers is very strong." Coming from the most senior official of China's officially recognized Protestant church, that comment was not intended as a compliment. But it serves to underline just how significant yet this "foreigner" has been in the emergence of today's Christianity in China.

ENGLISH TEACHERS IN CHINA

For all of the heroic—or, depending on your point of view, rash— adventures of Sutphen, Balcombe, and Chao, another sort of foreign Christian presence is making itself felt powerfully in hundreds, or even thousands, of individual ways. No foreign missionaries, of course, are permitted to work in China. But perhaps as many as 2,000–3,000 do so anyway, using the opportunity of being English teachers. For more than two decades several U.S.-based organizations have had continuing relationships with Chinese universities and colleges to provide qualified teachers of English. The open secret is that these teachers are not just *ordinary* teachers of English; they are often serious and committed Christians and are vocal about their faith. This often annoys Public Security Bureau officials monitoring the foreign presence across Chinese campuses. But over the years, China's higher education system has learned to appreciate the quality of the Christian teachers. They behave well, they don't get drunk, they don't flirt with the local girls, they don't have romantic relationships even with other foreigners, they are diligent, and they don't complain a lot.

Ken Wendling is founder of English Language Institute, China, and until his retirement in 2003 was the group's president. ELIC is by far the largest of all the foreign Christian groups that supply China with teachers—it has sent more than five hundred teachers in any given year either for one-year and two-year contracts, or for short-term summer teaching sessions. Wendling explains, "We want to send people to China who truly care about the well-being of the Chinese people, the well-being of China in a world that is increasingly small." The teachers are carefully selected, and thoroughly trained by previous teachers familiar with China, and are required to raise more that $10,000 of their own support. They are all highly motivated not just to live out a decent Christian life among Chinese college students who may never have met a self-styled Christian before, but also to use every opportunity to share some aspect of their faith. Careful to observe the niceties of not using their classrooms as forums for Christian propaganda, ELIC teachers tend to be most effective developing close, after-hours friendships with some of their students. The steady drip-drip-drip of one-on-one Christian evangelism by these earnest foreign teachers has had a deep impact among young Chinese intellectuals. Almost every urban young Christian I met in China had come to the Christian faith through a foreign, English-speaking teacher. Some had been baptized into the Christian faith in a bathtub in the teacher's apartment.

Nor is it just foreign teachers who have come to China with the desire to share Christianity. A sizable number of American students who have come to study Chinese at some of Beijing's and Shanghai's colleges are motivated by theology rather than Sinology to spend several months or one or two years in China. Many such students, some graduate students, have attended Beijing University, reaching right into the heart of the capital's urban intellectual elite. Others have attended less elite institutions such as Renda, or People's University.

Some of these students are sent by para-church organizations like Campus Crusade for Christ. That organization is not permitted any official presence in China, but it has regional leaders scattered all over the country. Campus Crusade students sometimes speak among themselves in a sort of English-language Christian slang to disguise what they are really saying. Here is a brief glossary of terms and their meanings:

_____

PRC—*"Pray to receive Christ," not People's Republic of China*
MT—*Mission Trip*
Rap—*Praise*
G—*God*
Dad—*God*
Book—*the Bible*
Bird—*the Holy Spirit*
Four Bugs—*the Four Spiritual Laws (a principle of explaining Christianity devised by and much used by Campus Crusade for Christ)*
Triple A—*Campus Crusade for Christ*
The Company—*Campus Crusade for Christ, not the CIA*

_____

The Southern Baptists is another American church Christian group that has been very active in China—again, quite clandestinely. For understandable reasons, the representatives of such groups are reluctant to identify themselves to outsiders, so it is hard to grasp the full dimensions of what is clearly a foreign missionary enterprise (in the old-fashioned sense) being carried on in China.

It would be unfair to say, however, that groups like Campus Crusade or the Southern Baptists have any intention to control or take over Christian activity in China. If there is one lesson that virtually every serious foreign Christian in China has internalized, it is that foreigners may evangelize, train, encourage, and nurture ordinary Chinese, but that is where it stops: China's Christian leadership, everyone agrees, must remain Chinese.

Still, this level of mature historical understanding hasn't stopped some eager young foreigners, especially Americans, from taking hit-and-run evangelism to remarkable extremes. One of these is "tract-bombing," the casting out of Christians tracts, in Chinese, where the largest number of people have a chance of reading them. Pat Caspary, fifty-two, originally from Englewood, California, no longer lives in China so he is willing to tell his story. A sometime beach bum and acid experimenter who was converted in the Jesus movement in 1972, Caspary found his way to a teaching job in Shenzhen, on China's border with Hong Kong, in 1988. "We were told flat out that it was absolutely forbidden to bring religion into China," he recalled with a chuckle. That didn't stop Caspary and six other American teachers from evangelizing for all they were worth. "We were leading men and women to the Lord," he said. "There were people weeping and being baptized in the bathtub."

One of Caspary's baptismal candidates was a young English-speaking Chinese woman called Wendy, who is now his wife. After bringing Wendy back to the U.S. for a brief visit to acquire her citizenship (through an obscure immigration and naturalization law provision that enables returning missionaries to acquire very quick citizenship for foreign-born spouses), Caspary, with Wendy guiding and interpreting, set off for some hair-raising evangelism and teaching in remote rural villages of Guangdong. "We took Bibles in and did underground teaching. We would be going to the bathroom with the pigs," he said. Caspary's "tract-bombing" would consist of standing by the open window of a bus, waiting until another bus was passing in the opposite direction, then pushing the Christian tracts as quickly as possible into the other bus through its open windows. "Often when we threw tracts out, they'd ask for more," Caspary says. Less dramatically, but sometimes more dangerously, Caspary, Wendy, and sometimes other foreigners would spend the wee hours of the morning placing tracts in the mailboxes of Chinese apartment dwellers. "I would walk into police stations all over China placing tracts there," Caspary said. He was never caught.

Most foreign Christians living in China are critical of things like "tract-bombing" and do not respect it very much. After all, throwing tracts at people isn't necessarily the best way of getting to know them, hearing them out, and winning their respect. It's questionable, too, how many ordinary Chinese ultimately respect this approach to bringing them an understanding of Christianity.

ORPHANAGES

There is, however, one category of foreign Christians in China for whom the Chinese have the very broadest respect. These are the many individuals and families who have dedicated their lives to bringing a greater quality into the lives of ordinary Chinese. They run everything from orphanages to relatively simple projects like providing irrigation cisterns or assisting in disaster relief. Several of these foreign Christian groups have been quietly accepted as legitimate because, though "Christian," their actions provide tangible benefit to China.

Take Chan Kit-yin, a Hong Kong Chinese Christian who started her Christian life with the Youth with a Mission short-term mission organization. Coming to China first in 1992, Chan took on the thankless and often depressing job of working in one of China's ill-equipped and often neglectful children's orphanages. In 1995 Kit-yin and representatives of the official orphanages of Nanning founded Mother's Love, an organization dedicated to providing care for orphans who are sometimes severely handicapped. The Mother's Love hospital is a spacious, clean-looking set of buildings where up to 150 Chinese orphans, ranging in age from infancy to a few years old, are taken care of under Chan's guidance. "We never hide our faith," she explained. "We show what we believe. We pray over babies in public. We see the miracles. They, *they* [the non-Christian Chinese workers] begin to pray." Most of the workers at Mother's Love are already Christian and more of them become so every month. Chan is gratified that 80 to 90 percent of the orphans handed over to Mother's Love are eventually adopted.

Christians staff several other orphanages in China, at least partially. One of them is in Kunming, capital of Yunnan Province. Kunming is climate-wise one of the most pleasant places to live in China—a land of permanent spring. It is also something of a Christian missionary base in China, with perhaps 400–500 foreigners working in the city who are essentially in some kind of missionary role. Interestingly, though, one of the most influential foreign Christians in Kunming, Robert Cheeley, is critical of those in the U.S. who, he says, constantly "bash" China on the grounds of religious persecution or lack of freedom. Cheeley is not naïve about the continuing suffering of many of China's Christians, but he takes a half-full-glass approach. "Chinese Christians will tell you without exception that they are gaining freedom," he insists. "We are just on the verge of something happening when Christianity is going to be completely tolerated. We say to government groups, 'Will you allow us to let the Chinese church into areas of orphanages, arts education?' Almost without exception, provincial departments say, 'Yes, but you have to get permission for it.' There is an acceptance of the idea that Christians are a group of people who can contribute something to China."

Cheeley heads Project Grace, an umbrella group that provides organizational cover for about twenty foreign Christian organizations (some Dutch, Scandinavian, and British, as well as American) involved in helping China's medicine, agriculture, education, AIDS prevention, and leprosy work. He has strong views of how Christianity is handled among local Chinese house churches, accusing some of the Henan networks of "sheep-stealing"—that is, trying to take over perfectly functional Christian communities in the city. But Cheeley believes that foreign Christians in China shouldn't expect the country to operate like a perfect, Western-style democracy before coming over and agreeing to work in all sorts of projects. "My question to some foreigners is, 'Did Jesus approach a worse situation in the same way you do?' He never said a word about the Roman government."

That is true, of course. And the Roman government did eventually change, and it was, according even to skeptical students of Christianity like Edward Gibbon, author of *The Decline and Fall of the Roman Empire*, largely Christianity that brought about the change.

Chapter Fifteen

CHINA'S CHRISTIAN FUTURE?

CHINA IS IN THE PROCESS OF BECOMING Christianized. That does not mean that all Chinese will become Christian, or even that a majority will. But at the present rate of growth in the number of Christians in the countryside, in the cities, and especially within China's social and cultural establishment, it is possible that Christians will constitute 20 to 30 percent of China's population within three decades. If that should happen, it is almost certain that a Christian view of the world will be the dominant worldview within China's political and cultural establishment, and possibly also within senior military circles.

What do I mean by a "Christian view of the world"? Of course, there is no uniform "Christian view" on many domestic and international issues. Christians differ with one another over political and social questions. But what I mean is an Augustinian sense of international responsibility. The word "Augustinian" derives from Augustine's calling in his major work, *The City Of God*, for a profound sense of restraint, justice, and order in the wielding of state power.

Both Britain and the U.S. have possessed this at the heights of their imperial power and influence, and the U.S. still possesses it. This does not, naturally, mean that national interests are placed aside in favor of the international community. No nation has even been totally unselfish in employing its national power. But some nations have been unusually generous and mindful of a real responsibility—in effect before God—to act wisely, justly, and generously in the international arena.

Though the perception of imperial power strategy among the nations of the world in the past two hundred years has rested on what might be called the "realist" framework of international affairs, there has, within the two great Anglo-Saxon empires of Britain and the U.S., been a strong component of human rights idealism. This would also come within the domain of that "Augustinian" consciousness I already mentioned.

The U.S. since World War II has certainly thought of itself as bound to proceed with such a duty to the world. America's continuing concern for religious and political freedom all over the world has often been carried on regardless of *realpolitik* assessments of its contribution to American power interests. Though America's diplomatic leadership has not been specifically Christian in recent decades, it has, always in public, and usually in private, spoken as though this "Augustinian" obligation applied to it. Though such a worldview is also rooted in Judaism, as Christianity itself is, it would not be amiss to call this sense of national obligation a "Christian worldview."

A MORE RESPONSIBLE POWER . . .

The Christianization of China is likely to be concurrent with China's emergence as a global superpower. A Christianized China may spend less time thinking of ways to outmaneuver and neutralize the U.S. than the military strategists of the current regime. This is not because they will have ceased to be patriotic, but because they will not see the world as a dog-eat-dog squabble between major powers.

Just as the U.S. emerged into a benevolent global imperial role after World War II and the decline of the British Empire, it is not implausible that a Christianized China, now an emergent global power, might find itself wanting to take on some of the burdens that the U.S. has carried for the past five decades. It is also possible that, for a period of time, the U.S. and China might find themselves sharing a common worldview on many thorny questions of international affairs, and in some ways cooperating closely to resolve them.

For example, a Christianized China would be unlikely to consent to any resolution of Middle East problems that allows for the elimination of Israel as a Jewish state. A Christianized China would seek to make the world safe for Christian missionary endeavor, especially within the Islamic domains. I do not think that China would try to bully its way into the hearts of Muslims in the way Western imperial powers tried to do into the hearts of Chinese in the nineteenth century.

If China becomes Christianized, the dominant form of its Christianity, at least initially, will be strongly evangelical in flavor. It was without question evangelicalism that was the main impetus behind both Britain's abolition of the slave trade within its own domains in 1833 and its insistence on trying to eliminate it internationally throughout much of the remainder of the nineteenth century.

Just as Britain's Royal Navy operated a successful global interdiction of the slave trade in the first six decades of the nineteenth century, a Christianized China might find itself eager to ensure international law and order wherever it had the capability of doing so: suppression of piracy on the South China Sea, for example, or in the Straits of Malacca. A Christianized China may also find itself in close cooperation with the rest of the world in the suppression of terrorism, or making a more conscientious effort than hitherto to prevent the proliferation of weapons of mass destruction.

... OR AN EMERGING MENACE?

However, the possibility of China's emergence as an aggressive global superpower menace should not be discounted. Many times in China's history since the seventeenth century, when the first significant Western contacts took place through the Jesuits, China has turned aggressively xenophobic after a long period of seeming to digest Western trade, science, technology and ideas. The Boxer Rebellion of 1900 was the most violent and fanatical of the episodes. In the 1920s, nationalistic anti-Westernism fueled strikes, protests, and a lingering antipathy to Western importations like Christianity. The years between China's entry into the Korean War in 1950 and Kissinger's visit of 1971 were another period when China closed in upon itself in great hostility to the major Western power of the day, the U.S.

More recently, the Chinese mobs that stoned the U.S. embassy in Beijing and burned down the U.S. consulate in Chengdu in 1999 after the U.S. bombing of the Chinese embassy in Belgrade indicated that there are thriving grass roots of populist nationalism (even if the government organized the buses to drive the demonstrators to the embassy).

Nor are these sentiments limited to the grass roots. Michael Pillsbury, one of America's most experienced and best-informed observers of China's military, has shown that among China's major military think tanks there is a deep-seated strategic speculation about the country's potential to become a supreme global military superpower in the current century. In *China Debates the Future Security Environment*, Pillsbury, who has personally known many of the Chinese theorists about whom he writes, reports how Chinese strategists have devised a system for denominating the powers of great nations called Comprehensive National Power. This system factors in matters like economic strength, military technology, national will, national weakness, and so forth. Pillsbury says that Beijing's prestigious military think tank, the Academy of Military Science, estimates that China's CNP will have matched that of the U.S. by the year 2020.[1] Another Chinese think tank, notes Pillsbury, which we have come across a few times already and which has generally had a much more pro-Western bent to it, the Chinese Academy of Social Sciences, has predicted that by the decade 2020–2030, the U.S. will grasp that China is about to overtake it as a global power.[2]

What Pillsbury and others have shown is, regardless of how realistic these predictions of China's rise to prominence may or may not be, Chinese strategic planners are currently envisioning the probable emergence of China as the number-one global superpower within a matter of decades.

It is certainly conceivable that, in the wake of a major economic collapse in China, or perhaps some military confrontation over Taiwan, China's political leadership could lurch in the direction of a dangerous and vengeful nationalism.

DEMOCRACY—BUT NOT SO FAST

Will China evolve into a political democracy? Will China permit genuine freedom of conscience? It's certainly desirable. The U.S. has no major security concerns with nations that practice freedom of religion. A China that is accountable to its own people through the political process is far less likely to lie—as the government did in the early stages of the SARS epidemic in 2003—or to be an international bully.

So how will China get from the one-party political dictatorship of today to the desirable multi-party democracy of tomorrow? There is a broadly based fear in China of the uncertainty and extreme violence that has often characterized regime change in China. Chinese, who have never enjoyed the experience of a functioning political democracy, aren't really sure that they have the needed self-discipline to make it work. They aren't sure if they have the needed *civic* virtues that all political democracies need in some measure. Can you have a viable democracy if you still have massive corruption? Can you deal with corruption effectively without first constructing a system for implementing due process under the rule of law? Which comes first, civic virtue or a new legal system? How do you ensure that you have a decent legal system without a solid core of people who are, well, *virtuous?*

In this context, China's house church Christians are uniformly patriotic and cautious: They do not want to see a breakup of China by the creation, for example, of an independent Tibet. They do not want to see a Taiwan that has declared sovereign independence from China (but they also don't want to see Communist military action toward Taiwan). They want to see religious and political freedom come to China, but in an evolutionary, reformist process, not through political violence against the authorities.

Yuan Zhiming, whose documentary *The Soul of China* has had a major impact among Chinese intellectuals in both China and the U.S., does not believe that political activism in and of itself is the best way to change China into a more humane society, not to mention a functioning political democracy. Yuan, both through *The Soul of China* and his most recent documentary, *The Cross*, hopes to demonstrate in an intellectually convincing way not just the compatibility, but the affinity, of traditional Chinese culture with Christian revelation.

Despite their designation by China's Communist Party as political oppositionists, many of China's Christian dissidents are only seeking moderate reforms. Unlike Wei Jingsheng and others, their primary goal is not to overturn Communism. Many do not believe China will be ready for any transition to political democracy in the next ten years. Some worry about the possible effect of complete religious freedom on the condition of the church.

"I think the next ten years is the best time [for Christianizing China]," says Zhang Boli, one Chinese student leader on the "most wanted list" after Tiananmen Square who is now a Christian clergyman. "If things are too open it is not good. Under hardship the Chinese church will be healthy. I am concerned that some day when things are totally open there will be corruption." Zhang, like Yuan, has seen some aspects of Christianity in the U.S. that have flourished in conditions of total religious freedom. And he doesn't like them: egotistical name-building by some clergy, an affluent lifestyle that pays no attention to the poor or to those who are suffering, a society plagued in some areas by theft and violence while others remain safe and uninterested in their suburban homes. Other Christian leaders are similarly cautious about desiring any regime change in China within the short-term future.

CHANGING THE FACE OF CHRISTENDOM

Also worth noting is how the emergence of China as a Christianized nation will affect global Christendom itself. Some have argued that, if China's Protestant Christian population is close to 70 million, it would make China's Protestants one of the largest such communities in the world. There is bound to be a consequence from the powerful position globally that China has come to occupy. A thoughtful biographer of Wang Mingdao, Thomas Alan Harvey, puts it this way:

> Regardless of which policy the Chinese government pursues, the church in China will profoundly affect the shape of Christianity worldwide for generations to come. With some thirty to seventy million souls and a growth rate of 7 percent annually, the number of Christians in China dwarfs the number of Christians in most nations of the earth. Like Christians throughout the developing world, Chinese Christians represent the vanguard of the church in the twenty-first century.[3]

Just as Christianity's spread in the West led to the dominance in global Christendom of the Western, or Roman, interpretation for centuries, so the spread of China into Asia and the southern hemisphere in the past two decades will probably affect Christianity on a global scale. This has been well illuminated by Philip Jenkins in his book *The Next Christendom*.[4] Already, the powerful weight of Third World evangelical theology within the global Anglican Communion has sought to counter modernist and liberal trends that some see as threatening to divide, if not ultimately destroy, the unity between the Anglican and Episcopal Churches in Britain, Canada, and the U.S. on the one hand, and the far larger group of member provinces of the Anglican Communion in the Third World. The sharp Third World Anglican criticism of the Episcopal Church in the U.S., after it approved the election of an active homosexual as the Bishop of New Hampshire in the fall of 2003, is only the most recent example of this trend.

It is worth considering the possibility that not just the numerical, but the intellectual center of gravity for Christianity may move decisively out of Europe and North America as the Christianization of China continues and as China becomes a global superpower.

In his book *Chinese Intellectuals and the Gospel*, Samuel Ling poses the question "Will the twenty-first century be China's century in the world? If China does become a world leader, will Christian ideas influence her direction? Her goals?" Then he goes on with a series of follow-up questions:

> What ideas will truly guide the "search for modern China"? Will China be anti-foreign, militant, and nationalistic people in the twentieth century? Will nihilism, materialism, and atheism be the governing ideas for the worldview of the Chinese people? Will Buddhism and folk religions rise again to dominate their thinking? Will a new version of Confucianism find a hearing among China's students and teachers? What is the place of the Christian gospel, the worldview based on the Old and New Testaments, in China's search for an all-comprehensive national ideology?[5]

It has been the contention of this book that Christianity will change the nature of China in many different ways over the next several decades, and in doing so, will change the world in which we live.

China's moment of its greatest achievement—and of the most benefit to the rest of the world—may lie just ahead. That moment may occur when the Chinese dragon is tamed by the power of the Christian Lamb. The process may have already started in the hopes and works of China's house church leaders.

UNITED APPEAL

A UNITED APPEAL OF THE VARIOUS BRANCHES OF THE CHINESE HOUSE CHURCH

(Translation revised and polished after consultation with Chinese scholars, October 12 1998.)

1. We call on the government to admit to God's great power, and to study seriously the new trends of development of Christianity. The government should ask itself, if it were not for the work of God, why would so many so churches and Christians be raised up in China?

Therefore, the judicial branch of the National People's Congress and the United Front system should readjust their policies and regulations on religion lest they violate God's will to their own detriment.

2. We call on the legal authorities to release unconditionally all House Church Christians presently serving in Labor Reform Camps. These include Presbyterians (who believe that if one is saved once, he or she is always saved), the Charismatic Church, the Local Church (incorrectly called the "Shouters' Sect"), the Way of Life Church (also called the Full Gospel Church), the Little Flock Church, the Pentecostal Church, Lutherans who do not attend the Three Self churches, and the Baptist Church. They should be released from prison if they

are orthodox Christians—as recognized by Christian churches internationally—and have been imprisoned for the sake of the Gospel.

3. There are approximately 10 million believers in the Three Self Church but 80 million believers of the home churches in the House Church. The House Church represents the main stream of Christianity in China. Therefore the government should face reality as it is. If Taiwan with its population of 22 million cannot represent China but the Mainland can with its population of 1.2 billion, so the Three Self Church cannot represent the Christian Church in China. The Three Self Church is only one branch. Moreover, in many spiritual matters there is serious deviation in the Three Self Church. The government should clearly understand this.

4. We call on the central leadership of the Chinese Communist Party to begin a dialogue with representatives of the House Church in order to achieve better mutual understanding, to seek reconciliation, to reduce confrontation, and to engage in positive interaction.

5. We call on the government to spell out the definition of a "cult." The definition should be according to internationally recognized standards and not according to whether or not people join the Three Self Church.

6. We call on the legal authorities to end their attack on the Chinese House Church. History has proven that attacks on Christians who fervently preach the Gospel only bring harm to China and its government. Therefore, the legal system should end its practice of arresting and imprisoning House Church preachers and believers, confining them in labor camps, or imposing fines as punishment.

7. The Chinese House Church is the channel through which God's blessings come to China. The persecution of God's children has blocked this channel of blessing. Support of the House Church will certainly bring God's blessing.

We hope the government will have a positive response to this united appeal by the House Church. The Holy Spirit has awakened our hearts. May God bless China!

Henan Province, August 22, 1998

CONFESSION OF FAITH

CHINESE HOUSE CHURCH LEADERS ISSUE CONFESSION OF FAITH AND DECLARE THE ATTITUDE TOWARD THE GOVERNMENT

Since late 1996 a leaders from some of the largest groups among house churches in Henan and Anhui have come together periodically to discuss matters of common concern. They were driven by a sense of the urgency of the Gospel at this juncture of Chinese history when the hearts of the people are open to the Gospel. A spirit of unity prevailed among them, believing that it pleases the Lord for them to come together as members of the same body of Christ and to promote spiritual unity among them for more effective evangelism in the next century. In the June meeting they came to the conclusion that they need to draft a common confession of faith as the Biblical basis for unity. Their understanding of unity is spiritual in nature, not organizational. By spiritual they mean that they recognize each other as members of the same body and called by the same Lord for the same purpose of bearing a testimony for Christ in China. Hence, they have decided not to criticize each other, but to help each other by sharing their different spiritual gifts. This has resulted in holding training sessions together and exchanging speakers with each other.

During November 24-26, sixteen members representing four large house church groups came together for a meeting in a village in North China to draft a confession of faith and also to issue a statement regarding their attitude toward the government, toward China's religious policy, and toward the Three Self Patriotic Movement. These documents are enclosed in this last issue of CNCR. Both the Chinese original and the English translations will also appear in web page of China Ministries International (*http://www.ccea.org.tw/~cmi*).

In drafting this confession of faith we are told that they wanted to put down only what they all agreed to accept, leaving points of disagreement for future discussion. Aside from their confession of the faith of historic Christianity, such as the affirmation on the authority of Scripture, the three persons of the trinity, and the redemptive work of Christ, these church leaders wanted their confession to reflect their refutation against some of current heretical teachings that currently prevail in China. Some of the heretical teachings include:

(1) that Christ has already come the second time, and He has done so in an incarnated form in the person of a Chinese woman called Ms. Deng in Zhengchou, Henan; this is the teaching of "Oriental Lightning."

(2) Some sects only accept certain books of the Bible and not all 66 books.

(3) Another group believes in a gradation in the trinity, namely, the Father is greater than the Son, and the Son is greater than the Holy Spirit.

(4) Still another group, called "Three Shifts of Servants," which believes in a gradation of priesthood and in which the head demands absolute authority over his smaller servants. These refutations are most included in the "we are opposed to..."

The second document on house church attitude toward the Chinese government, its religious policy, and the TSPM is partially a repeat of a document drafted in late August this year. What is new is the second and third section on why they do not register and why they do not join the TSPM. These declarations represent a new move on the part of the house churches in China. Whereas earlier they would remain silent when persecuted, now they want to make their cause known to the government, to the nation, and to the world; they want the government to understand what they believe to show that they are not cults as the government has labeled all those who refuse to register or join the TSPM. They also want the government to know why they take up such a position. In recent months they have also made events of persecution known through whatever media they are in contact with. This seems like the beginning of a surfacing of underground house churches, which seem to desire dialogue with the government.

CONFESSION OF FAITH OF HOUSE CHURCHES IN CHINA

INTRODUCTION

In order to arrive at a common standard of faith among house churches in China, in order to establish a common basis for developing unity among fellow churches in China and overseas, in order to let the government and the Chinese public understand the positions of our faith, and in order to distinguish ourselves from heresies and cults, top leaders of a few major house church groups have come together in a certain village in North China in November, 1998, to pray together, to search the Scriptures, and to draft the confession of faith as shown below.

I. ON THE BIBLE

We believe that the 66 books of the Bible to be inspired of God and that they were written by the prophets and apostles under the inspiration of the Holy Spirit. The Bible is the complete truth and without error; it will allow no one to change it in any manner.

The Bible clearly describes God's plan of redemption for man. The Bible is the highest standard of our faith, life, and service. We are opposed to all those who deny the Bible [as the Word of God]; we are opposed to the view that the Bible is out of date; we are opposed to the view that the Bible has error; and we are opposed to those who believe only in selected sections of the Bible. We want to emphasize that the Scriptures must be interpreted in light of their historical context and within the overall context of Scriptural teachings. In seeking to understand Scripture, one must seek the leading of the Holy Spirit and follow the principle of interpreting Scripture by Scripture, and not taking anything out of context. In interpreting Scripture, one ought to consult the traditions of orthodox belief left by the church throughout history of the church. We are opposed to interpreting Scripture by one's own will, or in by subjective spiritualization.

II. ON THE TRINITY

We believe in only one true God, the eternally self-existing triune God, Father, Son, and Holy Spirit who are the same in substance, equal in honor and glory, each having different personalities and each having different functional roles in the work of redemption: the Father plans salvation, the Son accomplished salvation, and the Holy Spirit implements salvation. However, there is no division among the Father, the Son, and the Holy Spirit, and the three are one in unity; the Son manifests the Father, the Holy Spirit manifests the Son; Father, Son, and Holy Spirit all receive our worship. We pray to the Father through the Son and in the Holy Spirit.

We believe that God created all things, and He created man according to his own image. God controls and sustains all things; He is the Lord of human history. The almighty God is just, holy, faithful, and merciful. He is omniscient, omnipresent, and omnipotent. He manifests his sovereignty in all of human history. God the Son and God the Holy Spirit are both eternal: the Son is eternally begotten of the Father and is not created; the Holy Spirit is sent by the Father and the Son. God is a spirit; He has no visible shape or form. Christians worship him in spirit and in truth. Aside from the trinity, Christians have no other objects of worship. We refute all mistaken explanations of the trinity, such as one entity with three modes of manifestation (such as water, ice, and steam); or one entity with three identities (such as a person can be son, a husband, and a father, or as the sun, its light and heat).

III. On Christ

We believe that Jesus Christ is God's only begotten son; He comes to the earth by way of incarnation (the Word became flesh). In His perfect humanity He was tempted, though without sin. He allowed himself to be crucified on the cross of his own will and there shed his precious blood in order to redeem those who believe in him from sin and death. He rose from the dead, ascended into heaven, and sat at the right hand of God the Father from whom He received the promise of the Holy Spirit, which He gives to all who believe in him. In the last day, Christ shall come again the second time and to judge the world. Christians receive the status of sonship, but they remain humans; they do not become God. No one knows the specific dates of the second coming of Christ, but we firmly believe that Christ will come again. We can also know some signs of his second coming. We are opposed to the teaching that Christ has come the second time in his incarnated form. We are opposed to all who claim to be Christ. All who claim that Christ has already come the second time should be declared heretics.

IV. On Salvation

Anyone who repents, confessing his or her sins, and believes in Jesus as the Son of God, that He was crucified on the cross for our sins, and that He rose again on the third day for the remission of our sins and for receiving the Holy Spirit, shall be saved through being born again. For by grace are we saved through faith: we are justified by faith; we receive the Holy Spirit through faith; and we become the sons of God through faith.

We believe that God will preserve his children in Christ to the end, and we also believe that believers should firmly believe in the truth to the end. We believe that receiving the Holy Spirit is the assurance (evidence) of being saved, and the Spirit of God bears witness with our spirit that we are the children of God. We are opposed to all who take specific phenomenon or personal experience as the objective criterion for being saved.

We are opposed to the belief that one can sin because He is under grace [contra "once saved, always saved, and hence one may sin freely]. We are opposed to the idea of multiple salvations [contra one can be lost if one fails to persist in faith, and hence must go through repentance and faith again]. We are also opposed to the belief that we can be saved by keeping the law.

V. ON THE HOLY SPIRIT

We believe that the Holy Spirit is the third person in the trinity. He is Spirit of God, the Spirit of Christ, the Spirit of truth, and the Spirit of Holiness. The Holy Spirit illuminates a person causing him to know sin and repent, to know the truth, and to believe in Christ and so experience being born again unto salvation. The Holy Spirit leads the believers into the truth, understand the truth, and obey Christ, and thereby bearing abundant fruit of life. The Holy Spirit gives all kinds of power and manifests the mighty acts of God through signs and miracles. The Holy Spirit searches all things.

In Christ God grants a diversity of gifts of the Holy Spirit to the church so as to manifest the glory of Christ. Through faith and thirsting, Christians can experience the outpouring and the filling of the Holy Spirit.

We do not believe in the cessation of signs and miracles or the termination of the gifts of the Holy Spirit after the apostolic period. We do not forbid the speaking of tongues and we do not impose on people to speak tongues; nor do we insist that speaking in tongues is the evidence of being saved. We refute the view that the Holy Spirit is not a person in the trinity, but only a kind of influence.

VI. ON THE CHURCH

The church is composed of all whom God has called together in Jesus Christ. Christ is the head of the church, and the church is the body of Christ. The church is the house of God, built on the foundation of truth. The church is both local and universal; the universal church is composed of all churches of orthodox faith currently existing in all parts of the earth and all the saints throughout history.

The administration of the church should be conducted according to principles laid down in the Scriptures. Its spiritual ministry shall not be directed or controlled by secular powers. Within the church all brothers and sisters are members of the same body, each fulfilling its role, and in love grow up in all things into Christ who is the head. In the Spirit the universal church should come to the unity of the faith and be united into one in Christ.

The missions of the church are: proclamation of the Gospel, teaching and pastoring the believers, training and sending them, and defending the truth by refuting heresies and bringing them to the correct path. Christians meeting in the name of Christ shall not be limited by number or location. All believers are priests, and they all have the authority and responsibility to preach the Gospel to the ends of the earth. We are opposed to the unity of the church and state or the intermingling of the church and political power.

We are opposed to the expansion of the church by relying on political power, whether domestic or international.

We are opposed to the church taking part in any activities that seek to destroy the unity of the people or the unification of the Chinese state.

VII. On the Lasting Things

We believe in the Second Coming of Christ and the bodily resurrection of those who are saved. Aside from the heavenly Father, no one knows the date of the Second Coming of Christ. When Christ comes again, He will come down from in the clouds from heaven with power and glory. The angels will blow the horn and those who are asleep in Christ shall be first raised from the dead, and the body of those Christians who have been born again and saved shall be changed, and they shall be lifted up to meet the Lord in the air, and they shall receive a glorified body. The saints and Christ shall reign for a thousand years. During this period of a thousand years, Satan shall be cast into the bottomless pit. After a thousand years, Satan shall be temporarily released to deceive all the people until he is cast into the lake of fire and brimstone. Then Christ shall sit on his throne and judge all nations and people. All the dead shall be raised again and they shall stand before the judgment seat. All those names not written in the book of life shall be cast into the lake of fire, and heaven and earth shall be consumed by fire, even death and hell shall be cast into the lake of fire.

Those whose names are written in the book of life shall enter into the New Jerusalem and be with God forever. We believe that as believers wait for the Second Coming of Christ, they should be diligent doing the work of the Lord, preach the Word of life, shine for the Lord on earth, and bear abundant fruit in word, deed, faith, love, and holiness. Those who do these shall receive all kinds of rewards.

As to the interpretation of whether Christ will come before or after the tribulation, we acknowledge that there are different views among different church groups and that we cannot absolutely endorse any view. The responsibility of Christians is to be alert and be prepared to welcome the Second Coming of Christ.

CONCLUSION

We praise and thank our almighty heavenly Father for leading us to draft this confession of faith. May the Holy Spirit work among more brothers and sisters to accept it, identify with it, and proclaim this Confession of Faith in church meetings. We pray that this Confession will be able to strengthen the faith of the brothers and sisters, resist heresies and cults, and together appropriate the great revival of the church in China.

May the Lord bless the unity of the house churches in China. May the Lord bless China, the Chinese peoples, and the Chinese Church. May praise and glory be unto our triune God. Amen.

(Signed)

Shen Yi-ping, representing China Evangelistic Fellowship

Zhang Rongliang, representing the Mother Church in Fangcheng, China

Cheng Xianqi, representing the church in Fuyang, China

Wang Chunlu, representing one of the other house churches in China
November 26, 1998
[Translation by Jonathan Chao, December 18, 1998]

ATTITUDE OF CHINESE HOUSE CHURCHES TOWARD THE GOVERNMENT, ITS RELIGIOUS POLICY, AND THE THREE SELF MOVEMENT

I. OUR ATTITUDE TOWARD THE GOVERNMENT

1. We love the Lord, the Chinese people, and the state; we support the unity of the nation and the unity of the peoples.

2. We support the constitution of the People's Republic of China and the leaders and the government of the people that God established.

3. Even though we are often misunderstood and persecuted by the government, yet we do not show a reactionary attitude, nor have we taken any reactionary action.

4. We have never betrayed the interest of the Chinese people; we only do what is beneficial to the people.

II. OUR ATTITUDE TOWARD THE RELIGIOUS POLICY OF THE GOVERNMENT:

Why do we not register?

1. Because the state ordinances on religion and demands of regulations for registration are contrary to the principles of the Scripture, such as the "three-designates" policy:

    a. Designated location: only in registered places we are allowed to conduct religious activities, otherwise such activities are considered illegal religious activities. But the Scriptures tell us that we meet anywhere and that so long as we meet in the name of the Lord, He will be with us.

    b. Designated personnel: only those who have been issued preaching licenses by the Religious Affairs Bureau are allowed to preach. But according to the teachings of Scriptures, so long as preachers are called by the Lord, recognized and sent by the church, they may preach.

c. Designated sphere: preachers are limited to preach only within the district for which they are assigned; they may not preach across villages or across the provinces. But the Bible teaches us to preach the Gospel to all the Peoples and throughout the ends of the earth, and to establish churches.

2. Because the state policy does not allow us to preach the Gospel to those under 18, or to lead them to Christ and be baptized. But Jesus said, "Let the children come unto me and forbid them not." Therefore, those under 18 should also have the opportunity to hear, and to believe in, the Gospel.

3. Because the state policy does not permit believers to pray for the sick, to heal them, and to exorcise demons out of them.

4. Because the state policy does not allow us to receive fellow believers from afar, but the Bible teaches us that elders should receive brothers and sister from afar.

5. Because the state policy does not allow us to have communication with churches overseas, but the Bible teaches us that the church is universal and that there is no division between Jews or Gentiles, and hence no division between Chinese and foreigners, for Christ has redeemed His people from all nations with His blood and that the believers are to love each other and to have communion with each other.

III. Why We Do Not Join the Three Self Patriotic Movement

Chinese House Churches do not join the TSPM for the following reasons:

1. The heads of the two are different:

a. Three Self churches accept the state as their governing

authority: their organization and administration are governed by the government's religious policy.

b. House churches take Christ as their head, and they organize and govern their churches according to the teachings of Scripture.

2. The ways church workers are established are different:

a. Religious workers in the TSPM churches must first be approved by the Religious Affairs Bureau before assuming office.

b. Workers in the house churches set apart their workers by the following qualifications: spiritual anointing, being equipped in the truth, possessing spiritual gifts, approved by the church, and having spiritually qualified character.

3. The foundations of the two are different:

a. The Three Self churches are products of the Three Self reform movement, which was initiated by the government; they were started by Wu Yao-tsung who propounded liberal social gospel type of theology; some of the initiators of the TSPM were not even Christians.

b. House churches take the Bible as the foundation of their faith; they developed from the traditions of the fundamentalists and evangelicals.

4. The paths of the two are different:

a. The Three Self churches practice the unity of politics and the church; they follow the religious policy of the state, and they engage in political activities.

b. House churches believe in the separation of the church from the state. They will obey the state when such obedience is in accordance with the Scriptures. When the two are in conflict with each other, they will "obey God rather than man." For such obedience they are willing to pay the necessary price, which is known as "walking the pathway of the cross."

5. The missions of the two are different:

   a. The Three Self churches can preach the Gospel and conduct pastoral ministry only within the designated places of religious activities.

   b. House churches obey the great commission of preaching the Gospel and plant churches.

IV. Our Attitude Toward Persecution

1. House churches are persecuted not because of political or moral issues, but solely because they refuse to register with the government and refuse to join the TSPM.

2. When house churches are persecuted, they do not hate the government, but to accept suffering as permitted by the Lord; they endure suffering silently; they yield to the government, and they intercede for the government and bless it.

3. When leaders and evangelists of house churches are persecuted, fined, interrogated, sent to labor instruction camps or labor reform camps, they do not complain; they still love their country and the government, waiting for God to grant them mercy.

4. The grassroots cadres who persecute the church can testify that the persecuted ones are innocent; these cadres have to execute their duties without choice.

5. The two reform institutions have a high estimate of believers and pastors who come under them; they trust them and are sympathetic with them. These all testify that the persecuted Christians have a heart that loves their country and people; they also testify that Christians have high moral integrity.

6. The faith of the house churches is orthodox; their model of ministry is in accordance with Scriptures, and they enjoy the presence of God. Therefore, although persecuted, the number of believers has increased rapidly—a force that cannot be resisted. The number of believers in all of China is by far larger than that in the Three Self churches. This is God's confirmation for us.

We sincerely appeal to the government

1. We appeal to the government to know the facts clearly and, in a truthful manner, correctly understand the nature of our faith and the purpose of our preaching, and no longer mistake us for cults.

2. We sincerely ask the government to stop its persecution against house churches, such as brutal beating, house searches, fines, detention, and labor camps; we sincerely petition the government to truly implement freedom of religion.

3. We ask the government to free all Christians and evangelists who are detained in the labor camps because of their faith or for preaching the Gospel and to do so as soon as possible.

As a matter of fact, wherever there are more believers, there is also greater social stability, higher spiritual civilization, better social atmosphere, and enjoying greater blessings from God. May there be peace in China and among her people. May God bless China abundantly.

By the representatives of the House Churches in China
November 26, 1998
[Translated by Jonathan Chao, December 18, 1998]

NOTES

CHAPTER 1: JESUS COMES TO BEJING

1. *China Daily*, December 18, 2002, front page.

2. And because you can buy anything in China if you have money, there are photographs of named officials doing just this. The Internet link is: *http://www.china21.org/simpChinese/news/031503pics/02.htm*

3. R.H. Tawney, *Religion and the Rise of Capitalism* (New York: Transaction Publishers, 1998). Originally published in 1926, his book looked into the connection between religious change in England in the sixnteenth and seventeenth centuries and the economic transformations in Europe that led directly to modern capitalism. Max Weber had already made the influential case in 1904 (*The Protestant Ethic and the Spirit of Capitalism*) that capitalism was a direct outgrowth of the Protestant Reformation, though Tawney took the view that Lutheranism conveniently adapted itself to a capitalist economy already taking shape. Many Chinese scholars of the role of Christianity in the rise of the West have accepted wholesale the Weberian thesis, a point noted in connection with Wenzhou in David S.G. Goodman and Gerald Segal, editors, *China Rising: Nationalism and Interdependence* (London and New York: Routledge, 1997), footnote 50 for page 40.

4. I cannot reveal the person who provided this anecdote, but I have met him, and he told the same story to two foreigners independently of each other.

CHAPTER 2: PATHFINDERS

1. In other versions they were digging a grave.

2. Peking is the name of China's capital city before the Communists renamed it Beijing in 1949.

3. Sometimes spelled Alopen in older historical accounts.

4. I am using the standard modern Chinese *pinyin* system for Romanizing Chinese characters. One of the oddities of this system to most people unfamiliar with China is that the letter combination qi corresponds approximately to the English sound chi-. So the Ching Dynasty, as China's last imperial (and Manchu) dynasty used to be referred to in most histories of China, in modern standard *pinyin* is rendered Qing Dynasty. By contrast, some Chinese names have become so much part of the English language in our time that I have not rendered them in *pinyin*. If I did so, it would not be clear who they were. For example, the founder of the Chinese Republic in 1911 is Sun Yatsen, the spelling that has been used for his name for a century. In *pinyin* his name would be spelled Sun Yixian. Similarly, his successor as leader of the Nationalist Party, which governed China until the Communist victory in the civil war of 1949, was Chiang Kaishek. If this former president of the Republic of China were spelled out in *pinyin*, he would appear as Jiang Jieshi, which almost no on would recognize.

5. An American missionary in Japan of Assyrian ancestry, Ken Joseph Jr., visited community members in Iraq just before the outset of Operation Iraqi Freedom. He admitted to a Fox TV anchor while being interviewed in Jordan that he had initially been anti-war, but had changed his views after being told by every Assyrian Christian he met in Iraq that they wanted the Americans to come and liberate Iraq from Saddam Hussein.

6. Ibid.

7. Palmer, *The Jesus Sutras,* passim.

8. Ibid., p. 226

9.　　Ibid., p. Martin Palmer, *The Jesus Sutras: Rediscovering the Lost Scrolls of Taoist Christianity* (New York: Ballantine Wellspring, 2001) p. 220 This is by far the best book on the Nestorian stele and the whole Nestorian presence in China. Palmer is particularly interested in the way in which some of the Nestorian-era Christian writings discovered in other parts of China in the past century or so reveal a Christianity that is rather hospitable to Buddhist and Daoist ideas.

10.　　Ibid., p. 236

11.　　Ibid., p. 18

12.　　Christopher Dawson, ed., *Mission to Asia: Narratives and Letters of the Franciscan Missionaries in Mongolia and China in the Thirteenth and Fourteenth Centuries* (New York: Harper & Row, 1966), p. 86

13.　　Samuel Hugh Moffett, *A History of Christianity in Asia, Volume 1: Beginning to 1500* (New York: Orbis Books, 1998), footnote, p. 420

14.　　Ibid., pp. 445-446

15.　　Sometimes spelled Chuanzhou, and named Zaitun in Western chronicles of this period.

16.　　Gavin Menzies, *1421: The Year China Discovered the World* (London: Transworld Publishers, 2002)

17.　　It is worth noting, by comparison, that the *Santa Maria,* the Portuguese carrack that bore Columbus across the Atlantic 60 years *after* the final Zheng He voyage, was a mere 92 feet long.　Even three hundred years later, flagship of the British fleet under Lord Nelson that defeated the French at the Battle of Trafalgar in 1805, the *Victory*, a warship of more than 100 guns with a crew of around 800, was only 186 feet in length.

18.　　Yale historian Jonathan Spence has written a fascinating book about this and other aspects of Ricci's life in China in Jonathan D. Spence, *The Memory Palace of Matteo Ricci* (New York: Penguin Books, 1984)

19.　　Quoted in Wolfgang Franke, *China and the West: The Cultural Encounter, 13th to 20th Centuries* (New York: Harper Torchbook, 1967), p. 39

20.　　Franke, ibid., p. 55

21.　　Translation provided by Meiling Sutphen. The two other poems, from *www.patriarchywebsite.com*, read as follows:

"The Poem on Truth"

Everything as seen by the eye is His creation.

He who has no beginning and no end, is three persons in one.

The heaven's gate was closed to the first man's sin and reopens through the Son.

Rid of all false religions, we should become real disciples admired by everyone.

"The Treasure of Life"

The treasure of heaven is comprised of Sun, Moon and Stars;

The treasure of earth consists of crops, gold and silver.

The treasure of a kingdom is to have righteous officials;

The treasure of a family is to have descendents with piety.

Yet, Gold, silver and jade are not as precious as one's life.

Hundred years of age is nothing compared to eternity.

Coming and going in life is like a dream.

The best food and clothing don't mean a thing.

It's no exception for someone born in a royal family.

The most important thing in the world is life.

Something that white jade, gold and silver can't buy.

Even plain porridge can be satisfying;

No cloth is fit to wear for a thousand years.

The heaven's gate was closed due to the first man's sin;

The path to salvation is through the Son only.

I would like to accept God, the Son, and the Holy Spirit;

And receive from thee my free gift of eternity.

22. Ibid., p. 57

23. Cited in A. J. Broomhall, *Hudson Taylor and China's Open Century: Barbarians at the Gate* (London: Hodder and Stoughton, 1981), p. 119

24. Stephen Neill, *A History of Christian Missions* (London: Penguin Books, 1986) p. 244

25. Broomhall, *Hudson Taylor and China's Open Century,* p. 286

26. Cited in Editors of Christian History Magazine, *131 Christians Everyone Should Know* (Nashville: Broadman & Holman, 2000), p. 253

27. Translated into Chinese, it is the *wanguo gongbao.*

28. Source: *www.intervarsity.org/ism/article_item/php?article_id=168*

29. By a curious historical coincidence, the May 4 incident occurred exactly

71 years before the shooting of four American student demonstrators at Kent State University in 1970.

30.   Particularly thoughtful and powerfully written is the trilogy by the British missionary, Geoffrey Bull, *When Iron Gates Yield* (London: Hodder & Stoughton, 1956), *God Holds the Key* (London: Hodder & Stoughton, 1954), *The Sky is Red* (London: Hodder & Stoughton, 1955)

31.   Franke, *China and the West*, p. 138

CHAPTER 3: PATRIARCHS

1.   In 1950 he published an autobiography of his first fifty years. This was later translated into English as *A Stone Made Smooth*. Wong Ming-Dao [Wang Mingdao], *A Stone Made Smooth*, (Southampton, England: Mayflower Christian Books, 1981). More recently, a biography of Wang was written by a Chinese who had been a member of Wang's church in Beijing, the Christian Tabernacle, and who had been arrested at the same time as Wang. Stephen Wang, *The Long Road to Freedom: The Story of Wang Mingdao* (Tonbridge, England: Sovereign World Ltd., 2002)

2.   *A STONE MADE SMOOTH*, p. 90

3.   G. Thompson Brown, in *Christianity and the People's Republic of China* (Atlanta: John Knox Press, 1986), p. 78

4.   Probably the most carefully compiled estimates are in Richard C. Bush, Jr., *Religion in Communist China* (Nashville and New York: Abingdon Press, 1970), p. 50

5.   Cited in *Christianity and the People's Republic of China*, p. 84

6.   James H. Taylor III, endnotes to *A Stone Made Smooth*.

7.   Allen Yuan, Autobiographical Letter (2001), featured on *www.idsi.net*

8.   Samuel Lamb, *Samuel Lamb's Testimony* (Guangzhou, China: n.p., 200), p. 31

9.   Ibid.

10.   The phenomenon of Christians (as opposed to homicidal lunatics who "hear" dogs telling them to kill people) claiming to hear an audible voice, in a variety of languages, depending on the person's nationality, is not as rare as it might seem. This author has met a British and an American Christian who each, on entirely unconnected occasions, claim to have had this experience.

11. Meeting of author with Moses Xie, Beijing, summer of 2002. (Exact date is omitted to avoid difficulties for Rev. Xie.)

12. The other three were Zhang Chunqiao, Wang Hongwen, and Yao Wenyuan. The Gang of Four was arrested after plotting a coup against Mao's "designated" successor team of Hua Guofeng and others, in early October 1976, just one month after Mao's death. Jiang Qing and Zhang Chunqiao were sentenced to life in prison in 1981 after their original death sentences were commuted. Jiang Qing committed suicide in prison in 1991. Wang Hongwen and Yao Wenyuan each received sentences of twenty years.

CHAPTER 4: UNCLES

1. That title used to belong to Sichuan, but the change of administrative status of Qiongqing to an autonomous urban unit promoted Henan.

2. Foot binding was a Chinese custom first popularized in the fourteenth century to shorten the length of a woman's foot – which supposedly rendered the woman more erotically enticing – by bending the toes back upon the arch and securing them in this position by a tightly wrapped cotton strip. The process was extremely painful when first applied in childhood and effectively prevented women from undertaking any physical activity requiring walking.

3. I met him along with fellow journalist Mark O'Keefe, then of *The Oregonian*.

4. Zhang Rongliang to the author, Zhengzhou, Henan Province, August 20, 1998, notebook #377, p. 106

5. Conversation with author, in June 2002.

6. Conversation with author, July 16, 2002, notebook #424, pp. 64-65

7. Xing Liaoyuan, in conversation with author, July 16 2002, notebook #424, p. 69

8. See Appendix, p. 293. The author has the original Chinese text of the United Appeal.

9. Ibid.

10. See Appendix, p. 293

11. Ibid.

12. Premillennialism is the belief that when Christ returns at the time of the

Second Coming, he will initiate a literal reign on earth of a thousand years. It has been the dominant interpretation of Biblical eschatology, or "end-times" events, among American evangelical Christians for approximately a century or more. Books like Hal Lindsey's *The Late Great Planet Earth* and the LaHaye and Jenkins' *Left Behind* series subscribe to the premillennialist interpretation of the Second Coming.

CHAPTER 5: AUNTS, NEPHEWS, AND NIECES

1. Wu Baixin is not his real name, as the Henan Public Security Bureau has intermittently wanted him because of to his close connections with the Fangcheng, Tanghe, and other fellowships. He is, besides Ding herself, the major source for the narrative in this chapter, and an additional source for many of the other events described in this book. Probably nobody in China knows more details about the various house churches than Wu Baixin.

2. Fanny Crosby (1820-1915), a blind hymn writer, had written more than 9,000 Christian songs at the time of her death, more than any other American before or since.

CHAPTER 6: SEMINARIES: TRAINING A NEW GENERATION

1. It is worth noting that church-arranged marriages are far more common in Christian communities in Third World countries than might be supposed. An Indian friend of our family, despite acquiring an M.A. in the U.S. and meeting plenty of attractive American women, was quite content to have his parents arrange for him to meet a "suitable" Indian bride once he returned to Bangalore.

CHAPTER 7: EARLY YEARS OF THE "STATE CHURCH"

1. Though in some parts of China those under eighteen have sometimes been discouraged from entering the churches—and Muslims under eighteen have been told that it is illegal to enter a mosque.

2. Tetsumao Yamamori and Kim-kwong Chan, *Witnesses to Power; Stories of God's Quiet Work in a Changing China* (Cumbria, UK and Waynesboro, GA: Paternoster Press, 2000)

3. Ibid.

4.   Amity website, *www.amityfoundation.org*

5.   Thomas Alan Harvey, *Acquainted with Grief: Wang Mingdao's Stand for The Persecuted Church in China* (Grand Rapids, MI: Brazos Press, 2002) p. 7

6.   Ron MacMillan, "Bishop K. H. Ting: Ally or Adversary of the House Church Millions," *News Network International*, Special Report, June 12, 1989, p. 6

7.   John Pomfret, "Protestantism Rises in the Land of Mao," *Washington Post*, December 24 2002, p. A 12.

8.   George N. Patterson, *Christianity in Communist China*, (Waco, TX: Word Books, 1969), p. 7

9.   Quoted in Harvey, *Acquainted with Grief*, p. 30

10. Patterson, *Christianity in Communist China*, p. 57

11. Ibid., p. 51

12. Ibid., p. 52

13. Ibid., p. 53

14. Cited in Lydia Lee, *A Living Sacrifice: The Life Story of Allen Yuan* (Tonbridge, England: Sovereign Books), p. 99

15. Documents of the Three Self Movement, p. 19

16. Ibid.

17. Ibid., pp 19-20

18. Ibid., p. 50

19. Documents of the Three Self Movement, p. iii

20. Ibid., p. 29

21. Cited in G. Thompson Brown, *Christianity in the People's Republic of China* (Atlanta: John Knox Press, 1986), p. 84

22. Cited in Patterson, *Christianity in Communist China*, pp. 11-12

23. Ibid., p. 12

24. Harvey, *Acquainted with Grief*, p. 67

25. As Wu put it, "Modernists consider the teaching about the Second Coming a form of poetic symbolism depicting the triumph of good over evil; they see the progress of the world taking place by gradual evolution." Documents of the Three Self Movement, pp. 100-101

26. Ibid., p. 103

27. Ibid., p. 104

28. Ibid., p. 105

29. Ibid., p. 106

30. Ibid.

31. Ibid., p. 109

32. It is a point of some curiosity why this piece was not included in Ding's selected English-language writings, called *Love Never Ends*, and published by the Amity Press in 2000.

33. G. Thompson Brown, *Christianity in the People's Republic of China*, p. 110

34. Ibid., p. 157

35. Ibid., p. 161

36. Cited in *Christianity in the People's Republic of China*, p. 109

CHAPTER 8: AFTER THE CULTURAL REVOLUTION

1. These committees typically composed of one army man, one party official, and a representative of "the masses" (perhaps a former Red Guard).

2. G. Thompson Brown, *Christianity in the People's Republic of China* (Atlanta: John Knox Press, 1986), p. 190

3. Quoted in *News Network International* (*NNI*), June 12, 1989, p. 9

4. *NNI*, June 12, 1989, p. 4

5. Document Number 19, in Donald E. MacInnis, *Religion in Chinga Today: Policy and Practice* (Maryknoll, New York: Orbis Books, 1989)), p. 10

6. Ibid., p. 12-13

7. Ibid., p. 14

8. Ibid., p. 18

9. Ibid.

10. Ibid.

11. Tony Lambert, *The Resurrection of the Chinese Church* (London: Hodder & Stoughton, 1991), p. 203

12. Ibid., p. 204

13. Ibid., p. 205

14. Cited ibid., p. 208

15. *NNI*, June 12, 1989, p. 6

16. *NNI*, February 15, 1989, p. 7

17. *NNI*, June 12 1989, p. 7

18. Lambert, *The Resurrection of the Chinese Church*, p. 215-216

19. Ibid., 230

20. Cited in Jason Kindopp, "The Politics of Protestantism in Contemporary China: Social Control, Civil Society, and Movement in an Authoritarian Party-State," Chapter Four: "Religion Policy in the Reform Era: From Control to Hegemony," Unpublished Ph.D. Dissertation, Department of Political Science, George Washington University, p. 26

21. Ibid., Chapter Seven, "Failed Hegemony: The Theological Construction Campaign," p. 2

22. Ibid, p. 4

23. Cited in Kindopp, op.cit, Chapter Four, p. 27

24. Ye Xiaowen text taken from website: *www.christianityinchina.org*

CHAPTER 9: CHINA'S "JERUSALEM"

1. Figures from the website of British Embassy, Beijing, in 2003: *www.britishembassy.org.cn*

2. Joe Studwell, The China Dream (London: Profile Books, 2002), p. 36

3. The oldest and most basic of all of the early Christian statements of faith, the Apostles' Creed may have been broadly accepted by Christian churches in the Mediterranean area before the end of the second century A.D. In China, it is regarded by the Three Self and the China Christian Council as a basic expression of Christian orthodoxy, and it has similarly long been accepted by the house churches. Its full text is as follows:

> I believe in God, the Father almighty, creator of heaven and earth;
> I believe in Jesus Christ, his only Son, our Lord. He was conceived by the power of the Holy Spirit and born of the Virgin Mary. He suffered under Pontius Pilate, was crucified, died, and was buried. He descended to the dead. On the third day he rose again. He ascended into heaven, and is seated at the right hand of Father. He will come again to judge the living and the dead.
> I believe in the Holy Spirit, the holy catholic Church, the communion of saints, the forgiveness of sins, the resurrection of the body, and the life everlasting. Amen.

4. Danyun, *Lilies Among the Thorns* (Tonbridge, England: Sovereign World, 1991)

CHAPTER 10: BACK TO JERUSALEM

1. "The Chinese Back-to-Jerusalem Evangelistic Band," prayer pamphlet, undated, but probably during the period 1947-1948. p. 4. This document was kindly made available by Dr. James Hudson Taylor III, great grandson of the founder of the CIM.
2. Ibid.
3. Ibid., p. 5
4. Report on *www.backtojerusalem.com*

CHAPTER 11: CATHOLICS

1. Inscription noted by author, in Beijing, August 2002.
2. Patterson, *Christianity in Communist China*, p. 103.
3. Quoted in G. Thompson Brown, *Christianity in the People's Republic of China*, p. 88
4. Ibid., p. 89
5. See website: *www.cardinalkungfoundation.org*
6. Statistics of China's population for the years 1959-1962 were revealed in Beijing in 1983. It was admitted that the total population of China had dropped between 1959 and 1962 in absolute terms by 27 million. Observers at the time estimated what the anticipated population would have been for 1962, and on that basis calculated that some 47 million Chinese perished of the famine that emerged from Mao's Great Leap Forward that was initiated in 1958.
7. Richard Madsen, *China's Catholics: Tragedy and Hope in an Emerging Civil Society* (Berkeley and Los Angeles: University of California Press, 1998), p. 62
8. Ibid., p. 53
9. Ibid., p. 57
10. Madsen, *China's Catholics*, p. 46
11. Ibid., p. 127
12. Quoted in ibid, p. 49
13. Madsen, *China's Catholics*, p. 44

14. This detail of John Paul II's career can be found in David Aikman, *Great Souls: Six Who Changed a Century* (Lanham, MD: Lexington Books, 2002), p. 291

15. *Xinhua News Service*, in English, September 28, 2000

CHAPTER 12: PERSECUTION

1. Subsequently amended to permit such things as transfer of land as property and in 1993 to characterize China's economy as "socialism with Chinese characteristics."

2. China's official government website in English, *http://www.china.org.cn/english/shuzi-en/en-shuzi/zz/htm/zj.htm*

3. Ibid.

4. *http://www.china21.org/simpChinese/news/031503pics/02.htm*

5. The four evangelical signatories were Tom White, director of the Voice of the Martyrs; Terry Madison, President of Open Doors with Brother Andrew; Jeff Taylor, managing editor of Compass Direct News Service; and Danny Smith, director of Jubilee Campaign U.K.

6. Time Asia, November 5, 2001, from website: *http://www.time.com/time/asia/news/magazine/0,9754,181681.00html*

7. Cited by Tony Lambert, "Lightning from the East: A Satanic Cult Exposed," in *China Insight Newsletter*, September/October 2001, p. 3

CHAPTER 13: ARTIST, WRITERS, AND ACADEMICS

1. Yuan Zhiming, "The Dream of Those Years: Beginning from a Reassessment of River 'Elegy'," in *Soul Searching: Chinese Intellectuals on Faith and Society* (Wheaton, IL: China Horizon, 1997), p. 9

2. Ling, Chinese Intellectuals and the Gospel, p. 48

3. Yuan, Soul Searching, p. 16

4. Ian Buruma, *Bad Elements: Chinese Rebels From Los Angeles to Beijing* (New York: Vintage Books, 2002), p. 50

5. Unpublished English-language narrative of "Land of God," p. 7

6. Yuan Zhiming keeps an updated account of the progress of this project on his website, *www.chinasoul.org*

7. Chan Juinming, "Liu Xiaofeng: Contours of His Thought," unpublished paper written for China Horizon (La Mirada, CA) 1999, passim

8. Edwin Hui, "The 'Cultural Christian" Phenomenon in Immediate Context, with Theological Reflections," in *Chinese Intellectuals and the Gospel*, p. 110

9. Ravi Zacharias is the author of several books, including *Can Man Live Without God?* and Light in the Shadow of *Jihad: The Struggle for Truth*

10. Campus Crusade for Christ developed the film project *Jesus* as a multi-language evangelistic tool. The actual film was made, in English, in 1978 and was shown extensively in the English-speaking world. Since the 1980s, however, it has been translated into more than eight hundred languages and, according to *www.jesusfilm.org*, shown worldwide to more than 5 billion people in 236 nations and territories. A Mandarin Chinese version of the Jesus film has been available since the 1990s.

CHAPTER 15: CHINA'S CHRISTIAN FUTURE?

1. Michael Pillsbury, *China Debates the Future Security Environment* (Washington DC: National Defense University Press, 2000), p. xxv

2. Ibid., p. xxix

3. Thomas Alan Harvey, *Acquainted with Grief* (Grand Rapids, Michigan: Brazos Press, 2002), p. 159

4. Philip Jenkins, *The Next Christendom: The Coming of Global Christianity* (Oxford and New York: Oxford University Press, 2002).

5. Ling, *Chinese Intellectuals and the Gospel*, pp. 1-3 passim

ACKNOWLEDGMENTS

IT IS VERY HARD TO REMEMBER ALL of the people who, over a three-decade period, have played a role of some kind or other in the writing of this book. It is nevertheless important that I try. If there are a handful of individuals who feel their names ought to be represented here and yet are not, I convey to them my apologies in advance. Believe me, I am aware of help from incredibly numerous and diverse sources.

I am most grateful to Regnery Publishing, and in particular to former president Mr. Al Regnery, for taking on this project in the first place and for continuing to support it through the closing processes of book preparation and book launch. Also at Regnery, my editors Bernadette Malone, Trish Bozell, and Xiaochin Yan are owed many thanks, along with executive editor Harry Crocker and Regnery's current president and publisher, Marji Ross. I am very grateful to Paul Elie, senior editor of Farrar, Straus & Giroux, for urging me to write the book in the first place.

First, on very practical matters, I would like to thank the Smith Richardson Foundation for providing a grant to cover the cost of research and completion of the writing of this book. I would like to thank Mr. and Mrs. David Saunderson, of London, England, for a generous research grant at the outset of the project, enabling me to fly off to Hong Kong and China for reporting, the Mclellan Foundation of Tennessee for travel grants, Fieldstead and Company for a writing grant and an amazingly generous couple somewhere in the U.S., who do not want to be named, for setting in motion the final stages of the book with a display of remarkable spontaneous largesse.

In Hong Kong, Mr. and Mrs. David Sutherland very generously lent me their beautiful Hong Kong apartment on a hill facing the South China Sea while they were away during the summer to use as a base between China reporting trips. Mr. and Mrs. Bob Kuenzli also graciously let me stay in their apartment at the beginning and toward the end of the Hong Kong sojourn. Ms. Jackie Pullinger, a longtime friend and a true worker of miracles in Hong Kong, kindly let me on arrival in Hong Kong use an apartment in the fine New Territories main building of the Society of St. Stephen. On our return to the U.S., Mr. and Mrs. Bill Sargent kindly had my wife and me to stay several days in their home. Mr. and Mrs. Paul Klaassen very generously made available their guest house during the initial stages of writing.

Mr. Mark Zhou, my researcher and translator, provided invaluable guidance and counsel on the China scene and in locating important research material for the book. I am very grateful to him for this work, as well as for helping make our chocolate Labrador, Chip, one of the few bilingual (Mandarin and English) obedience-trained dogs in Loudoun County.

It would be invidious, and perhaps unwise, to indicate precisely in which way so many people helped me enormously with different facets of this book over many years and on at least three continents: advance preparation, contacts, advice, friendship, information, material, judgment, but I certainly think I should name as many of them as I safely can, and place them in alphabetical order:

Rev. Dennis Balcombe, Ms. Jan Berris, Mr. Jeff Book, Rev. David Boyd, Mr. Werner Burklin, Mr. John Cao, Dr. Kim-kwong Chan, Dr. Jonathan Chao, Mr. Robert Cheeley, Mr. Michael Cromartie, Rev. Loren Cunningham, Mr. John Davies, Dr. Lon Diehl and Louise and

Seth Diehl, Bishop Ding Guangxun, Dr. Audrey Donnithorne, Mr. Wright Doyle, Mr. Tom Farr, Mr. Feng Jianguo, Ms. Charlene Fu, Dr. Brent Fulton, Rev. Rich Gao, Mr. Robert Glover, Dr. and Mrs. Billy Graham, Mr. Wayne Graham, Dr. Os Guinness, Mr. and Mrs. Andy Hamilton, Dr. Carol Hamrin, Mr. Han Dongfang, Mr. Han Wenzao, Ambassador John Hanford, Rev. Tom Herrick, Mr. Hong Yang, Mrs. Meiyun Chen Hoyle, Mrs. Roberta Hromas, Rev. Ji Tai, Dr. Jason Kindopp, Mr. and Mrs. Jimmy Lai, Mr. Mark Lambert, Dr. Tony Lambert, Rev. Samuel Lamb, Rev. Li Tianen, Bishop Li Du'an, Dr. Samuel Ling, Mr. K.C. Liu, Paul Liu, Dr. Richard Madsen, Mr. Ron Macmillan, Dr. Paul Marshall, Ms. Stacy Mattingly, Rev. Ellyn McInnis, Mr. Peter McInnis, Mr. Miao Xuefeng, Rev. Miao Zhitong, Rev. Martyn Minns, Dr. Richard Mouw, Ms. Becky Neufeld, Mr. Dwight Nordstrom and Mrs. Jewell Nordstrom, Monsignor Eugene M. Nugent, Dr. Diane Obenchain, Mr. Don Parett, Mr. Scott Pollock, Ms. Donna Rosenthal, Mr. Gary Russell, Mr. Mark Simon, Mr. and Mrs. Paul Steward, Mr. Timothy Su and Bai Ling, Ms. Harmony Sun, Mr. Doug Sutphen and Mrs. Meiling Sutphen, Dr. James Hudson Taylor III, Mr. T. K. Thong, Mr. and Mrs. Phil Tolstead, Dr. Joseph Tong, Mr. Rolf Towe, Ms. Lynn Turpin, Ms. Elaine Vitaly, Dr. Ambrose Wang, Rev. David Wang, Mr. Eric Watt, Rev. and Mrs. Ken Wendling, Mr. Chris Wilde, Mr. Xiao Dongfang, Rev. Moses Xie, Dr. Edward Xu, Ms. Xu Yongling, Rev. Xu Yongze, Dr. Danny Yu, Mr. Yu Jiade, Miss Mandy Yu, Mr. Yuan Zhiming, Rev. Yang Hong, Professor Yang Huilin, Rev. Allen Yuan, Bishop Joseph Zen, Rev. Zhang Boli, Fr. Francis-Xavier Zhang, Mr. Zhang Jinglong, Fr. John-Baptist Zhang, Mr. Zhang Rongliang, Mr. Zhang Yinan, Mr. Zhen Datong.

I owe a lasting debt of gratitude to the late Dr. Donald Treadgold of the University of Washington for his unique and immense insights into China and into the Christian faith while I was studying under him in graduate school.

INDEX